Orthodox Christianity

A collection of essays

Orthodox Christology

A collection of essays
Second Edition

Father Peter Farrington

THE ORIENTAL ORTHODOX LIBRARY

Copyright © 2014 Father Peter Farrington

All rights reserved.

No part of this publication may be reproduced, stored in a retrieval system or transmitted in any form or by any means electronic, mechanical, photocopying, recording or otherwise, without the prior written permission of the author.

Printed in the United Kingdom

First Printing, 2010

Second Edition 2014

The Oriental Orthodox Library

264 Upper Fant Road

Maidstone, Kent, United Kingdom. ME16 8BX

www.orthodox-library.com

Contents

Preface	7
Introduction	9
An introduction to Orthodox Christology	15
Eutyches and the Oriental Orthodox tradition	37
The Orthodox view of Ibas of Edessa	69
The Orthodox Christology of St Severus of Antioch	93
The Humanity of Christ in St Severus	121
Hypostasis in St Severus of Antioch	141
St Timothy Aelurus of Alexandria	155
After Chalcedon - Orthodoxy in the 5th/6th Centuries	195
The Rejection of Chalcedon – An Introduction	209
The Intercession of the Archangel Michael in St Severus of Antioch	223
Some Brief Thoughts on the Eucharist from St Jacob of Serugh	227
A Syrian monk as educator	235
Natural disasters in the Sixth Century Chronicle of Pseudo-Joshua	241
The Apostle Thomas and the Origins of the Orthodox Church in India	259
The Orthodox Tradition and the Councils	271
Penal Substitution	291
Conversation About the Will of Christ	301
Accepting the Eastern Orthodox Councils?	327

Preface

This extended collection of articles makes no claim to originality, or to any great academic quality. Indeed in the years since I became a Coptic Orthodox Christian it has become clear that the more I learn, the less confident I feel in daring to present any of my opinions as being worth the time and attention of fellow Orthodox.

Nevertheless, His Eminence Abba Seraphim, the Metropolitan of Glastonbury has always been an encouraging and supportive spiritual father, and has published many of these articles in the British Orthodox publication, the Glastonbury Review. They are, to some extent, a record of my studies in Orthodox theology over the last decades.

It is said that the best is often the enemy of the good, and therefore rather than wait indefinitely until I have gained a perfect knowledge of the things written about in this collection, it seems better to make available what has already been produced in a convenient format so that if there is anything of value it might be a blessing to others now rather than later.

It is my hope that as other Orthodox Christians read these articles they will be encouraged to study these matters for themselves, and produce written explanation of our Faith which surpass these efforts, so that our Orthodox communion might see a renaissance of patristic studies. Over the years since this volume was first published it has been a great pleasure to discover that just such a renaissance seems to be beginning.

Father Peter Farrington
August 2014

Introduction

The Oriental Orthodox communion draws together Christians from a wide variety of ethnic and cultural backgrounds. These diverse backgrounds are reflected in the various liturgical and canonical traditions of each community. But within this colourful proliferation of rites there is an essential unity of faith which is rooted in a common patristic understanding. This collection of articles reflects my own interest in this common theological tradition, and describes my own efforts as a convert to Orthodoxy to understand more completely the faith I had embraced.

In my first years as an Orthodox Christian it was relatively difficult to locate material in English which was relevant to the study of Oriental Orthodoxy. There were indeed a number of translations of selected works produced in the 19th century, but before the widespread availability of texts on the internet these volumes were difficult, if not impossible, to locate. The first major primary work I was able to find in translation was an edition of some of St Severus' letters. Far from satisfying my desire to dig deeper into the Oriental Orthodox theological tradition, reading these letters made me all the more determined to find more texts in English, and then in French, so that my commitment to the Orthodox Faith might be rooted in a patristic study and not simply in the reading of modern Orthodox writers.

The internet has transformed the opportunities for researching and studying the substance of Oriental Orthodox theology. Of course the future will provide even more comprehensive access to the global library of written texts, but even at the time of writing it is possible to conduct very serious study by means of documents available in online theological collections.

These collected articles have been previously available in a variety of publications as they have been written. Many have been published in the Glastonbury

Review, the journal of the British Orthodox Church within the Coptic Orthodox Patriarchate. Others have only been available on particular websites. One article was submitted to the World Council of Churches. Another is the unpublished text of a lecture on Christology. This is the first time they have been collected together in a convenient format.

The first article in this volume, an Introduction to Orthodox Christology, was presented as a lecture at a British Orthodox study day. It is a brief overview of the three early challenges to an Orthodox description of Christ. These were the Arian, Nestorian and Eutychian christologies, each of which has been robustly condemned by the Oriental Orthodox communion.

The second article was first published in the Glastonbury Review, and is a consideration of the person and Christology of Eutyches. He is shown to be a much more complex person than usually presented, and although the Christology which bears his name is undoubtedly heterodox, this article suggests that it is not entirely clear he always held that position.

The third article deals with another controversial figure from the same period in the 5th century, Ibas the bishop of Edessa. This article was also first published in the Glastonbury Review. The article describes Ibas' career, and explores the nature of his heterodoxy. He is a figure who must be considered in relation to the ecumenical dialogue between the Eastern and Oriental Orthodox since he was received as an Orthodox bishop at Chalcedon, and then found his infamous, and heretical, letter to Maris the Persian condemned at Constantinople in 553AD.

These first three articles, although written over a number of years, describe the false Christologies which the Oriental Orthodox have always resisted and repudiated. The next three are all articles about the life and teachings of St Severus of Antioch, certainly the greatest of all post-Chalcedonian theologians. The fourth article in this collection provides an overview of the life and teaching of St Severus, while the fifth is concerned especially with his teaching on the continuing integrity of the humanity of Christ. The sixth considers his use of the term hypostasis and explores the nature of the union of humanity and divinity in Christ.

The seventh article is a major piece on St Timothy Aelurus of Alexandria, the successor to St Dioscorus as archbishop of that city, and leader of the Church in Egypt. It was also published in the Glastonbury Review, and since there seem to be very few articles indeed about this important figure it was written to provide a description of his life, and an overview of his Christology.

The eighth article was one of the earliest which I produced. It seemed to me, even in the first years of my life as an Orthodox Christian, that the historical narrative of the 5th century which was being promoted by many Eastern Orthodox was simplistic and one-sided. This article is concerned with some of the efforts which were made to reconcile the two parties within the Church in the 5th and 6th centuries before the separation became permanent. Although the division between the Oriental Orthodox and the Eastern Orthodox is popularly dated to 451 AD there are many reasons for considering the date of the division to be within the 6th century, and even as late as 565 AD.

The ninth article considers some of the reasons why the Oriental Orthodox reject the Council of Chalcedon. It describes the anathemas which St Dioscorus issued against the council, and which were reiterated by succeeding generations of bishops. This article is an introduction to the topic, but it does show that the rejection of the council was not willful, and was certainly not due to the acceptance of any heresy, but was rooted in a concern that the council had fallen into a Nestorian manner of speaking about Christ.

These first nine articles are all concerned directly with the Orthodox Christology of the Oriental Orthodox, or with the positions held by those whom they opposed as heretics. The final five articles are on a more varied range of topics, but are all concerned with historical aspects of Oriental Orthodoxy. The tenth article was first published on the erkohet.com website. It is a shorter piece which considers the power of the intercession of St Michael as described in one of the homilies of St Severus.

The eleventh article was first published on the same website, and provides some thoughts on the eucharist from the writings of St Jacob of Serugh. These early materials are useful since they describe the liturgical setting of the eucharist at this time, and also confirm that the Church professed a clear belief in the real presence of Christ in the eucharist. The twelfth article, a third written for the same website, uses a passage from the Lives of the Eastern Saints by John of Ephesus to consider the relation of one Oriental Orthodox monastic leader with his local secular community, and especially the interesting system of education which he established for the local children.

The thirteenth article was written to gain a place on the World Council of Churches Global Platform for theological reflection. This was a conference held at the WCC offices in Geneva, with an invited group of participants, who gathered from a variety of backgrounds to consider the manner in which the Bible was used in the face of crisis and catastrophe in the world. I chose to write on the disasters which struck Syria in the 6th century and which were documented in the Chronicle of Pseudo-Joshua.

The final article was written most recently. My bishop, Metropolitan Seraphim, led a pilgrimage to the sister Churches of Kerala in India. The Orthodox Christians of India have therefore been on my mind, and becoming aware of certain criticisms of the apostolate of St Thomas I began to study the patristic testimony about his life and death and wrote this article which shows clearly that the Fathers had always considered him completely a member of the Apostolic college, and a recipient with all the other Apostles of the grace of Apostleship.

I hope that those who read these articles will find them interesting and helpful. But it is more important that those who read these simple materials are inspired to study the patristic tradition of the Oriental Orthodox communion for themselves.

Father Peter Farrington

May 2010

An Introduction to Orthodox Christology

Why worry about doctrine?

Growing up in an Evangelical Protestant home, and playing an active role in my local Evangelical Church, I often heard people complaining that we needed a lot more love and a lot less doctrine! I knew what they meant. They were rejecting narrow and intellectual faith in words and concepts rather than in Christ Himself. But even as an Evangelical I disagreed, because I understood that if we don't know what we believe, and why, then we may well end up believing all manner of things about God, about the Christian life, about our very salvation, many of which may not be true at all.

If doctrine is the description and explanation of what we believe to be true then it is important that we seek to have a right understanding. Doctrine is a spiritual medicine, or rather it is a description of the spiritual treatment which will heal us. Think how dangerous it is if the wrong medicine is prescribed to a patient, or the wrong amount is administered. Remember the recent drug trial which went so terribly wrong and left several men damaged for life. Describing and understanding our faith using the wrong doctrines is just as likely to cause harm, though it may be spiritual rather than physical.

Perhaps we can briefly consider a manifestly false doctrine, but one which has had some influence in the past decades. The 'Health and Wealth' Gospel teaches that God wants all Christians to be healthy and wealthy. More than that, if you are not healthy and wealthy then it is a sign that you lack faith. What sort of a Christian does this doctrine create? Surely one whose eyes are set on material gain. One who is taught to condemn and disparage those who are less well off because they have brought their poverty upon themselves by lacking faith. We can barely recognise this teaching as being Christian, but it is a Gospel for our modern, consumer society, and it has many hundreds of thousands of adherents, even millions, many of whom are found in the Third World and who hope that by praying more, attending Church services more, naming and claiming what material goods they desire, somehow God will grant them all. Yet the authentic Gospel teaches us 'take up your Cross and follow me'.

So right and true doctrine matters because doctrinal error can cause us spiritual harm, and even prevent us becoming Christian. The Mormon Church considers itself Christian but its teachings are contrary to those of the New Testament. Is it enough that it considers itself Christian, or should there be some lines in the sand which define the boundaries of that which is truly Christian and Orthodox teaching?

This has certainly always been the opinion of the Church, and we find St Paul warning his young Christian disciples to keep away from those who were bringing them another, different Gospel. There is a Christian truth, and the Orthodox Church has been committed to preserving that truth since the beginning. Certainly not because it lacked the imagination to think of new teachings, certainly not because it was merely old fashioned, but because it has always believed that 'the truth shall set you free', and that Christian doctrine is a means of finding salvation, a spiritual map. Not the same as salvation certainly, not the same as knowing Christ, but the means by which we find the true Christ and enter into the fulness of the Christian life.

It is easy to be misled, and the desire to find doctrinal truth is not separated from Christian love, as some of my Evangelical friends thought, but it is the means by which we enter fully into that love. He who said He was the way and life also said He was the truth, and we neglect the truth at our spiritual peril.

Why is Christology important?

We can imagine that at the heart of all the controversies over doctrine is the teaching about the incarnation, passion, and ministry of Our Lord Jesus Christ. It should be no surprise that our enemy, Satan, will wish to compromise the very Gospel itself, if he can. Therefore Christology, the study of the doctrine of Christ, can appear as though it is so mired in argument and disagreement that it is best left alone. Nothing could be farther from the truth, because in fact the true understanding of Christology is salvation itself, and if we can make a little effort to see our way through the fog of many words and contradictory teachings then we will come to a place of light and life.

Christology deals with the question which Christ Himself posed to His disciples..

"Who do you say that I am?"

He seems to have asked them only a few direct questions which are recorded in the scriptures, and seems rather to have spent His time constantly explaining to them what He was doing and what His teaching meant. But on this occasion he asked them a serious question and therefore it is shown to be of central importance.

"Who do you say that I am?"

Already in the Apostolic Age we can see that the issue of Christology had a central place in the reflection of the Church. In fact the first answers of the Apostles provide some of the diversity of responses which can still be heard…

"Some say that you are John the Baptist, others say that you are Elijah, while others say that one of the prophets of long ago has come back to life."

This is a Christological answer. Indeed if we consider Islam as a Christian heresy, a form of Christianity which has gone wrong, then Islamic Christianity provides this same answer. Jesus Christ is a prophet. There are plenty of modern people who consider themselves Christian but who believe no more than this. That Jesus was a good man, perhaps no more than a good man, a prophet of sorts.

But it is not the only answer. When Jesus Christ asked his disciples who THEY thought he was, Simon Peter answered boldly....

"You are the Christ, the Son of the Living God".

This is a different Christological answer to the same question. But it has the advantage that Jesus Christ Himself acknowledges it as the true answer.

"Blessed are you, Simon Bar Jona; for flesh and blood has not revealed this to you, but my Father in heaven."

These words of our Lord point out the difference between a Christology which is developed solely according to human logic and philosophy, as is the case with the Christological heresies, and that which derives from Scripture, from prayer and from revelation.

So we cannot escape Christology. It seeks to answer, hopefully with humility and a due sense of the limitations of all human thought about God, those central questions about the life of Christ and our salvation which can be summed up in the question..

"Who do you say I am?"

The answer matters a great deal. We cannot be saved by a prophet or a good man. Our spiritual sickness is altogether too grave, indeed it is a spiritual death, separating us from God. Christology matters because Jesus Christ, the Word of God become flesh matters. Indeed the incarnation is the very central point of the whole of creation. All that precedes it is leading up to it, and all that follows is consequent upon it.

A brief overview

We cannot hope to consider all the answers that Christians have produced over the centuries out of their reflection on this question, but we do need to consider several key moments in time, and several important figures, who have shaped the landscape of Christological thought. As is often the case, the greatest periods of doctrinal controversy and deliberation have been times when there has been a challenge to the truths which have been taught about Christ.

So we will consider very briefly the three Christological heresies of Arianism, Nestorianism and Eutychianism; and then we will turn to one of our own non-Chalcedonian Fathers and will an important historical statement of faith which confirms that our own Christological faith is entirely that of the Apostles, and the great Orthodox Fathers of the following centuries.

Arianism

For a while it was enough for the Church to understand that Christ was 'the Son of the Living God'. We should not think that simply because the Church had not developed a complex Christological language at the beginning this means that it did not have a complex and developed Christology. We should careful to understand that from the very beginning, from the time of the Apostles, the content of the Orthodox faith in Christ was always the same. Justin Martyr, writing in about 150 AD shows this early appreciation of all that an Orthodox Christology should describe when he says..

"Jesus Christ is the only proper Son who has been begotten by God, being His Word and first-begotten, and power; and, becoming man according to His will, He taught us these things for the conversion and restoration of the human race."

He was 'the Word become flesh who dwelt among us'. Emmanuel, God Himself with us. We will turn to the scriptures as we consider these three Christological heresies and we will find that the Apostles had already expressed themselves in ways which the Orthodox doctrines, even as they became more terminologically complex, had already described. These Biblical phrases, and may others like them, contain three important concepts which an Orthodox, that is a true and proper Christology must always contain.

These are firstly that Jesus Christ is truly God the Word, secondly that he is one with us in the fulness of our own humanity, and thirdly that He has Himself, and no other, truly become human. Of course each one of these concepts is liable to all manner of misunderstanding and misinterpretation, but these concepts were there from the beginning and it is not possible for us to agree with those who suggest, for instance, that it was only at some later date that Christ was understood by the Church as being God.

Now over the first centuries there were many assaults on one or other of these Christological foundations.

The first serious Christological controversy which we will consider, and which posed a threat to the whole Church originated in the early 4th century. An Alexandrian presbyter, Arius, basing his ideas on earlier false teachings, started to preach that though the Word was the Son of God He could not be considered the same as God. Indeed Arius and those supporting Him essentially denied that the Word of God was God at all. They insisted that only the Father could be properly called God, and that before time He had begotten the Son and Word as His first creation, who had Himself in due course created the Holy Spirit.

Why should the Arians, as they came to be known, wish to hold such a Christological position? One of their surviving writings shows that they used 1 Corinthians 8:5-6 as a proof text. It says…

"To us there is but one God, the Father, of whom are all things, and we in Him, and one Lord Jesus Christ, by whom are all things, and we by Him".

The Arians were strict monotheists, and if we take this verse out of context then we can see how attractive the Arian position might sound. It saves all manner of complicated Trinitarian thinking. There is one God, the Father. The Son is his first and highest creation; and the Holy Spirit is the creation of the Son to help Him in his works. Not only is God able to divorce Himself from the messy business of running the universe, but there is no need to consider the inconceivable idea that He had become man.

According to this view Jesus Christ Himself could not genuinely be considered God. He was little more than a body which was moved and used by the created Son of God. Simply put the Christology of Arius was that the Son of God was a created being, although the greatest, and that Jesus Christ was therefore not God. Indeed it was not even a complete humanity which this created Son had taken, but the shell of a man.

It was Athanasius, bishop of Alexandria, who found himself leading the response of the Orthodox party to this challenge. It was certainly not easy for him, and he found himself exiled far from Alexandria on several occasions. The Emperor Constantine had granted some important rights to the Christian Church, but it was not always clear which Christian Church he was going to support, and often those who stood out firmly for doctrinal truth looked like troublemakers, and were treated as such.

There is not the time to go into all that he wrote about these important Christological matters, but he developed two important principles which have always guided a proper and Orthodox Christology ever since. These were…

"That which is not assumed is not healed"

And

"God became man so that we might become gods"

We can see that these two principles are not teaching anything new, but they are explaining and defining more clearly the three foundational concepts we have already described.

The first principle, "That which is not assumed is not healed", allows us to understand that when we say that the Word became flesh we must mean that the flesh He became is our own humanity, and it must be a complete humanity, saving only sin. As it is written in Hebrews…

"But we see him who for a little while was made lower than the angels, namely Jesus, crowned with glory and honor because of the suffering of death, so that by the grace of God he might taste death for everyone…. Since therefore the children share in flesh and blood, he himself likewise partook of the same things, that through death he might destroy the one who has the power of death, that is, the devil, and deliver all those who through fear of death were subject to lifelong slavery. For surely it is not angels that he helps, but he helps the offspring of Abraham. Therefore he had to be made like his brothers in every respect, so that he might become a merciful and faithful high priest in the service of God, to make propitiation for the sins of the people."

We can see once again from this passage that the Scriptures contain a complex Christology, and these verses teach us to understand that Christ is completely human in all regards, and more than this it shows us that it was necessary for our salvation that he become fully and completely human, like his brothers in every respect, so that He might represent all mankind before God, as the High Priest represented the people of Israel in the Holy of Holies.

We see that even at the time of the Apostles it was clearly understood that it was by truly becoming man and dying our human death that God willed to liberate man from the power of death.

Someone who is not fully human cannot represent humanity. There was a need, according to the will and purpose of God, for a human to once and for all live a perfect and obedient life before God, the life that Adam should have lived, and in dying a death that was not the punishment of his own sin to be able to break the bonds and power of death and sin by His own divine authority and by the power of the Holy Spirit.

If God were incarnate in anything less than a complete humanity then that which was not assumed by God could not be brought through death to resurrection. The Arian Christ was not the Biblical Christ because He did not assume all of our humanity. The mind and soul were replaced by the Son of God.

We can easily see how this explanation fails to safeguard our salvation. When we reflect on our own spiritual lives before God we surely must conclude that the root of our sinfulness is not found in our foot, or our elbow, or our shoulder, but is found in our mind and will and soul. It is these which need to be redeemed even more than flesh and bone.

"What is not assumed is not healed" and "He became like his brothers in every respect…to make propitiation for our sins". These are expressing the same Christological principle.

But St Athanasius' other principle is also scriptural, and is also necessary to preclude an Arian Christology. He says that "God became man, that we might become like God".

What a startling and perhaps provocative statement. But it is a necessary one because it insists that the one who became man was indeed God. Not a creation of God, but God Himself. And it insists equally that we are brought into a new relationship with God, as sons of God, by grace of course and not by the changing of our human nature into His divinity, but sons and daughters none the less.

The scriptures are clear, not least in passages such as

"Behold what manner of love the Father hath bestowed upon us, that we should be called the sons of God."

And

"For as many as are led by the Spirit of God, they are the sons of God."

During the Arian controversy the Church was having to consider what language and terminology it should use to preserve the authentic doctrine about Jesus Christ, about God the Father, the Son and the Holy Spirit.

Greek terms were used with a variety of subtle but important differences in meaning.

Some said that the Son was *homoi-ousios,* which has the meaning 'of a similar essence', while the Orthodox insisted that Christ was *homo-ousios,* which means 'of the same essence'.

These two descriptions are a world apart. The one says no more than Arius would agree to, that the Son of God was certainly like God, indeed had been mae by God and shared many of his characteristics, but was, essentially, NOT God. The other says that the Son is truly God of God, of the same essence and therefore to be considered God as much as the Father because both were of the same essence.

If it is not God Himself who has become truly man for our sake then we are not saved. This is the heart of all Christological controversy. We are not saved by angels, nor by God avoiding becoming a complete man, but by Emmanuel, God with us, and God in us.

Arianism, for all its temporary worldly success, was not a Christian Christology, and it was therefore rejected by the Church which found that it failed to adequately describe and explain what had always been believed. The Nicene Creed is witness to the Orthodox rejection of Arianism, and to the preservation of an Apostolic and Biblical Christology.

"We believe in one Lord Jesus Christ, the only-begotten Son of God, begotten of the Father before all worlds, God of God, Light of Light, Very God of Very God, begotten, not made, being of one substance with the Father by whom all things were made; who for us men, and for our salvation, came down from heaven, and was incarnate by the Holy Spirit of the Virgin Mary, and was made man, and was crucified also for us under Pontius Pilate. He suffered and was buried, and the third day he rose again according to the Scriptures, and ascended into heaven, and sitteth on the right hand of the Father. And he shall come again with glory to judge both the quick and the dead, whose kingdom shall have no end."

The second serious Christological error also erupted in the East, and is named after its most well known defender, Nestorianism. For several generations there had been scholars, bishops and theologians who had increasingly described Christ as being the union of God with a man. There reasoning was that since God was utterly other to His creation it was impossible to say that He had Himself become man, it was necessary to say that He had united Himself in some external sense to a man.

Their desire to preserve the integrity of the Divine nature from change was commendable, but the explanation of the incarnation which they proposed meant that it was not in fact possible to speak of the Word becoming flesh in a substantial sense at all.

The controversy came to a head when Nestorius, the bishop of Constantinople, heard a sermon which described the Virgin Mary as Theotokos, or God-bearer. He objected to this term and insisted that she was only anthropo-tokos, the man-bearer, or christo-tokos, the bearer of Christ. He refused to allow that it could be said that God had been born, or that God had been nursed as a baby.

But his Orthodox opponents, not least St Cyril of Alexandria, asked who had been born if not God the Word? It it were indeed some other person, united to God in some manner, then it was not God who was crucified and it was not God who was raised from the dead. And if that were so then the Word had not become flesh and had not given us the right to become children of God, as the Gospel of John states.

The teaching of the Apostles in the Acts, and throughout the New Testament is clear. It is the Word who has become incarnate, who has been made man, and therefore Christ is the Word become flesh, not a man in some relationship of grace with the Word.

St Cyril clearly understood the implications of Nestorius' position. No less than that of Arius it denied that God had Himself become man for our salvation, and while preserving the divinity of the Word, unlike Arius, it nevertheless denied that He had become fully and properly man.

St Cyril says...

"Man therefore was He truly made, through Whom God the Father made the worlds too; and was not (as some suppose) in a man, so as to be conceived of by us as a man who has God indwelling in him. For if they believe that these things are really so, superfluous will seem to be the blessed Evangelist John, saying, And the Word was made Flesh. For where the need of being made man? or why is God the Word said to be Incarnate, unless was made flesh means that He was made like us, and the force of the being made man declares that He was made like us, yet remained even so above us, yea also above the whole creation?"

It could be said by the Nestorians that He was in a man, or was united to a man, or dwelt in the man as in a temple, but He was not that man in the sense of having the same identity. In the Nestorian incarnation there were not only two natures in Christ in the sense of two ways of being, the human and the divine, but there were two subjects, the man and the Word.

The same objections which were raised against Arianism apply to Nestorianism. If God has not Himself become man then we are lost because it is not the incarnate Word who has been crucified and it is not the incarnate Word who has been raised from the dead. It is no more than a good man.

St Cyril spent much of his episcopal career writing and preaching against this false Christology. He often used the phrase 'one incarnate nature or hypostasis of the Word'. By this he meant that there was only one subject in Christ, only one identity, and that was of the Word made flesh. There was not 'the Word' and 'a man', but rather the man whom children embraced and soldiers beat was Himself the incarnate Word and no-one else.

In Christ, according to our Orthodox Christology and the teaching of St Cyril, there is only one 'WHO' in Christ, even while we understand that He is fully and perfectly God and fully and perfectly man, without sin. If we were blessed to see Him in the street and someone asked who He was, we could truly answer that He is the incarnate Son and Word of God. There is no other Orthodox answer. He is not Jesus, if by that we mean that He is a man called Jesus who is united in some way to the Word of God, rather this man Jesus is the incarnate Word of God, and the incarnate Word of God is this man Jesus.

While he lay in His mother's arms, at the same time He held the whole universe in His own divine embrace. The one as being truly human, the other as being unchangeably Divine. When He walked it was as a man, because God does not walk, but when He walked on water He showed that He was more than a mere man but rather God incarnate.

This unity and identity of being is no more than the Apostles had expressed, though St Cyril has to state it much more forcefully and clearly because of his circumstances. But he says no more than St John in his Gospel, "the Word became flesh" when he speaks of 'one incarnate identity or person or subject of the Word'.

In his twelfth anathema St Cyril declares…

"Whoever does not acknowledge God's Word as having suffered in the flesh, being crucified in the flesh, tasted death in the flesh and been made first-born from among the dead because as God He is Life and life-giving shall be anathema!"

This sums up so much of what St Cyril understands the Bible and the Church to have taught as true and saving doctrine.

We must confess that it is God the Word Himself and no other who suffers and dies, but He suffers and dies according to the humanity which He has made His own and not according to His unchanging and unchangeable divinity. If we will not confess God the Word Himself and none other to be Jesus Christ then we cannot say that He has Himself risen from the dead, trampling down death by death, at best we can say that He has raised a man from the dead. A miracle indeed but not enough to gain our salvation.

Unlike Arianism, which in the denial of Christ's divinity remains a popular modern option but lacks a formal Church organisation, the heresy of Nestorianism would appear to persist among the Church of the East, who especially venerate Nestorius' teachers, Diodore and Theodore of Mopsuestia. But more than that it remained an active tendency in the Roman Empire, and even today, when pushed, there are those who claim to be Orthodox but who tend towards a separation of the humanity and Divinity in

Christ which amounts to Nestorianism. The same desire to prevent any sense of change or mutability attaching to the Divine nature may still produce the same unbalanced response even today.

The **third period of major Christological controversy** erupted in the decades after the first council of Ephesus in 431 AD. This had succeeded in producing a dogmatic statement about Nestorius and his teaching, but it had failed to overcome the tendency towards Nestorian ways of thinking, which was still prevalent in both the East and West.

After the council of Ephesus there were major communities of Christians, not least those of the See of Antioch under their bishop John, who were out of communion with the wider Orthodox communion, and with St Cyril of Alexandria. It was not until 433 AD that a measure of reconciliation was effected, but this was itself rather illusory because both sides interpreted the reconciliation as being the capitulation of the other. Thus many Antiocheans believed that St Cyril had given up his confusing language of 'one incarnate nature' and was now confessing that Christ was 'in two natures', while St Cyril hoped that the Antiocheans confessed the true union of God and man in Christ, and had given up confessing 'two independent natures'.

This third controversy developed because the issue of Nestorianism, or at least the Nestorian way of thinking about and describing Christ, had not been completely dealt with.

In 449, Eutyches, the famous and elderly archimandrite of a monastery in Constantinople, was called before the local synod of Flavian, the Patriarch of Constantinople, and accused of teaching that after the union of humanity and Divinity in Christ there was only one nature. Flavian, and some of his bishops, used Antiochean terminology and understood 'one nature' as meaning either that the Divinity and humanity were mixed into some third nature, or else that the humanity was not present in the union. Of course Eutyches, not a very competent theologian, was wanting to insist that when the Word of God became incarnate He remained one subject and was not two subjects, the Son of God and a man.

His accusers saw this as an opportunity to both attack St Cyril's language of 'one incarnate nature' and also to curtail the influence of Eutyches in the Imperial court. He was condemned and the local synod expressed the view that it was necessary to say that Christ was two natures, not one, thereby setting themselves at odds with the teaching of St Cyril, and against the settlement of Ephesus in 431.

At Ephesus St Cyril's anathemas had been received, which say in part..

2. If anyone does not confess that the Word from God the Father has been united by hypostasis with the flesh and is one Christ with his own flesh, and is therefore God and man together, let him be anathema.

3. If anyone divides in the one Christ the hypostases after the union, joining them only by a conjunction of dignity or authority or power, and not rather by a coming together in a union by nature, let him be anathema.

4. If anyone distributes between the two persons or hypostases the expressions used either in the gospels or in the apostolic writings, whether they are used by the holy writers of Christ or by him about himself, and ascribes some to him as to a man, thought of separately from the Word from God, and others, as befitting God, to him as to the Word from God the Father, let him be anathema.

5. If anyone dares to say that Christ was a God-bearing man and not rather God in truth, being by nature one Son, even as "the Word became flesh", and is made partaker of blood and flesh precisely like us, let him be anathema.

There is not the time to describe the second council at Ephesus in 449 which defended Eutyches when he presented an Orthodox confession of faith, and which condemned those like Theorodet and Ibas who were teaching that St Cyril had an heretical Christology. Nor to investigate the council of Chalcedon and the Tome of Leo, which both weighed in on the side of the 'two nature' terminology.

But we should take note of the reason why the non-Chalcedonian Orthodox Churches are not Eutychian, and indeed have repudiated him from the beginning. There were times when he presented an Orthodox Christology, but it would also appear that he failed to fully comprehend that of St Cyril, even though he spoke of 'one nature'.

St Cyril always spoke of 'one incarnate nature', meaning one individual, the Word, who has become incarnate. Eutyches spoke simply of 'one nature' and therefore may well be considered as failing to properly safeguard the incarnation. Jesus Christ is not simply the Word, he is the Word made incarnate, without ceasing to be what He is as God.

More than this, on occasion Eutyches also refused to confess that Christ was consubstantial with us in His humanity. This was a seriously damaging position. He rejected the idea that the humanity of Christ had come down from heaven, but if it was not completely our own humanity then he is found to damage one of the foundational principles of an Orthodox Christology, which is, of course, that God the Word became completely human for our salvation.

Eutyches would appear to have adopted a more Orthodox Christology at Ephesus in 449, whether in appearance or in reality and with conviction, but his rather incoherent Christology found some followers and over the next two centuries it was occasionally necessary for it to be repudiated, and various clergy to be excommunicated.

In fact the origins of our own non-Chalcedonian Orthodox communion is rooted in the events which took place before, during and after the council of Chalcedon, which we have understood as confirming a form of Nestorianism, or at least failing to preserve the Cyrilline standard of Orthodox Christology. Eutyches has never been considered a father of the Church, and Eutychianism, that confusing of the humanity and Divinity, or the failure to preserve the integrity of the humanity of Christ, has always been rejected as a heresy. If we are non-Chalcedonians it is because we reject the dividing up of Christ into God and a man which we have understood that council to describe, rather than because we have any commitment to Eutyches and his false Christology.

What do these three examples teach us?

We can see that the principles of an Orthodox Christology are always diminished or degraded by a false Christology. These three principles bear repeating. They are that God the Word Himself became man; that He became truly and completely man as we are; and that He authentically became man, not only in appearance, or by uniting to Himself some other human person.

In the case of Arius, he denied that Christ was truly God. In that of Nestorius, he denied that God had Himself become man; and in that of Eutyches, that God had become truly man as we are. Almost all of the Christological errors throughout history can be understood as falling into one of these categories.

Why does this matter?

The preservation of a right way of thinking about Christ has already been described as having spiritual and eternal consequences. If it is not God the Word who is incarnate then Christ has no power to save us, and His death and resurrection are only his own, effected upon him by some other external Divine power. Death is not trampled down by the death of a man. But if he is not completely and wholly a man like us in every way except sin then our broken and weak humanity is not completely and wholly healed and we remain under the power of those human elements which such a Christ had not assumed. And finally if God the Word has not truly become man then it is a man apart from God who has suffered and died, and again we are not redeemed and have only the example of a good life lived by a good man to follow.

Our Orthodox Christology teaches us that God Himself has come down to enter into our human existence, while remaining without change as God. How comforting this is. We may believe that He knows our frailty because He has shared in the experience of hunger, tiredness and even the fear of death.

"For we have not an high priest which cannot be touched with the feeling of our infirmities; but was in all points tempted like as we are, yet without sin."

But He did not become man simply to extend a sympathetic understanding towards us. Rather in becoming man and living a life of obedience to the will of God he overcame the curse which had afflicted humanity, and in truly experiencing death and overcoming it from within as it were, He has won the right to grant to all those who share

His humanity the grace of the Holy Spirit and a life lived in union with God, if they have faith in Him.

How important an Orthodox Christology is, and how much a right understanding urges us to enter into the life that Christ, the incarnate Word, offers us. We worship no distant God, nor do we follow a good teacher, a prophet perhaps. But we have been made brethren of Emmanuel, God with us, and God in us, and are sons and daughters of God with Him.

What about our own Christology?

What of our own non-Chalcedonian Christology? We are often accused of being Eutychians and denying that Christ is truly man. Yet all that we have considered shows that this is not the case. Perhaps we can read one statement of faith from the non-Chalcedonian Patriarch of Constantinople, Anthimus, written in the 6th century. It describes clearly both the content of our own Christology, and its exact agreement with the Orthodox Christology of St Cyril.

He says….

"I confess that God the Word, the only Son, who was begotten of the Father in eternity, through whom all things were made, Light of Light, living image of the Father and sharing His nature, in the last times became incarnate by the Holy Spirit and of Mary the Virgin, and became a man perfectly without variation and confusion, in everything like unto us except sin; and He remained God immutable, and, when He assumed our attributes, He was not diminished in His Godhead; and that which was derived from us He made His own by dispensation by a natural union. For He who was begotten without time and without a body of God the Father, the same underwent a second birth in flesh, inasmuch as in an ineffable manner He became incarnate of a virgin mother; and, after she had borne Him, she continued in her virginity; and we justly confess her to be the Theotokos, and that He who was born of her in the flesh is perfect God and perfect man, the same out of two natures one Son, one Lord, and one Christ, and one nature of God the Word who became incarnate; and each one of the natures which combined to form an indivisible unity remained without confusion. And so He is very rightly one of the holy and connatural Trinity, both before He took flesh and after He took flesh, and a fourth number was not added to the Trinity; and He is impassible in that He is of the nature of the Father, but passible in the flesh in that He is of our nature. For God the Word did not suffer in His own nature, but in flesh of our nature; and He who personally united this to Himself suffered in our likeness. And Gregory the Theologian defined the matter and called Him impassible in His Godhead, passible in the assumption of flesh. And He is one in the miracles, and also in the passions, and by dispensation He made our passions His own, voluntary and innocent ones, in flesh which was passible and mortal after our nature, endowed with a soul and an intellect, and passible and mortal all the time of the dispensation; for He suffered not in semblance but in reality, and in flesh that was capable of suffering He suffered and died on the cross; and by a Resurrection befitting God He made and rendered it impassible and immortal, and in every way incorruptible, since it came from the union of the womb, which was holy and without sin. While recognising, therefore, the distinction between the elements which have combined to form the unity of nature, I mean between the Godhead and the manhood, we yet do not separate them from one another; also we do not cut the One into or in two natures, nor yet do we confound Him by rejecting the distinction between the Godhead and the manhood, but we confess Him to be one out of two, Emmanuel."

This passage surely shows very clearly that our own Orthodox faith preserves an authentic and Orthodox Christology. Christ is indeed understood in this statement of faith as being God the Word incarnate, as having Himself become man, and as having become truly man, of our own nature, without change.

An Orthodox Christology is the very heart of an Orthodox Faith; and by avoiding the errors of Arius, Nestorius and Eutyches, our Orthodox Church, which includes those of us in the British Orthodox Church, has been preserved from false doctrine and remains truly a source of life in Christ Jesus, the incarnate Word and Saviour of the world.

Eutyches and the Oriental Orthodox tradition

The Oriental Orthodox communion has been regularly and routinely accused of following the teaching of Eutyches, the controversial archimandrite of Constantinople. Historical sources, such as the Catholic Encyclopaedia, conflate the teaching of Eutyches with monophysitism, and then insist that all those who speak of one nature may be indifferently called Eutychians or Monophysites[1]. Of course, this understanding would mean that St Cyril of Alexandria must also be called a Eutychian since he speaks of the 'one nature of God the Word incarnate'. Nor is this a new tendency, since the early opponents of St Cyril also accused him of confusing the Divinity and humanity in Christ[2], and from the beginning of the post-Chalcedonian period those who refused to say that Christ was 'in two natures' were accused of being the followers of Eutyches[3].

Eutyches appears as a monk of Constantinople during the crisis surrounding the first council of Ephesus, held in 431 AD. In the History of the Patriarchs, under the section describing the patriarchate of St Cyril, there is a description of the difficulties which were placed in the way of the Orthodox party sending any information to the emperor and their supporters at Constantinople. The Patrician Candidian had put guards on the roads to prevent any word of the situation reaching the court. In the end St Cyril and his fellow bishops had to disguise a member of their party, and place a message to the emperor inside a

---

[1] Chapman, John. "Eutyches." The Catholic Encyclopedia. Vol. 5. New York: Robert Appleton Company, 1909. 18 Mar. 2009

[2] Bulgakov, S. (2008). *The Lamb of God.* : Wm. B. Eerdmans Publishing. p.756

[3] The Parastaseis Syntomoi Chronikai (Brief Historical Notes) of the 8th century, as just one example, describes the later followers of the Cyrilline position of mia physis as being 'disciples of Eutyches'.

hollow walking stick![4] When the messenger reached Constantinople he gave the message to two monks, Dalmatius and Eutyches, who had contacts in the court and were able to pass the message to the emperor. It would seem that even in 431 AD Eutyches already had important friends.

Eutyches was not a great theologian, and his importance was rather limited to the monastic circle in Constantinople where he was the respected and powerful archimandrite of a monastery outside the city walls. He was the godfather of the eunuch Chrysaphius, one of the most influential ministers in the court of the emperor Theodosius II. Despite his lack of learning he was resolutely opposed to the heresy of Nestorius, and those who thought like him, and considered himself a disciple of St Cyril.

Eutyches becomes more than a minor footnote in monastic history because by 448 AD, a few years after the death of St Cyril and the succession of his archdeacon Dioscorus[5], it was clear that the teaching of Nestorius had not been rooted out. In fact Nestorius was not the chief proponent of this Christology, and was himself a disciple of the much more significant Theodore of Mopsuestia, whom Nestorius, Theodoret of Cyrus, Ibas of Edessa, and others, all considered a great teacher of the Church[6]. By 448 AD Ibas of Edessa was facing great opposition in his own see of Edessa, where he had set about translating the works of Theodore of Mopsuestia into Syriac. Theodoret was restricted to his own see by imperial decree, because he was also attempting to revive the Theodorean Christological position[7].

---

[4] History of the Patriarchs, p. 440

[5] Haas, C. (2006). *Alexandria in Late Antiquity.* : JHU Press. p.316. Dioscorus was an important supporter of St Cyril in his lifetime, but had to deal with the opposition of some of Cyril's family members, who had expected to continue to benefit from their position in the Church.

[6] Ibas describes him as a Doctor of the Church in his infamous Letter to Maris the Persian.

It was clear that the agreement between St Cyril of Alexandria and John of Antioch in 433 AD had not really resolved any of the underlying tensions. Indeed it was interpreted by some, such as Ibas of Edessa, as being the complete reversal of St Cyril's Christology and his acceptance of that of Theodore of Mopsuestia[8]. Theodoret had also written his polemical work, *Eranistes*, possibly directed at Eutyches, but also criticising the Christology of St Cyril. This being the case, it is understandable that the issues should come to the surface again.

One of those flash points was Constantinople. Early in 448 AD Eutyches had written to Pope Leo of Rome advising him that a revival of Nestorianism was taking place. Leo replied to him in a letter which commends Eutyches for his concern about the situation, and promises some action when the details are more fully known[9]. It is thought that Eutyches had accused Domnus of Antioch and Theodoret of Cyrus of being sympathetic to the teaching of Nestorius. Domnus retaliated by writing to the emperor and accusing Eutyches of reviving the heresy of Apollinarius. The emperor appears to have also sensed that there were moves to re-establish the Christology of Nestorius, and he issued instructions to burn the writings of Nestorius, wherever they were found, and to depose Irenaeus, the bishop of Tyre and a close friend of Nestorius.

At the home synod of Flavian of Constantinople, held in November 448 AD, Eusebius of Dorylaeum, who had also been accused by Eutyches of a covert Nestorianism, took the opportunity to openly accuse Eutyches of heresy. Flavian

---

[7] Urbainczyk, T. *Theodoret of Cyrrhus*. (2002). Univ. of Michigan Press. p. 26

[8] Ibas said that opponents of Theodore such as Cyril were 'now teaching the very opposite to their former Doctrine'.

[9] Library of the Nicene and Post Nicene Fathers, Second Series, Vol XII, p. 72

seems to have attempted to counsel a more cautious approach, but Eusebius insisted on pressing his charges, not least because he believed that if he failed he was laying himself open to a counter-charge of false accusation.

Eutyches was accused by Eusebius of having become corrupt and a source of corruption. He refused outright to visit Eutyches to try and come to an agreement, but insisted that the matter be dealt with in the synod without delay. The other members of the synod appear to have criticised Eusebius for lacking respect to his archbishop, but it was agreed that Eutyches should be called to the synod since the charges against him were so grave.

Eutyches was summoned to attend the synod, but was hesitant to do so since it was clearly being dominated by his enemies[10]. First he said that he had made a vow never to leave his monastery; then he pleaded illness. But on the third summons he knew that he must attend or be condemned and so he appeared in person.

The synod began without him though, and in the first sessions some of the letters of St Cyril were read out. Clearly the bishops did not fully comprehend the teaching of St Cyril which they acclaimed, because after reading his letters they then went on to insist that Christ should be 'acknowledged in two natures'. First Basil of Seleucia made such a statement, and then Seleucus of Amasia anathematized anyone who did not say that Christ was 'defined in two natures'[11]. The other bishops present at the synod then agreed to these statements. There is a clear Theodorean tinge to their position. Indeed Eudoxius of Bosporus makes this clear when in his statement he says, 'God.. assumed a perfect man for our salvation'[12]. Everyone present agrees with St

---

[10] Price, R. *Acts of the Council of Chalcedon* (2005). University of Liverpool Press. Vol I, p.26

[11] Price, R. *Acts of the Council of Chalcedon* (2005). University of Liverpool Press. Vol I, p.191

Cyril, but it is not clear that the St Cyril they agree with is being properly represented.

At the beginning of the third session Eusebius asks that the messengers who were sent to call Eutyches should report back to the synod. They reported that Eutyches insisted that since the beginning he had bound himself by a rule that he would never leave his monastery, but treat it as a tomb. Nevertheless he did make several statements. Firstly, and as seems quite clear, Eusebius of Dorylaeum had long been an enemy and was simply seeking to slander him. Secondly, that he was ready to assent to the teachings of Nicaea and Ephesus. Thirdly, that after the incarnation he worshipped one nature in Christ, that of God made man. Finally, that he had never said that the humanity of Christ came down from heaven. He added that he did not find that the fathers spoke of Christ being formed of two natures united hypostatically, and that while he acknowledged Christ as perfect God and perfect man, he could not say that the Word had flesh which was consubstantial with us.

Eutyches was clearly basing his Christology on that of St Cyril, and his understanding of the term 'nature' was in accordance with that of St Cyril and the Alexandrians. Christ is not formed from two natures, when that term is used in the sense of an identity or subject. But his position was certainly weak in regards to denying the double consubstantiality of the Word. He was trying to avoid any idea that the humanity of Christ was a man on its own, but this took him beyond St Cyril, and certainly into ambiguity, even while his intent did not seem to be heretical[13].

At the next session Eusebius reported that Eutyches was circulating a tract around the other monasteries and was

---

[12] Price, R. *Acts of the Council of Chalcedon* (2005). University of Liverpool Press. Vol I, p.197

[13] Perry. Acts of the Second Council of Ephesus (1881)Orient Press p.423

trying to gain support for his position. Eusebius insisted that the synod should send to all of the monasteries and report if Eutyches had contacted them. Even while he was urging this action on the synod the messengers returned who had been to call Eutyches a second time to appear before the bishops.

The brothers of Eutyches' monastery had told the messengers that he was ill, but eventually they were able to give their message to him in person. He repeated his statement that nothing would cause him to leave his monastery save death, although he did wish to read a statement of faith to the messengers which they refused to hear. Then he said that he would send his statement of faith to the bishops.

Eusebius, who does appear a rather unpleasant character even from the sympathetic records of the synod at Constantinople, urged that he be brought to the synod by force and condemned. But the other bishops wished him to have one more chance to appear of his own accord.

At the fourth session some of the Eutychian brethren appeared at the synod, and related that Eutyches had been unwell all night and was unable to appear. Flavian was willing to give Eutyches the weekend to recover, but it is telling that even without an investigation of Eutyches having been conducted he spoke of Eutyches as having led many into error, and of persisting in the wrong. It would seem that he had prejudged the case, and even went so far as to prepare a written condemnation of Eutyches before he had a chance to speak.

Then at the fifth session, because this controversy was taking up many days, Eusebius spoke up again demanding that Eutyches be condemned. He insisted that there could be no defence open to Eutyches. His aim was clearly that Eutyches be deposed, and his opinion was clearly that there was no need for Eutyches to defend himself. Flavian agreed and stated that in his opinion also Eutyches was already liable to deposition for holding opinions contrary to the faith[14]. But unlike Eusebius he wanted him to have one last chance to appear.

Eusebius prepared his case at the sixth session and drew up a list of witnesses he wanted to appear on Monday morning, when Eutyches was finally expected to present himself. While this preparatory session was underway some of those who had previously taken messages to Eutyches were ordered to report other parts of their conversations. The main evidence was that Eutyches refused to say that Christ was from two natures, even though he insisted that Christ was perfect God and perfect man. This again should be understood as reflecting his use of the term 'nature' as an identity or subject and not in the sense of an ousia or underlying substance. It is clear that he did confess that the humanity of Christ was perfect but he did not wish to call it a nature, in the sense of a distinct subject.

Another messenger reported a similar conversation, and added that Eutyches had spoken of the Word made flesh, but did not want to speculate about which nature of Christ had raised humanity to life. Indeed the very words of the messenger again point to a Theodorean perspective. St Cyril would also have rejected saying that one or other natures had saved man. The messenger appeared to have wanted Eutyches to agree that it was the human nature of Christ which saved man, but the very division of natures in Christ in such a way is not Cyrilline at all.

At last the final session arrived and Eutyches did appear before the bishops. It was agreed that the minutes of the previous sessions be read out. When the letter of St Cyril was read out which spoke of Christ being consubstantial with the Father and consubstantial with us, Eusebius could not contain himself. The very last thing he wanted was for Eutyches to agree with what was being read.

---

[14] Price, R. *Acts of the Council of Chalcedon* (2005). University of Liverpool Press. Vol I, p.212

'I have proved him guilty', he shouts out, 'He is convicted already'[15].

Eusebius' great concern was that Eutyches would be able to convince those present that he held to the faith, and would therefore jeopardise his own position. If at all possible he wished to prevent Eutyches from accepting the position presented to him for approval. Flavian agreed that Eutyches was guilty as charged – though he had not yet spoken. And comforted Eusebius with a promise that even if he accepted the faith of the synod he would be still be convicted for his past statements.

Flavian finally questioned Eutyches and asked him if he acknowledged that Christ was a union from two natures. 'Yes, from two natures' Eutyches replies. This is indeed a Cyrilline position, and if he had resisted this previously then it weakened his Christology. Eusebius pressed his own position however and insisted that Eutyches confess two natures after the incarnation, and that Christ is consubstantial with us in the flesh.

Eutyches is unwilling to enter into an argument and asks that his statement of faith be read. Flavian requires him to read it himself, which he then does. His confession is short but worth repeating in full. He says,

'This is what I believe: I worship the Father with the Son, the Son with the Father, and the Holy Spirit with the Father and the Son. I acknowledge that his coming in the flesh was from the flesh of the Holy Virgin, and that he became man perfectly for our salvation'[16].

As far as it goes this statement is Orthodox. It confesses the Trinity, the incarnation of the Son, his

---

[15] Price, R. *Acts of the Council of Chalcedon* (2005). University of Liverpool Press. Vol I, p.218

[16] Price, R. *Acts of the Council of Chalcedon* (2005). University of Liverpool Press. Vol I, p.220

becoming perfectly man of the Virgin Mary. Flavian explores the difficulty which Eutyches had perceived in saying that Christ was consubstantial with us according to his humanity. On this occasion Eutyches is willing to say that the humanity is consubstantial with us because the bishops insist on it. He does explain his reticence, and it lies in the fact that he wishes to say that the perfect and complete humanity of Christ is the body of God the Word rather than the body of another man. When it has been explained to him that to say that the Virgin is consubstantial with us, and that the humanity of Christ is from the Virgin, then it is necessary to say that the humanity is consubstantial with us he is willing to agree.

The discussion then passes to the refusal of Eutyches to acknowledge two natures after the incarnation. He asks the bishops to read the teachings of St Athanasius were they would discover that he did not speak of two natures after the incarnation. The bishop Basil insisted that if he did not accept two natures after the incarnation then he must imply confusion and mixture. Of course St Cyril also refused to speak of two natures after the incarnation and he was not guilty of any confusion of mixture, though he was also often accused of it.

As St Cyril says,

'But who will be thus distraught and unlearned as to suppose that either the Divine Nature of the Word has been turned into what it was not, or that the flesh went over by way of change into the Nature of the Word Himself (for it is impossible)? but we say that One is the Son and **One His Nature** even though He be conceived of as having assumed flesh with a rational soul. For His (as I said) hath the human nature been made, and He is conceived of by us none otherwise than thus, God alike and man'[17].

---

[17] Pusey, P.E. Cyril of Alexandria: That Christ is One. (1881). p.264

At this point many of the bishops started shouting out condemnations of Eutyches, and Flavian rose up to issue the synodal condemnation. He accused him of being riddled with the heresies of Valentinus and Apollinarius, and forthwith deposed him and excommunicated him, and threatened to excommunicate anyone who even spoke to him.

This all seems a little unfair. Eutyches had been willing to go so far as to speak of Christ as being 'from two natures'. He had even accepted that the humanity of Christ could be spoken of as being consubstantial with us. He confessed that the humanity of Christ was 'perfect', and that it was God the Word who had become flesh of the Virgin Mary. Though his earlier statements could be criticised, even condemned, nevertheless during this session the sole issue which remained a point of difference was whether or not Christ could be spoken of as one nature after the incarnation or two.

Since Eutyches had rejected any sense that the humanity of Christ had come down from heaven, and had insisted on its perfection, it seems unreasonable to accuse him of the heresy of Valentinus who denied the physical body of Christ. And since Eutyches insisted on the perfection of the humanity of Christ, there is little basis for accusing him of the heresy of Apollinarius. It would seem that the sole point on which he was condemned was that of speaking of one nature of Christ after the incarnation, rather than two.

If the position of Eutyches, as presented in the hostile minutes of the home synod, still seems to allow him to just about fit into a Cyrilline Orthodoxy, though his earlier position as reported was certainly defective, then it also raises questions about the dyophysite position adopted by Flavian and his synod. Some of the bishops certainly seemed to understand their two nature Christology in an equally unbalanced manner, especially those able to speak of the Word 'assuming a perfect man'.

Immediately Eutyches appealed to Rome, and he clearly hoped that Leo would support him rather than Flavian. He also sent letters to other important figures, not least the emperor himself. His complaint was that the record of events at Constantinople had been doctored and that he had not received a fair trial. He says,

'I read yesterday the minutes concocted by the most devout bishop Flavian against me, and I found it contained in the document things contrary to the proceedings; for neither does it contain what he said to me, nor have they recorded in these minutes what I said'[18].

This had some significant results because the emperor ordered that a hearing be conducted in Constantinople to verify whether or not the minutes published by Flavian were a true record of the events. The official notaries were required to come before the bishops and officials but were very hesitant in producing the minutes as required. One of them says,

'Let him who caused and initiated the investigation of this matter give us an opportunity to justify a decision whether to produce the minutes or not'[19].

What a strange comment from a clerk? Why would he be so concerned about producing what should have been simply the record of the council meeting? The notaries were even accused of using 'delaying tactics', and they expressed their fear of being liable to penalties. Eventually they were instructed to produce the minutes without any further delays.

The reading and discussion of the minutes proceeded with some arguments and minor disagreements over the

---

[18] Price, R. *Acts of the Council of Chalcedon* (2005). University of Liverpool Press. Vol I, p.234

[19] Price, R. *Acts of the Council of Chalcedon* (2005). University of Liverpool Press. Vol I, p.235

record of the messengers conversations with Eutyches. As he had been deposed and excommunicated he was not allowed to be present, but was represented by a small group of monks. Eventually the process reached the record of the more important final session. At this point some interesting, and subsequently important differences between the written minutes and the recollections of those present became known.

For instance, the minutes showed that Florentius, the patrician who had been involved in the synod, had said, 'He who does not say 'from two natures' and 'two natures' is not Orthodox in his beliefs'. But now he insisted that he had said no such thing, and would not have done so because it was a matter of faith. The notaries replied that he had been able to read the minutes before and had never complained, but he interrupted them and asserted that he had never been given the minutes to read, or had them read to him.

Then came the crucial point at which Eutyches had been condemned. Constantine the Deacon, who was representing him, pointed out that the grounds for his deposition were missing from the record. He said,

'The Lord our Archbishop made this demand of him, "Say two natures after the union and anathematize those who do not say it!". It was when he refused to anathematize, saying, "Woe is me if I anathematize the Holy Fathers" that he carried out his deposition.'[20]

This would make much more sense in terms of the condemnation given by Flavian. In the minutes it seemed that Eutyches had gone a long way in agreeing with the synod. But when this final demand is written back into the record it becomes clear that he could never have agreed to it. As St Cyril said, 'We say that the Son is one, and one is His nature'. Flavian and Eusebius were pushing for a position

---

[20] Price, R. *Acts of the Council of Chalcedon* (2005). University of Liverpool Press. Vol I, p.260

that was certainly not Cyrilline in language, and were overturning the fragile agreement of 433 AD by insisting that the continuing dynamic duality of humanity and divinity in Christ must be described as 'two natures' to the exclusion of St Cyril's own language. What did Flavian and Eusebius mean by 'two natures'? Certainly Eutyches understood them as describing a Theodorean unity of two identities, which he could never admit.

At this point in the review bishop Basil also spoke up. He claimed that he had mentioned that St Athanasius also used the phrase 'one incarnate nature of the Word'. Other witnesses remembered that at this point they had recommended that their own statements of faith, recorded in the earlier sessions, should be read out to see if Eutyches was in agreement with them. None of this was recorded in the minutes. The patrician reminded the bishops that even though this had been proposed, the deposition of Eutyches had in fact been read out straight away.

Basil then added to his statement. He remembered that when Eutyches had been unable to confess two natures he had tried to be helpful and had said,

'If you say from two natures before the union but say one nature after the union without qualification, you incur the suspicion of implying confusion and mixture..If you ascribe to God the Word one nature incarnate and made man, you say the same as we and the Fathers'.[21]

Basil said that he had made these comments to try and calm Flavian down, who was obviously himself becoming agitated, and also said that when he had tried to find a way forward Eusebius also became angry with him. It seems that a reconciliation and agreement between Eutyches and the synod was the last outcome which some participants wanted.

---

[21] Price, R. *Acts of the Council of Chalcedon* (2005). University of Liverpool Press. Vol I, p.261

The notary complained that he could not be expected to write everything down, but these missing comments do show rather clearly that the issue was finally whether it was proper to anathematize those who spoke of one nature and refused to speak of two. Much more discussion took place between the bishops, about whether or not Flavian or Eusebius had made this the sticking point, and the bishop Longinus had to declare that during the synod 'those who were at the back didn't know what was going on at the front'.

Finally, Constantine the Deacon complained that after the sentence of deposition had been read out against Eutyches he had appealed to the synods of Rome, Alexandria, Jerusalem and Thessalonica and that this was also not in the minutes. Florentius the patrician remarked that Eutyches had indeed made such a comment to him softly and that it had seemed important enough for him to tell the archbishop Flavian. Basil remembered that Eutyches had mentioned that he would only affirm two natures in Christ if the fathers of Rome and Alexandria ordered him to but he hadn't heard his appeal.

This official review of the minutes, under Imperial instruction, does not change a great deal. It would seem that the issue was entirely whether or not Eutyches would accept two natures after the incarnation, and would anathematize those who spoke of one nature. It also seems clear that the final session was rather uproarious and not all the bishops had a very clear idea of what was taking place. Both Flavian and Eusebius seem to have become heated in their exchanges, and Basil felt the need to try and be conciliatory, a response not very well received by Eusebius.

We are fortunate to also have information about why Eutyches was able to receive this official review of the minutes. When he wrote to the emperor, after the synod, he claimed that Magnus the Silentiary, one of the court officials, who had been sent to accompany Eutyches to the synod, had heard some important matters which should be reported. It is worth quoting Magnus' testimony as it has a bearing on Eutyches' appeal to the other synods.

He said,

'I was sent many times by our most divine and pious master to Archbishop Flavian concerning the presence of the most magnificent and glorious former prefect, former consul and patrician Florentius at the synod which was about to take place in the Episcopal palace of this imperial city. The archbishop postponed it, saying, "There is no need for the same most magnificent former prefect, former consul and patrician Florentius to take the trouble to come here, for a sentence has already been delivered on the case, and the monk Eutyches has been deposed because he did not heed a second summons". They finally brought me a document containing his deposition....I have already said that it was prior to the synod that he showed me Eutyches' sentence of deposition'[22].

This does seem to show that from the beginning it had been the intention of Flavian and Eusebius to condemn, depose and excommunicate Eutyches, whatever he said at the synod. Certainly there was evidence that his Christology was weak, though not necessarily fatally flawed, but at the synod he seemed willing to go most of the way towards accepting some sort of compromise position with the bishops. The sticking point seemed to be that he was not willing to anathematise those who spoke of one nature, since as far as he was concerned this would require him to anathematise St Athanasius and St Cyril.

There was no possibility that the situation could be allowed to rest with the deposition of Eutyches. Flavian had laid down the gauntlet before the whole Alexandrian tradition of St Cyril. In anathematising all of those who

---

[22] Price, R. *Acts of the Council of Chalcedon* (2005). University of Liverpool Press. Vol I, p.268

spoke of one nature he was responsible for re-opening the Christological controversy much more than Eutyches. Flavian was after all the archbishop of the imperial city and his attitudes and actions had an effect across the empire. Therefore after the synod Eutyches was able to gain support for a review of the minutes, and then for a new council, an ecumenical council, to consider the controversy which had broken out into clear view again.

The letters of the Emperors to the Second Council of Ephesus show the concerns which moved the Imperial authority, and what were expected to be the main issues to be dealt with. They were essentially that the matter of doctrine which Flavian of Constantinople had raised against Eutyches be concluded, and that the heresy of Nestorius be finally rooted out of the Church. If some of the Eastern Orthodox have wished to describe the Council of Chalcedon in anti-Eutychian terms only, then it is reasonable to ask that the Second Council of Ephesus be understood as an anti-Nestorian council, and as seeking to complete that elimination of Nestorianism which the First Council of Ephesus wished to see take place, but which circumstances prevented.

This article is not concerned primarily with the Second Council of Ephesus, apart from the reception and restoration of Eutyches. He had already written to the Emperors, and in his letter he insisted that he had not said those things of which he was accused, and that the minutes of the Flavian's Synod had been falsified. The court was already aware that Flavian appeared to have condemned Eutyches even before he had been able to appear before the synod. One of the reasons which the emperors gave for calling the council was to discover exactly what had taken place. The emperor wrote to St Dioscorus, to Leo of Rome, and to other bishops, calling them to assemble at Ephesus so that the whole controversy might be investigated and resolved, and that the Orthodox faith might be confirmed. The emperor also instructed that since there were certain bishops 'said to be infected with the impiety of Nestorius' who were troubling the cities of the East, (and he must mean Ibas and Theodoret, with their supporters), Barsumas, a leading archimandrite from Syria, would also be invited to attend as a representative of the monks of the East.

Eutyches had prepared a written statement of his faith, which was presented to the bishops. He says that from his childhood he had only wished to live a life of quiet, but had been disturbed by the intrigues of others. He declares that he entertained no opinions contrary to the Fathers of Nicaea. Then he writes out the creed of Nicaea into his statement and asserts that he has always held this Faith, and will always hold it. He reminds the bishops that the First Council of Ephesus had canonised the same creed, and had condemned those who should change it. He was even able to state that he held in his hands a copy of the Declaration of the First Council of Ephesus which St Cyril had had sent to him. Then he goes on to denounce publically a list of heretics, naming Manes, Valentinus, Apollinarius and Nestorius, as well as those who say that the flesh of the Lord Jesus descended from heaven.

On the one hand, it would seem clear that Eutyches wishes to be known as being faithful to the Nicaean Faith, and rejecting all heresies and heretics. The fact that he wishes to write out his statement, and that he has wished to have a statement read out at the Home Synod, suggests that he was not comfortable in public speaking, and that it is reasonable to conclude that he was not entirely confident in theological disputation.

On the other hand, Eutyches wants it made clear that his enemies, especially Eusebius of Dorylaeum, had intrigued with Flavian so that he was condemned and deposed even before he had been accused. He writes,

'He called me a contemptible heretic without advancing any specific heresy in his libel, when, suddenly in the altercations of dispute I committed those lapses of the tongue so customary in such confusion and through strong voices, I fell into mistake.'[23]

We find a useful description of Eutyches in this short passage. Not only must he write out his statement to the bishops, but he recognises that he often slips up and makes mistakes when he gets into a theological argument. We can hardly imagine St Cyril describing himself in the same way. The lapses of the tongue might be customary to Eutyches, but this illustrates his lack of ability as a controversial theologian.

Eutyches describes his position several times in his statement as being that of Nicaea and Ephesus. In one sense he is correct, that was his position. The Nicaean creed spoke of Christ as being consubstantial with the Father, and as having been made man of the Holy Spirit and the Virgin Mary. This was exactly what Eutyches confessed. And just has he had not found the creed using the term 'consubstantial with us', so he also hesitated to use it. He has rightly been described as an 'Old Nicaean', although it was a weakness in his Christology not to have embraced the complete terminology of St Cyril, since he claimed to be a disciple of the great Alexandrian.

The Second Council of Ephesus properly begins with St Dioscorus reminding the bishops that the faith had been defined at Nicaea and at Ephesus and that those who went beyond what had been decreed should be excommunicate. The bishops gathered together all agree, 'We all say the same, let him who rejects them be excommunicate'[24]. St Dioscorus wishes these two councils to be the basis of this new council, and he wishes it to be clear that the council has not gathered to define the faith again, but to determine

---

[23] Perry. Acts of the Second Council of Ephesus (1881) Orient Press p.414

[24] Perry. Acts of the Second Council of Ephesus (1881) Orient Press p.419

whether in the present controversy anyone goes beyond the definition of the faith already laid down. St Dioscorus proposed that first of all the transactions from the various meetings in Constantinople be heard, and then the letter of Leo of Rome.

The minutes of Constantinople were then read out, and the bishops at Ephesus found some of the recorded statements disturbing. Those passages which seemed especially troubling were those which have already been referred to such as that of Julius of Cos who confessed two natures in one person, and Eudoxius of Bosporus who had said that the Word had taken a perfect man. The Ephesine bishops began to murmur that those who held such view were at odds with the Fathers. Then the statement by Seleucus was read out in which he said he believed in two natures after the incarnation and excommunicated anyone who thought differently. The bishops started calling out now, and their comments are written into the record.

'Nobody proclaims our Lord to be two after the incarnation - nobody divides that which is indivisible - Nestorius did this'[25].

The council then heard some of the transcript of Eutyches' testimony, especially where he had said that he worshipped one incarnate nature of God, and that the Lord was of two natures before the union but that he confessed one nature after the union. They also heard him affirm the perfect humanity and divinity of Christ. There were undoubted weaknesses, not fatal ones however, in his comments, but the last passage they heard was his confession of one nature after the union, and this resonated with the Cyrilline mood of the council. The members of the council affirmed, 'We all assent to this – yes, all of us'.

---

[25] Perry. Acts of the Second Council of Ephesus (1881) Orient Press p.422

Then the council heard the passages where Eutyches confessed that Christ was 'of two natures', and where Eusebius had insisted that he confess two natures after the incarnation. Many of the bishops cried out at this point. The council had been asked to consider those statements which described Christ as being two natures, and those which described him as one, and they were sure that the Orthodox faith required that the former be rejected, while the latter be affirmed.

The members of the council all cried out together, 'Whoever affirms two natures let him be anathema!'

At this point bishop Basil, hearing his own testimony being read out and criticised, made it clear that he wished to repudiate his earlier language, saying,

'I worship one nature of the divinity of the only, begotten Son, who became incarnate and assumed corporeity'.

Seleucus also spoke up and rejected his previous statement, and anathematized all those who spoke of two natures after the union.

It seems clear that the issue surrounding Eutyches, both at Constantinople and Ephesus, comes down to whether or not it is proper to speak of Christ as two natures, excluding the language of one nature; or as one nature, excluding the language of two natures. It would seem that a bishop such as Basil of Seleucia could find Orthodoxy in Eutyches' insistence on speaking of one nature – as indeed St Cyril did – by drawing attention to the language of 'one nature of the Word made incarnate'. He was also able to repudiate the language of two natures which he used at Constantinople, and use the language of one nature at Ephesus, without seeming to find any great difference in his own understanding of these phrases. What seems important to him is an affirmation of the presence of a real humanity and divinity in Christ.

There is no evidence that any of the other bishops at Ephesus rejected this duality of humanity and divinity in Christ, even though they rejected the use of the concept of two natures, which for them had the Theodorean sense of two identities and subjects. This is made very clear from the statements they make as they give their opinions of Eutyches.

Juvenal of Jerusalem speaks first, and accepting the repeated statement of Eutyches that he follows the definitions of Nicaea and Ephesus proposes that he be restored to his ministry. Then Domnus of Antioch states that he had only signed the deposition of Eutyches when it was sent to him by Flavian because of the documents he had received. Now that he had heard Eutyches assent to the Faith of Nicaea and Ephesus he believed that he should be restored. Stephen of Hierapolis agrees that what he has heard from Eutyches shows that he is Orthodox. John of Massana said that Eutyches had not gone beyond Nicaea and Ephesus. The other bishops then gave similar opinions. Finally Dioscorus also gives his approval to the restoration of Eutyches to his ministry. In all one hundred and thirteen bishops, together with Barsumas representing the monks, agree to Eutyches being restored.

Eutyches is therefore accepted as Orthodox because he accepts the Faith of Nicaea and Ephesus, and for no other reason. His views are not considered a definition of the faith, or as modifying it at all. What matters is that he confesses the faith of Nicaea and Ephesus. The monks of Eutyches' monastery, who have been excommunicated along with him, then present themselves, asking to be released from the discipline laid upon them by Flavian. They also insist that they and Eutyches held to the faith of Nicaea and Ephesus, and that Flavian wished to overthrow it. The monks are required to state their own faith so that it can be understood whether or not they were worthy of such penalties. They state,

'As our religious archimandrite informed your holiness in his plaint, our beliefs accord with the decrees of the holy fathers at Nicaea, which the holy council here confirmed, and we have never conceived or held anything contrary to this creed'[26].

St Dioscorus then questions them more closely and asks,

'Regarding the coming of the Saviour in the flesh, do you believe the same as the blessed Athanasius, the blessed Cyril, the blessed Gregory, and all the bishops?'

The monk Eleusinius replies,

'We believe the same as the holy fathers who met at Nicaea, and those who assembled here'.

St Dioscorus asks again,

'The most devout presbyter and archimandrite Eutyches has sent a document. Do you agree with what he has written? Do you follow his faith?'

The monk insists that he does, that he does not offend against it in any way, and that they all believe the same.

It is on this basis, of receiving the faith of Nicaea and Ephesus, that Eutyches' monastic community is then received back into communion. Dioscorus is clear that it is only with the assent of the bishops that they are released from the penalty which had been placed on them. Just as Eutyches also was restored to his priesthood and monastic leadership only by the assent of the bishops at Ephesus.

Thalassius of Caesarea and several other bishops then suggest that the creed of Nicaea and of Ephesus be read as the substance of their Orthodoxy. These are read out in great detail, together with the writings from the fathers which supported the Orthodox position at Ephesus I, and the

---

[26] Price, R. *Acts of the Council of Chalcedon* (2005). University of Liverpool Press. Vol I, p.295

writings of Nestorius which were condemned. It is interesting that the Greek manuscript tradition of the Acts of Chalcedon in which these minutes are found has removed almost all of the statements made by the various bishops in favour of restoring Eutyches, and all of this review of the documents of Ephesus I, though these have been fortunately preserved in the Latin manuscripts. This allows us to see clearly that the Acts of Chalcedon are not a simple verbatim record of the events, but are themselves an edited text to be used to support the a particular position.

Dioscorus asks whether the bishops are agreed that no-one should go beyond this faith of Nicaea and Ephesus, and one by one the bishops state such things as said, for instance, by Stephen of Ephesus,

'The decrees and definitions of the 318 fathers who assembled in the city of Nicaea are clear, and were confirmed by the ecumenical council that met in the metropolis of Ephesus. Therefore if anyone utters what is contrary to the decrees, let him be anathema, because this is the true and orthodox faith'[27].

Even Julius, representing Leo of Rome, agrees 'The apostolic see holds this'. While Hilary, also representing Leo, says, 'That which has just been read, partly from the creed of those who met at Nicaea and partly that which was confirmed at the holy council held previously at Ephesus, the apostolic see teaches and reveres'.

The rest of the bishops then make it clear that they also hold the same views.

It is necessary to summarise what has been considered so far. Eutyches was found to have certainly expressed himself in an ambiguous manner, but when questioned at Constantinople it seems clear that he confessed the perfect and true humanity of Christ the incarnate Word,

---

[27] Price, R. *Acts of the Council of Chalcedon* (2005). University of Liverpool Press. Vol I, p.342

and did not believe in a humanity come down from heaven. It would also seem clear that Flavian and Eusebius had determined to depose and excommunicate him, even before he appeared before the synod, and that he was excommunicated on the basis that he refused to anathematise those who spoke of Christ as being one nature.

At Ephesus he was restored to his ministry on the basis of his affirming the faith of Nicaea and Ephesus, and then the bishops at the council, including those representing Leo of Rome, and some of those who had been present at the synod in Constantinople, stated very clearly that the basis of the Orthodox faith was that same faith as proclaimed at Nicaea and Ephesus. This is not the place to go on to describe the deposition of Flavian and Eusebius, save to say that the record shows that this was entirely because they were understood as having perverted the doctrines of Nicaea and Ephesus. Indeed during the statements made by the bishops as they condemned Flavian and Eusebius there is no mention of Eutyches.

Of course Flavian did appeal to Leo of Rome, and had already sent letters to him discussing the controversy with Eutyches. These letters were the cause of Leo's Tome which he sent to Flavian. It is necessary to make a few comments about this Tome as it relates to Eutyches. It is clear that Leo failed entirely to comprehend Eutyches' position. When Eutyches said that before the union he confessed two natures, and after the union he confessed one, he was essentially echoing St Cyril, who had said,

'In respect of the elements from which is the one and only Son and Lord Jesus Christ, as we accept them in thought, we say that two natures have been united, but after the union, when the division into two has now been removed, we believe that the nature of the Son is one'[28].

---

[28] Cyril of Alexandria *Select Letters*, 48

Leo of Rome is setting himself against St Cyril when he says in his Tome, against Eutyches,

'It is just as impious to say that the only-begotten Son of God is from two natures before the incarnation as it is unlawful to assert that after the Word became flesh there is one nature in him'[29],

Once again the issue is that the opponents of Eutyches, and now of St Dioscorus, wish to exclude all use of the 'one nature' language, even though it is that of St Cyril. It is not at all clear that Eutyches is being used as anything more than a representative figure of the 'one nature' Christology of St Cyril and of the Alexandrians.

Now it is necessary to consider whether or not St Dioscorus is a Eutychian, and what that might mean. The accusation was raised at Chalcedon by the disturbing character Eusebius of Dorylaeum, who was now intriguing against Dioscorus, as he had against Eutyches. He proposed that even though Eutyches flatly denied that the humanity of Christ was from heaven, he did not clearly say where it did come from – though in fact he did say several times that it was from the Virgin Mary.

This prompted St Dioscorus to state that, 'if Eutyches holds opinions contrary to the doctrines of the Church he deserves not only punishment but hellfire. For my concern is for the catholic and apostolic faith and not for any human being'[30].

Now this has been taken by some as if St Dioscorus was already withdrawing his support from Eutyches[31], but it

---

[29] Price, R. *Acts of the Council of Chalcedon* (2005). University of Liverpool Press. Vol II p.23

[30] Price, R. *Acts of the Council of Chalcedon* (2005). University of Liverpool Press. Vol I p.159

[31] Price, R. *Acts of the Council of Chalcedon* (2005). University of Liverpool Press. Vol I p.159 n.120. Richard Price thinks this shows

is much more consistent with everything else we know of him to read it as simply showing that the controversy was not about Eutyches at all, but about the faith. Eutyches was only accepted at Ephesus II because he affirmed the faith of Nicaea and Ephesus, and it was this same faith which was being assaulted at Chalcedon, as far as St Dioscorus was concerned.

Even after Chalcedon, when the council sent a letter to the Emperor Marcian, they chose to describe St Dioscorus as supporting Eutyches who had said, 'I acknowledge that our Lord Jesus Christ was from two natures before the union, but after the union there is one nature'. Yet we have seen that this is the teaching of St Cyril. St Dioscorus is also accused of having restored Eutyches to his monastic ministry without waiting for a conciliar decree, yet the evidence produced in the minutes of Ephesus II showed clearly that he had waited until the bishops all affirmed that his restoration should take place. Eutyches was already becoming simply a pawn in the Chalcedonian strategy of excluding the Cyrilline language of 'one incarnate nature'.

In exchanges of letters in the following years all those who resist Chalcedon are accused of being followers of Eutyches. Yet this is manifestly false. At Ephesus II Eutyches only featured because in standing up for the one nature of St Cyril he was opposed by those who insisted on the 'two natures' terminology. The bishops present there spent most of their time considering the faith of Nicaea and Ephesus. That of Eutyches was only of importance as it showed itself to be an affirmation of the faith of the fathers. At Chalcedon Dioscorus also made clear that the personal beliefs of Eutyches were irrelevant when it came to the defence of the faith.

---

that Dioscorus was ready to abandon the cause of Eutyches, but it shows no such thing, rather that in the mind of Dioscorus the issue was never about Eutyches, and always about the faith.

In a letter from Leo of Rome to the council members, sent in 453 AD, he speaks of the 'impious teaching of Eutyches and Dioscorus', but by this he can only mean the Cyrilline teaching of 'one incarnate nature' which he showed great difficulty in comprehending. The issues at Ephesus I, Constantinople, Ephesus II and Chalcedon seem to be essentially about the same thing. Whether or not the Cyrilline language of one incarnate nature, or the duality language rooted in the Theodorean tradition, should predominate. Eutychianism, as far as this process is concerned, seems to be defined simply and polemically as a use of the one nature language and the rejection of the two nature language.

St Dioscorus certainly did not doubt the reality of the humanity of Christ. Writing from his exile in Gangra he said,

'No man shall say that the holy flesh, which our Lord took from the Virgin Mary, by the operation of the Holy Spirit, in a manner which He Himself knows, was different to and foreign from our body. And, indeed, since this is so, they who affirm that Christ did not become incarnate for us, give the lie to Paul. For he has said, 'Not from angels did He take (the nature), but from the seed of the House of Abraham'; to which seed Mary was no stranger, as the Scriptures teach us. And again,' It was right that in everything He should be made like unto His brethren,' and that word 'in everything' does not suffer the subtraction of any part of our nature: since in nerves, and hair, and bones, and veins, and belly, and heart, and kidneys, and liver, and lungs, and, in short, in all those things that belong to our nature, the flesh which was born from Mary was compacted with the soul of our Redeemer, that reasonable and intelligent soul, without the seed of man, and the gratification and cohabitation of sleep....For if, as the heretics think, this was not so, how is He named 'our brother,' supposing that He used a body different from ours ? And how, again, is that true which He said to His Father, 'I will declare Thy name to my brethren?' Let us not reject, neither let us despise, those who think in this way. For He was like us, for us, and with us, not in phantasy, nor in mere semblance, according to the heresy of the Manichaeans, but rather in actual reality from Mary, the Theotokos. To comfort the desolate and to repair the vessel that had been broken, He came to us new. And as Emmanuel, indeed, He is confessed; for He became poor for us, according to the saying of Paul, 'that we, by His humiliation, might be made rich.' He became, by the dispensation, like us; that we, by His tender mercy, might be like Him. He became man, and yet He did not destroy that which is His nature, that He is Son of God; that we, by grace, might become the sons of God. This I think and believe; and, if any man does not think thus, he is a stranger to the faith of the apostles.'[32]

If this teaching of St Dioscorus is the same as that of Eutyches then neither may be considered to have departed from the position of Nicaea and Ephesus. But St Dioscorus never defined himself on any occasion as a follower of Eutyches. Even if Eutyches Christology was different, even heretical, then it cannot diminish the entirely Orthodox Christology of St Dioscorus. Nevertheless the name of Eutyches came quite quickly to be associated with a weak Christology and his name gathered up a variety of errors which had already been current both in the time of St Cyril, and even before. The Chronicle of Zachariah, written in the time of St Severus, described a certain John the Rhetor who sought to make a name for himself in Alexandria at the time of the usurping bishop Proterius. This man is accused of failing to confess the natures from which the one Christ appeared, and of sometimes denying that Christ took anything from the Virgin Mary. Certainly this is a defective Christology, and it is given the name of Eutyches, but in fact as we have seen he was always careful to insist that the perfect humanity of Christ was taken from the Virgin Mary.

---

[32] Zachariah of Mitylene, *Syriac Chronicle* (1899). Book 3.

In the time of St Timothy of Alexandria, the proper successor of St Dioscorus, there was a need for him to write against a group of clergy based in Constantinople whom he calls Eutychians. Eventually he excommunicated them from his exile. They had been spreading the report that St Timothy was of their opinion, but in his letter he said,

'Accordingly, let no one, thinking to honour God, insult His mercy by refusing to obey the doctrine of the holy fathers, who have declared that our Lord Jesus Christ is of the same nature with us in the flesh, and is one with His flesh. For I have heard also the holy apostle teaching and saying, 'Forasmuch as the children were partakers of the flesh and the blood, He also (partook of the same) in like manner; that by means of death He might destroy the power of death, who is Satan; and might deliver all who were held in the fear of death, and were subject to bondage, that so they might live forever. For He did not take (the nature) from angels, but He took it from the seed of Abraham. And it was fitting that He should be made in all points like unto His brethren, and that He should be a merciful priest and faithful with God; and that He should make reconciliation for the sins of the people. For in that He suffered being tempted, He is able to succour them that are tempted.' For this expression, 'He was made like us in all points,' teaches all who desire to be meet for the blessings of heaven and to be redeemed, that they must confess the Incarnation of our Lord Jesus Christ as being from Mary the holy Virgin and Theotokos; Christ Who was of the same nature with her and with us in the flesh, and is of the same Nature with the Father in His Godhead' without change God the Word, One Person who became flesh'.

It is also said that when St Timothy was recalled from his exile and stayed in Constantinople, he was able to show that both Nestorianism and Eutychianism were two sides of the same heresy. 'For the one, indeed, making objection declares that it would be a degradation to God to be born of a woman, and to be made in all points like as we are, by becoming partaker of flesh and blood; whereas He was only partaker by identity of name, and by power and indwelling, and by operation. But the other, indeed, for the purpose of liberating and exalting God, so that He should not suffer degradation and contempt by association with a human body, publishes the doctrine that He became incarnate from His own essence, and that He assumed a heavenly body; and that just as there is no part of the seal left upon the wax, nor of the golden signet upon the clay, so neither did there cleave to Christ any portion of humanity whatsoever'.

It would seem that this identification of Eutyches with definite Christological heresy arises during the episcopate of St Timothy. What could this be based upon? Perhaps Eutyches had indeed developed his weak Christology in a more advanced manner and had slipped into a real heresy, although he always seemed to affirm that the humanity of Christ was truly of the Virgin Mary? Perhaps those who followed him and used his name developed the heretical position which St Timothy wrote against? In the time of St Timothy it would not have appeared very important to consider whether Eutyches held the views of those who proposed what seemed a similar Christology. Perhaps Eutyches, like Nestorius, had already become a useful symbol for a particular Christology, irrespective of what he actually believed.

What is clear is that the heretical and defective Christology attributed to Eutyches, which was certainly present in a weak form in his own statements, though without appearing to have gone so far as definite error was never held by St Dioscorus, or St Timothy. Indeed turning to the writings of St Severus we find the same rejection of this false Christology under the name of Eutyches.

In one of his letters he addresses the issue of how Eutyches had come to be received at Ephesus II if he actually held an heretical Christology? On the one hand he explains that the council had only been interested in dealing with those who held the teachings of Nestorius, and taught nothing new with regard to the faith. On the other hand, with the information before them, both the minutes of Constantinople and the petition of Eutyches, there was nothing which was contrary to the faith, even if heresy was hidden in his heart. In another letter he suggests that perhaps Eutyches had 'returned to his vomit'. In some of his other writings St Severus compares Julian of Halicarnassus, who taught that the humanity of Christ was glorified from the moment of the incarnation with Eutyches because he diminished the reality of the humanity of Christ.

This indeed is what the name of Eutyches has come to represent. Any Christology which causes the reality of the humanity of Christ to be minimised in some way. Yet this false Christology has always been condemned by all those who follow the teaching of St Cyril. It plays no part in the Orthodox Christological tradition of those Churches which have rejected the council of Chalcedon. The reason for the rejection of Chalcedon has nothing to do with Eutyches at all, but is entirely to do with the belief that Chalcedon was soft on the error of Nestorianism, and contrary to the Christology of St Cyril. Eutyches has never been considered a saint, his teaching, such as it is, has never been promoted, or transmitted, his error is not very clear. The Church of St Dioscorus, St Timothy and St Severus cannot be considered Eutychian.

Orthodox view of Ibas of Edessa

Introduction

Most modern Byzantine descriptions of the Council of Chalcedon, and its relationship to the Oriental Orthodox, or non-Chalcedonian communion, tend to be based almost universally on the point of view that the Council is beyond criticism, and that the end of any ecumenical activity must result in the Oriental Orthodox accepting the council as Ecumenical. Even those Byzantine and Roman Catholic historians and theologians who are willing to consider Chalcedon with a welcome degree of reflection still tend to describe the Oriental Orthodox objections as being substantially without merit.

But the anathemas which were issued against Chalcedon in the 5th century, and have been briefly considered in a previous article, still stand without any comprehensive or sympathetic response from the supporters of Chalcedon, now divided into the Byzantine and Roman Catholic communities. This particular paper will consider just one of these anathemas in rather more detail than was possible previously. It raises the most interesting case of an Eastern bishop, who had been deposed at the council of Ephesus in 449 AD. for his Nestorianism, was then restored at Chalcedon in 451 AD.

One of the six anathemas of Dioscorus refer to this bishop by name. It is in fact the fourth anathema which says,

Chalcedon is anathematised because it has accepted the communion of the partisans of Nestorius, such as Ibas.

This anathema helps us to see why it is worth spending a little time studying this particular bishop. As far as the non-Chalcedonians have been concerned, he is a representative of the Nestorian way of thinking about Christ, and therefore his acceptance at Chalcedon suggested that the council was soft on that false Christology. The ecumenical dialogue with the various Chalcedonian communities – Roman Catholic and Byzantine – requires that Chalcedon be comprehensively reconsidered, and this must include the historical events which took place there, as well as the documents which it produced.

In many ways the documents are easier to deal with. It is possible to understand even the Tome of Leo in an Orthodox manner, acceptable to our communion, since a document can be understood in a variety of ways. It is likely that we can find an Orthodox meaning to which all parties can agree in good conscience. But an event is perhaps harder to change without becoming guilty of historical revisionism. This short study of Ibas will help us to see how far the history of Chalcedon remains an obstacle to the acceptance of that council as authoritative and ecumenical.

Biography

Ibas, (or Hiba in Syriac), was a priest of the important Roman city of Edessa. The local Christians were particularly impressed by the teachings and writings of Theodore of Mopsuestia, a priest of Antioch, who had become the bishop of Mopsuestia, a town in what is now South-Eastern Turkey. Theodore was himself a disciple of Diodore of Tarsus. These two were particularly concerned to combat the heresy of Apollinarius of Laodicea, who had suggested that the Word of God had united Himself to a human nature in such a way that He took the place of the intelligent soul. Against this error Diodore, and Theodore after him, stressed the complete humanity of the man Jesus, but often in a way which seemed to make him a man separate from God, even while they insisted this was not their intent.

Theodore had written, "The man assumed from us had had such free access [to God] that he became an ambassador on behalf of the whole race, so that the rest of humanity might become partners with him in this special transformation".[33]

This description of the incarnation, suggesting that the Word had assumed a man, had always seemed liable to the objection that it failed to adequately take account of the fact that "the Word became flesh".[34] But its aim was to protect the impassibility of the Divinity from the equally defective Christology of Arius and Apollinarius, who had, for their part, described Christ as being a humanity in which the mind and spirit were not that of man but of God.

Ibas, together with many other Antiocheans and Eastern Christians, found the teachings of Theodore entirely satisfactory. Indeed Ibas became well known even while a priest as a translator of the works of Theodore into Syriac from Greek. He attended the council at Ephesus in 431 AD in the party of John of Antioch, and wrote to a friend afterwards that Cyril of Alexandria and his party had,

"..assented to the Twelve Chapters written by Cyril, just as if they were consonant with, while they are in reality adverse to, the True Faith".[35]

His own bishop, Rabulla, attempted to prevent the spread of Theodore's writings, both banning them and expelling Ibas from Edessa. But because Ibas seems to have had the support of the nobility in the city, he was elected bishop as successor to Rabulla in about 435 AD. He had supported the reconciliation between the Antiocheans under John of Antioch, with Cyril of Alexandria, in 433 AD, but a letter he wrote some time afterwards shows that he understood the reconciliation entirely fromn a Theodorean point of view, and says of Cyril that he and his party,

"have become abashed, apologizing for their folly and teaching the very opposite to their former Doctrine. For

---

[33] Fairbairn, Donald. Grace and Christology in the Early Church. Oxford: Oxford University Press, 2003. p. 43

[34] John 1:14

[35] S.G.F. Perry. Second Synod of Ephesus. Orient Press. 1881. p. 115

no man ventures now to affirm that there is One Nature only of the Divinity and humanity of Christ, but men openly avow the Temple and Him who dwells in it to be the One Only Son Jesus Christ".[36]

This is a description of the incarnation which is completely consistent with the thought of Theodore of Mopsuestia. The use of the phrase 'the Temple' to refer to the humanity of Christ excludes the Cyrilline idea that the Word Himself had become flesh. It is important to note that Ibas was clearly committed to the Christology of Theodore and condemned Cyril's Twelve Chapters against Nestorius[37], even while in the same letter he was able to condemn Nestorius' terminology. Ibas needs to be understood as a disciple of Theodore, not Nestorius, and this even after he considered himself reconciled to Cyril.

Ibas was clearly a bishop who could condemn Nestorius for his terminological excesses, while also venerating Theodore of Mopsuestia as the greatest of theologians, and who could be reconciled with Cyril, while also considering his teaching of the Twelve Chapters, and about the 'one nature' to be unadulterated heresy. It is clear that the rejection of Nestorius and the apparent reunion with Cyril do not preclude a commitment to the false Christology of Theodore.

Proclus, who became archbishop of Constantinople after Nestorius was deposed, mentions Ibas in one of his letters, to John of Antioch, and describes him as a wolf, and as someone who perverts the sense of scripture in order to devour the faithful.[38] He was active as an advocate of the

---

[36] S.G.F. Perry. Second Synod of Ephesus. Orient Press. 1881. p. 119

[37] These were twelve propositions which excluded the defective Christology of Nestorius, but also precluded that of Theodore. For that reason Ibas rejected them and indeed considered them heretical. In 433 AD Ibas was still describing Theodore as 'that preacher of the Truth, that Doctor of the Church'.

teaching of Theodore of Mopsuestia for the whole period between Ephesus I in 431 AD and Ephesus II in 449 AD.

Finally, in about 448 AD, some of his own clergy sought to bring the content of his preaching, and a number of administrative and moral irregularities at Edessa, to the attention of Domnus, the successor of John at Antioch. They found themselves summarily excommunicated. Further complaints taken to Constantinople led to an enquiry, but this seems to have been intended simply as a means of resolving the conflict at Edessa, not dealing with the charges themselves.

Eventually dissent became so vocal, with large numbers of citizens voicing their opposition to Ibas, from many different community groups, that the civil authorities had to take notice, and he found himself detained while his teaching was examined.

Ibas and the Second Council of Ephesus

During this same period there was also a controversy raised concerning the Christological opinions of Eutyches, the aged and famous archimandrite of a monastery in Constantinople. He had been accused of teaching that the humanity and Divinity of Christ were confused, and at a local synod he had been deposed by his bishop, Flavian.

Eutyches insisted that he had been misrepresented and that he was in fact only professing the unity of subject in Christ which was the teaching of Cyril. He was certainly powerful enough to be able to complain to the emperor, to Pope Leo of Rome and to Dioscorus of Alexandria, the successor to Cyril.

The confused situation of the times seemed to demand an ecumenical council to settle the various controversies. Thus, despite the resistance of Leo, a council

---

[38] Nicholas Constans. Proclus of Constantinople and the Cult of the Virgin in Late Antiquity. Brill 2003. p. 113

was called to gather at Ephesus in 449 to consider the case of Eutyches and Flavian, and of importance for this study, in the second session it took time to review the status of Ibas of Edessa.[39]

The council had received a letter from the Emperor which drew attention to the reports which were being made from the people at Edessa about their bishop Ibas. There were also monks from the East who had been instructed to attend the council by the Emperor. They bore letters from the Emperor which describe 'certain bishops of that land who, infected with the impious tenets of Nestorius, have rendered themselves infamous..'[40]

This can only refer to Ibas, Theodoret and those who held their opinions. It is clear that the opinions of these bishops were not simply privately and discretly held, but on the contrary were notorious for being in sympathy with that of Nestorius. The investigation of Ibas at this council was not simply a matter of ecclesiastical intrigue but was required by the public controversy which their teachings provoked.

The bishops Photius, Eustathius and Uranius were asked to report on their own investigations into Ibas. They briefly referred to the great commotion which had been evident in Edessa over the previous year and stated that after their investigation into Ibas they had refused to be in communion with him.[41]

At this point the official records of the recent events in Edessa which had led to Ibas' arrest began to be read. A civil investigation had been ordered by the Emperors and this was conducted by Chaireas, the Civil Governor of the region of Osrhoene, in which Edessa was situated. His visit

---

[39] The record of this second session is found in S.G.F. Perry. Second Synod of Ephesus. Orient Press. 1881.

[40] S.G.F. Perry. Second Synod of Ephesus. Orient Press. 1881. p. 39

[41] S.G.F. Perry. Second Synod of Ephesus. Orient Press. 1881. p. 43

to Edessa began on April 12th, 449, just a year after the investigation of the three bishops mentioned above had concluded at Tyre, in February 448. There was still no peace in Edessa.

Indeed on his arrival the Governor was greeted by crowds of Edessans shouting out acclamations, as was their custom. This was not a mob, but rather one of the normal means of ordinary people making sure that their opinions were heard.

Among the praises offered to the Emperor were repeated criticisms and condemnations of Ibas.

"All of us are of one mind – nobody accepts Ibas. No man wants a Nestorian bishop"

"No man wants the enemy of Christ"

"An Orthodox bishop for the Metropolis – let Ibas take his departure"[42]

Of course it is the case that supporters of Ibas might well have wished to stay away from such a crowd, but these acclamations, and the others like them, are taken from official, not Church records, and certainly show that there was a significant proportion of the population who were offended by what they understood as Ibas' Nestorian sympathies.

A couple of days later the Governor held a meeting in the Council Chamber to which various clerics, monks and vowed people came to present depositions in writing. But the record shows that workmen and inhabitants of the city again came to make their voice heard, and having been admitted they shouted out their views which were duly recorded.

"No one accepts Ibas as bishop"

"No man wants a depraver of Orthodoxy"

---

[42] S.G.F. Perry. Second Synod of Ephesus. Orient Press. 1881. p. 49

"Ibas alone has robbed the Church"

"Ibas has corrupted the faith of Ephesus"[43]

"Ibas has carried off possessions that are the common property of all"[44]

Some of these acclamations have reference to the accusations made against him over the previous year that he had used Church property for his own ends, and had preferred his own family and friends. Other refer clearly to the apparently widespread opinion that he was opposed to the Orthodoxy of the First Council of Ephesus and of Cyril of Alexandria.

There are a great many of these acclamations, all duly recorded in the official minutes.

Chaireas had felt obliged to report to his consular superiors, and therefore at this point in the proceedings of the Second Council of Ephesus his letter to them is read into the record. Chaireas describes how all of the priests, together with the leaders of the monks and wise-men,[45] had gathered to ask him to consider a petition which had also been signed by various tradesmen and even labourers.

The petition states that Ibas had been respected for many years as a bishop even when it became clear that he had maladministered the property of the Church. But on his being accused of heresy, and the proof of his opinions being found in the testimony of many witnesses, and even in the letters which Ibas had written to Persia, then it was necessary for the clergy and people of Edessa to reject him. In fact the people of Edessa have to go further and petition

---

[43] That is the first council of Ephesus in 431, at which Nestorius was condemned and the Christology of Cyril accepted as the measure of Orthodoxy.

[44] S.G.F. Perry. Second Synod of Ephesus. Orient Press. 1881. p. 51

[45] Possibly various officers in the educational communities which were present in Edessa.

that Ibas not be allowed to invoke the military power of the Empire to force himself upon the city.

An even larger group of citizens are recorded as having subscribed to this petition. They include the Clergy, the Archimandrites, the Monks, the Vowed Brethren, the Municipal Authorities, the Roman Officials, the schools of the Armenian, Persian and Syrian communities, as well as the Artizans.

As the official record states, "Every person, with his own hand, subscribed and assented to these transactions and to the presentation of the petition."[46] Even if this is an exaggeration, it does seem clear that the vast majority of the population considered Ibas to be an heretic, and wished themselves rid of him.

The whole city was then in uproar for three or four days while the people persisted in making acclamations against Ibas. Chaireas was in rather a difficult situation since he felt that he could not continue to trouble the Imperial authorities with the problems in Edessa, not least because we can imagine that it would have reflected badly upon his abilities as Governor of the region. With this in mind, and since the clergy seemed united in wishing some resolution to the turmoil then overwhelming the city, he decided to proceed with a further examination of the case of Ibas so that he could report more fully to his superiors. This second enquiry is now read at the Second Council of Ephesus.

This second enquiry seems to have been forced after the local civil leader, Count Theodosius, together with the Governor, Chaireas, had to come to the cathedral to settle the population of the city who had gathered there for the Liturgy. Theodosius had to promise that the charges against Ibas would be made public, and so the clergy, monastics and community leaders gathered before Chaireas again to hear the substance of the accusations made public.

---

[46] S.G.F. Perry. Second Synod of Ephesus. Orient Press. 1881. p. 67

Count Theodosius entreats Chaireas to put an end to the tumult in the city which "the accusation made against Bishop Ibas, in the city of Berytus[47], has occasioned, through which the people have learned that he has uttered a host of blasphemies, and that he has committed many acts subversive of the laws and adverse to the christian faith."[48]

Once again a long list of clergy, civil leaders and citizens append their names or speak out publically in support of the request for some action to be taken immediately. Finally, after a week of unrest, the investigation gets under way and the original accusers of Ibas are called to give testimony. These were the priests Samuel, Maras and Cyrus. Samuel is their spokesman and he gives a detailed account of what had taken place, from his point of view, during the previous investigations of Ibas' teachings and behaviour.

He accuses Ibas of 'everywhere scattering gold' so that it was almost impossible to get their complaints heard, and it would appear that even the minutes of the meetings held with the bishops Photius, Uranius and Eustathius were being kept secret. There seems to have been a consistent desire to sweep the whole problem of Ibas under the carpet.

Samuel the priest described how at the very beginning the dispute was taken to Domnus of Antioch, the senior bishop of the See, but that after they had testified about many points he simply sent them away without taking any action at all. So they had to go to the capital and present their complaint before Flavian, the archbishop of Constantinople, and the Emperor Theodosius. Samuel

---

[47] This was the investigation conducted by the three bishops Uranius, Photius and Eustathius in 448, and which took place in Berytus and Tyre. Although accusations were made against Ibas it seems the bishops had the objective of trying to prevent scandal and discord rather than investigate Ibas' Christology.

[48] S.G.F. Perry. Second Synod of Ephesus. Orient Press. 1881. p. 90

repeats before Chaireas the same charge which he laid before Flavian.

Ibas had said,

"I do not envy Christ becoming God, for in so far as he has become God I have become so, for he is of the same nature as myself."

This rather clearly suggests that he maintained the views held by Theodore of Mopsuestia, that Christ was a human subject, apart from the divine Word, who became God in some sense. It would seem that Ibas dealt with this criticism by excommunicating those who objected to his teaching, and then claimed that as excommunicates they could not testify against him. A rather clever ploy that allowed him to avoid being investigated. Indeed at the enquiry in 448 he had objected to all those clergy from Edessa who came to testify against him by claiming that they were excommunicates or associated with excommunicates. It is no wonder that Ibas had not been found guilty of heresy previously, if he had managed to silence all those who had anything relevant to testify.

Things were rather different during the inquiry under Chaireas however, and all those who could throw light on the controversy surrounding Ibas were invited to speak. Many priests, deacons, monks and vowed persons now did just that.

Many repeated that they had clearly heard Ibas say,

"I do not envy Christ's becoming God; for I am become so no less than he, since he is of the same nature as my own."[49]

Or reported that they had heard him say,

---

[49] S.G.F. Perry. Second Synod of Ephesus. Orient Press. 1881. p. 101

"That God the Word, in His foreknowledge, knew that Christ would justify himself by his works, and therefore dwelt in him."[50]

This is an equally Theodorean description of Christ as a man in whom God the Word dwelt. Another Theodorean type of statement used by Ibas was,

"In the beginning was the Word, but Matthew the Evangelist has said – The Book of the Generations of Jesus Christ, the Son of Abraham, the Son of David – is not the former one thing and the latter quite another?"[51]

Others reported hearing him dismiss the idea of Hell as a figure of speech used to threaten people, and said that he had copies of the works of Nestorius, and that he had said in the Church during a homily that the Jews had only crucified a mere man.[52]

One witness, John, a vowed person, testifies most clearly to the essentially Theodorean foundation of Ibas' teaching in this period just before the Second Council of Ephesus and that of Chalcedon, when he reports,

"I heard Ibas, when expounding in Church, say:- 'It was one person who died, and another who was in heaven, and that was one person who was without beginning, and that was another perdon who is subject to a beginning; and he was one person who is of the Father, and he was another who is of the Virgin."[53]

This is the Christology of Theodore, Nestorius and clearly also that of Ibas. Many other clergy continue to give their own recollections of things which Ibas had said which had troubled them, and which they had not been able to

---

[50] S.G.F. Perry. Second Synod of Ephesus. Orient Press. 1881. p. 101

[51] S.G.F. Perry. Second Synod of Ephesus. Orient Press. 1881. p. 104

[52] S.G.F. Perry. Second Synod of Ephesus. Orient Press. 1881. p. 105

[53] S.G.F. Perry. Second Synod of Ephesus. Orient Press. 1881. p. 106

raise in public before, for fear of joining those who had so spoken and been excommunicated.

The Count Theodosius, one of the local civil leaders, asks that all of these testimonies be forwarded to the Imperial authorities, and to the Archbishops of Constantinople, Alexandria and Antioch. But he also asks that Ibas' letter to Maris the Persian also be read into the official record and placed among the Acts of the investigation being conducted by Chaireas.

This letter to Maris has been mentioned before. It is most important as showing the substance of Ibas' opinions after he had apparently entered into union with Cyril of Alexandria. This reconciliation is often taken by writers of the Eastern Orthodox Church as showing that there was a unanimity in the Church based on a balanced reading of Cyril's Christology. But a few brief excerpts from the letter will allow us to conclude that Ibas was, and remained to this period just before the council of Chalcedon, a determined supporter of Theodore of Mopsuestia and an opponent of the substance of Cyril of Alexandria's Christology.

The main points to concern us in this brief consideration of Ibas are that,

i. He is able to condemn both Nestorius and Cyril for uttering blasphemous statements. The one because he rejected the phrase 'Mother of God', and the other for saying that 'God, the Word, became man'.

ii. He describes the Twelve Chapters which Cyril had written to Nestorius as being impious and contrary to the True Faith.

iii. He uses the Theodorean concept of Christ being the 'Temple' in which God dwells.

iv. He warmly praises Theodore of Mopsuestia as being a Doctor of the Church.

v. He describes Cyril as having abandoned his errors and having now accepted the Christology of Theodore, speaking of 'the Temple and Him who dwells in it'.[54]

Now all of these points represent the opinion of Ibas *after* he had been 'reconciled' with Cyril of Alexandria. It is abundantly clear that his perception of this reconciliation is one in which Cyril has abandoned his Christology and that of Theodore has been adopted by all. This letter was written in about 433. It allows us to see that at the First Council of Ephesus in 431 Ibas had been a disciple of Theodore of Mopsuestia, and that in 433 he remained a disciple of Theodore. His other spoken comments, testified to by a great many clergy from Edessa, as well as the statements of important bishops such as Proclus of Constantinople, and the fact that Ibas had been exiled from Edessa by his bishop Rabulla, all demonstrate that he never ceased to be a disciple of Theodore, and at the time of this present investigation before Chaireas, and during the Second Council of Ephesus in 449, there was no evidence at all that he had changed his Christological opinion.

Perhaps it will be suggested that Ibas might not have been the author of this letter, and that it had been associated with him simply out of mischief and a desire to do his reputation some damage. But this was also considered by the inquiry we are examining. When the presiding judge asked that those who had been present at the preceding and rather neutered investigation should certify if this letter had been acknowledged by Ibas a number of clergy stepped forward and made statements such as,

"I was there at Berytus when Ibas owned in my presence that the letter was his, by saying – 'I acknowledge it

---

[54] S.G.F. Perry. Second Synod of Ephesus. Orient Press. 1881. p. 116-119

to be so' – and I have believed this to be the case up to the present day, and if the Emperor were to decree and order me to be cut in pieces, I should still believe it to be so."[55]

After other clergy had testified in a similar manner, the Governor Chaireas brought these considerations of Ibas to a close and promised to forward all of the materials to the Imperial authorities, as Count Theodosius and the great crowd of the people had been urging.

This brings us back to the events at Ephesus in 449. The case of Ibas was being discussed because of the investigation held under Governor Chaireas and because of the uproar against Ibas which had taken place in Edessa once his views became public.

Once his written and spoken opinions had been read out before the council of bishops there was no excuse found for him. He was unworthy of the episcopate, indeed he should be excommunicate since his opinions were contrary to the faith of the Church.

Dioscorus spoke first, saying,

"Ibas, who has estranged himself from the honours of the episcopate by those such great impieties on which he ventured and by those unmeasured statements contrary to the truth of the nature of our Redeemer which he has advanced, has brought upon himself .. condemnation."[56]

Others were more than willing to make the same judgement. Indeed the words of Ibas himself left the bishops no other option. He had exalted Theodore and condemned Cyril. He had confessed the Temple and he who dwelt in him.

Juvenal of Jerusalem, Thalassius of Caesarea, Stephen of Ephesus, one by one the bishops give their opinions.

---

[55] S.G.F. Perry. Second Synod of Ephesus. Orient Press. 1881. p. 121
[56] S.G.F. Perry. Second Synod of Ephesus. Orient Press. 1881. p. 134

Eustathius of Berytus, one of those who had been part of the investigation at Tyre-Berytus in 448, states that,

"Ibas has given proof that he agreed with, if he did not precede, Nestorius, and has become a teacher of that impious heresy."[57]

This is indeed the only conclusion that a reading of the material gathered by Charieas could allow. One by one the bishops speak out, making the same judgement, until Dioscorus asks that the rest of the bishops should show whether they agree with what had been decided. The Acts of the Council show that the bishops indicated by various comments that indeed they did agree,

"The same things all of us say – this is the decision of us all – all of us reject him."[58]

Now what do all of these proceedings over the period of 448-449 tell us? Certainly we do not need to insist that all of the clergy and people at Edessa had turned against their bishop. Nor that all the bishops at Ephesus were entirely happy with the deposition of Ibas. But it does seem clear, not least because much of the evidence used in the final judgement was determined at a civil enquiry, that Ibas was and remained a follower of Theodore of Mopsuestia. Though he had been able to use various machinations to prevent his Christology coming under too strict an investigation, in the end, as the bishops decided, it was his own views which judged him unworthy of the episcopate.

Ibas and the Council of Chalcedon

Now if matters had remained as the Council of Ephesus in 449 left them, then Ibas' successor at Edessa, Nonnus, would have remained in undisturbed possession of his see. Ibas would have been no more than a less well known heretic of the same sort of views as Nestorius.

---

[57] S.G.F. Perry. Second Synod of Ephesus. Orient Press. 1881. p. 137

[58] S.G.F. Perry. Second Synod of Ephesus. Orient Press. 1881. p. 145

But when the emperor Theodosius fell from his horse and died, his sister Pulcheria abandoned her vows as a nun, and took the aged general Marcian as her husband, making him emperor. These two were much less inclined to support the Christology of Cyril over that of Leo and the Eastern bishops, and so at their council of Chalcedon the restitution of Ibas was one of the matters which was placed on the agenda.

Ibas approached the council and insisted that he had not been found guilty of any heresy, and that bishop Uranius had contrived that certain clergy should be assembled to accuse him. This argument does not bear much weight. If Uranius had contrived to assemble Ibas' accusers at Tyre-Berytus then why did he and his fellow investigating bishops not allow any of them to testify at that investigation? Likewise, if Uranius had desired above all to see the deposition of Ibas then why did his enquiry allow Ibas to make various promises about his future behaviour and essentially allow him to avoid any theological questions?

The main request which Ibas presented to Chalcedon was that,

"all the proceedings at Ephesus in my absence be declared void and that my rights be respected since I have been found guilty of nothing."[59]

This was an entirely disingenuous argument. Of course he had been found guilty of both heresy and mismanagement of his see. Both in the investigation under Chaireas, and then at the council of Ephesus in 449. No wonder he wanted the investigation at Ephesus to be declared void, since it was at that council that the material was presented which showed he was a disciple of Theodore of Mopsuestia.

---

[59] Richard Price and Michael Gaddis. The Acts of the Council of Chalcedon. Translated Texts for Historians. Vol 45. Liverpool University Press. Vol III. p. 260

The Roman legates at Chalcedon took the lead and asked that the judgement of the proceedings which had taken place at Tyre-Berytus be read. Ibas had a copy conveniently to hand.

The judgement hardly clears Ibas from the condemnation which was imposed on him at Ephesus and which represented the opinion of the clergy and people at Edessa. The bishops Uranius, Photius and Eustathius appear to have been pleased that Ibas declared himself willing to anathematise Nestorius publically in his own city, accept the faith contained in the letter of reconciliation between Cyril and John of Antioch, and to accept the substance of the council of Ephesus in 431.

In actual fact we have already shown from the letter of Ibas to Maris the Persian that it was entirely possible for Ibas to condemn Nestorius and accept the reconciliation with Cyril, according to his own erroneous interpretation of that reconciliation, while all the time being a committed disciple of Theodore of Mopsuestia and his Christology. There is also no evidence whatsoever that Ibas ever followed through in his promises and anathematised Nestorious in public at Edessa or showed any inclination to change his opinion of Cyril's teaching.

This being so, the judgement at Tyre-Berytus was worthless. It had, as the council of Ephesus in 449 showed, entirely failed to address his theology, and was no more than an attempt at a white-wash.

After the reading of this weak judgement the Roman legate Paschasinus asked that the council express its will concerning Ibas. We read in the Acts that "all the most devout bishops remained silent."[60]

---

[60] Richard Price and Michael Gaddis. The Acts of the Council of Chalcedon. Translated Texts for Historians. Vol 45. Liverpool University Press. Vol III. p. 264

It was just impossible for the bishops to swallow the idea that Ibas should be exonerated. Many of them had been at Ephesus a couple of years earlier and had heard the wider evidence against him. The 'most magnificent officials' declared that the council would give its opinion the next day. His reputation as a disciple of Theodore preceded him and undoubtedly there was a need for a busy night to convince the bishops that Ibas should be restored. It certainly was not their opinion at the end of the first session concerning him.

The second session appears to have been well stage-managed.[61] It begins with Ibas reminding the bishops that he had not been able to defend himself at Ephesus. This allowed the bishops to declare that all of the proceedings at Ephesus against Ibas should be annulled. There then followed a suggestion by Patricius of Tyana that the judgement of Photius and Eustathius should be accepted, the weak judgement which failed to investigate his Christology. The Eastern bishops of Antioch were happy to accept this, since it also meant that there would be no theological judgement required.

A small group of accusers of Ibas were allowed to enter the council. The charge that Ibas had said that he did not envy Christ becoming God was repeated. Photius, one of the bishops who had been happy to exonerate Ibas in 448, insisted that since Ibas swore he had not said anything like this, and seeing that those who had come to accuse him were all excluded, he must be innocent. Therefore the basis for their positive judgement is seen to be entirely based on the statement of Ibas himself that he was innocent, and on the exclusion of anyone who said anything different.[62]

---

[61] Richard Price and Michael Gaddis. The Acts of the Council of Chalcedon. Translated Texts for Historians. Vol 45. Liverpool University Press. Vol III. p. 274

[62] Price notes that the accusers of Ibas had been excommunicated in an attempt to prevent them appearing against him. He seems to

The Acts of the proceeding at Tyre-Berytus were now read up to and including the letter of Ibas to Maris the Persian. We have already seen that it clearly shows that Ibas was a Theodorean. Price also detects omissions in the Acts of Chalcedon at this point which seem to serve to suppress any discussion of this controversial letter.

After the letter had been read, the 'magnificent officials' suggested that the proceedings of Ephesus in 449 be read out so that there would be a complete account of all of the circumstances in which Ibas was concerned. But these damaging documents, which must have made his true opinions public, were not even to be mentioned! The Roman legates insisted, "it is clearly pointless to read out the proceedings there...the proceedings there have been made null by the most blessed and apostolic bishop of the city of Rome."[63]

Of course it is interesting that Leo of Rome considered that he had the authority on his own to set aside a council of the Church. But it is also clear that there was no desire at Chalcedon to investigate the teaching of Ibas. On the contrary, anything that might seem liable to condemn him appears to have been simply written out of the historical record. Once the bishops had decided that nothing which took place at Ephesus in 449 should be considered at all, then there seemed nothing standing in the way of Ibas being restored to his see.

Paschasinus and Lucentius, with Boniface, speak first on behalf of Leo of Rome. We have already seen that Leo considered that he had the authority to make binding decisions for the whole Church. They speak with his authority and say,

---

have used this ploy several times.

[63] Richard Price and Michael Gaddis. The Acts of the Council of Chalcedon. Translated Texts for Historians. Vol 45. Liverpool University Press. Vol III. p. 303

"from the reading of his letter we have found him to be Orthodox."[64]

This is an important judgement. The representative of the Roman See, giving a judgement on behalf of Leo, and concerning which Leo never shows any objection, say that they have read Ibas' letter to Maris the Persian and after having read it they conclude that he is Orthodox!

Anatolius, archbishop of Constantinople, speaks next and says,

"the reading of all the accompanying material prove the most devout Ibas innocent of the accusations brought against him."[65]

Then Maximus of Antioch speaks, and he also states clearly that he has heard what has been read, including his letter to Maris, and,

"from what has just been read it has become clear that the most devout Ibas is guiltless of everything charged against him; and from the reading of the transcript of the letter produced by his adversary his writing has been seen to be Orthodox."[66]

So the representatives of the great Sees of Rome, Constantinople and Antioch all agree that having read the letter of Ibas to Maris the Persian they believe that this shows him to be Orthodox. Does it not also show that they consider their own Orthodoxy to be in accord with the letter if Ibas to

---

[64] Richard Price and Michael Gaddis. The Acts of the Council of Chalcedon. Translated Texts for Historians. Vol 45. Liverpool University Press. Vol III. p. 305

[65] Richard Price and Michael Gaddis. The Acts of the Council of Chalcedon. Translated Texts for Historians. Vol 45. Liverpool University Press. Vol III. p. 306

[66] Richard Price and Michael Gaddis. The Acts of the Council of Chalcedon. Translated Texts for Historians. Vol 45. Liverpool University Press. Vol III. p. 306

Maris the Persian? What does that mean in terms of the Orthodoxy of Chalcedon? Surely it requires that all of the statements of that council be read with the Christology of the letter to Maris in mind. The letter which considers the Christology of Cyril to be heresy, and the teaching of Theodore of Mopsuestia to be Orthodox.

Even at this point in the session there were still bishops who were not convinced by this very impressive display of support for the erstwhile bishop of Edessa. They cried out demanding that he anathematise Nestorius. Of course we already know that Ibas is happy to anathematise Nestorius, even while he remains a disciple of Theodore. Nothing has changed. The anathema against Nestorius has no value if it is made by one who continues to follow Theodore.

Worse than that, at the same time he also anathematises all those who say 'one nature', and the council accepts this statement, and the one against Nestorius as being enough to prove his Orthodoxy.

But if we turn briefly and for a final time to the letter to Maris, which has just been read at Chalcedon, then we find that the anathema against those who speak of 'one nature' includes Cyril and his Christology. For Ibas had written,

"Cyril wrote the Twelve Chapters..asserting that there is one nature of the Godhead and manhood of our Lord Jesus Christ... No one now dares to say that there is one nature of Godhead and manhood but they profess belief in the temple, and the one who dwells in it."[67]

It is clear that Ibas, in this final jibe at the session which exonerated him, has in mind not only Eutyches but Cyril himself. It was, after all, Cyril who had been his

---

[67] Richard Price and Michael Gaddis. The Acts of the Council of Chalcedon. Translated Texts for Historians. Vol 45. Liverpool University Press. Vol III. p. 296

opponent for the past decades, not Eutyches. It was Cyril who had taught the 'one nature' of Christ, and whom Ibas considered mired in heresy until he accepted the teaching of Theodore.

Ibas and the Rejection of Chalcedon

At the beginning of this paper we considered the anathema issued against Chalcedon by Dioscorus in 451. It said,

Chalcedon is anathematised because it has accepted the communion of the partisans of Nestorius, such as Ibas.

Perhaps we are now better placed to see that there is weight in this argument. Ibas was well known in the decades between Ephesus in 431 and Chalcedon in 451, as a disciple of Theodore of Mopsuestia and his heretical Christology. He was quite able to condemn Nestorius while remaining a committed follower of Theodore. He was also quite able to enter into communion with Cyril on the false assumption that Cyril had abandoned his 'one nature' Christology, and Ibas always considered this 'one nature' or 'mia-physis' Christology to be heresy.

He appears to have been reasonably condemned at Ephesus in 449 on the basis of a civil investigation at Edessa which seems to have been conducted in an unbiased fashion by the Governor of the region whom we may conclude acted in a neutral manner. These investigations, and his own written and spoken words, were and are clear enough evidence that he was, as all knew him to be, a disciple of Theodore, and therefore a 'partisan of Nestorius', who was equally a disciple of Nestorius.

At Chalcedon it is clear that the Roman representatives of Leo had already determined his innocence. By excluding the negative evidence against him the council hoped that it would be reasonably easy to restore him to his see. Why allow the letter of Ibas to Maris to be read? Surely because it was considered positive not negative evidence in the case. The representatives of the three leading Sees all stated in their judgements that they and read the letter and after reading the letter concluded that Ibas was Orthodox.

This seems evidence that their Orthodoxy was the same as that of Ibas and his letter. There was nothing which Ibas said at Chalcedon which changes in even the smallest point the position which he had presented in his letter. The anathema against Nestorius does not preclude his continuing as a Theodorean, and his anathema against those who speak of 'one nature' excludes his being in any sense a Cyrilline.

It seems entirely reasonable to criticise Chalcedon as having accepted the partisans of Nestorius such as Ibas. In their haste to reject all that had taken place at Ephesus in 449, the way was opened for those whom Ephesus had rightly condemned to find a place in the Church.

The Orthodox Christology of St Severus of Antioch

St Severus of Antioch is one of the great Fathers of the Oriental Orthodox Churches. In the decades after the Council of Chalcedon in 451 AD it was he, more than any other theologian, who expressed most forcefully and clearly the Orthodox Christology of the Oriental Orthodox Churches. He grew up in the confused environment of the Church produced by Chalcedon and intermittently exacerbated by imperial persecution of those who rejected the decisions of that council. Yet despite his opposition to Chalcedon he always remained as tolerant and irenic as possible, being willing even to accept the phrase 'in two natures' as long as the union of Divinity and humanity in Christ was confessed. Yet the Eastern Orthodox have accused St Severus of being both a Nestorian and a Eutychian and the latter Eastern Orthodox councils have anathematised him together with St Dioscorus.

The actual teachings of St Severus have become unjustly obscure, both among the Eastern Orthodox and even the Oriental Orthodox, who should value him more. Yet his manifest reliance and dependence on the teaching of St Cyril of Alexandria, and the clarity of his thought, should make him a useful exemplar of the Christology of the Oriental Orthodox. The Christological teachings of the Eastern Orthodox are widely known and published, but in this time of ecumenical dialogue it seems that most of the Oriental Orthodox Christology that Eastern Orthodox learn is derived from second-hand and erroneous accounts that twist and distort what Oriental Orthodox have always believed. The teachings of St Severus, answering many of the same objections as are heard today, are an antidote to such misinformation and promote the dialogue between the Churches.

St Severus was born in Sozopolis in Pisidia in 465 AD. He came from a wealthy family and was sent to Alexandria to study. He continued his studies in Beirut where he came under the influence of a group of Christian students. He began to study the writings of Sts Gregory of Nazianzen and Basil and at some time in this period he was baptised.

After his baptism his outlook became increasingly ascetical and he spent much of his time in Church. Finally, after he had qualified as a lawyer, he decided to become a monk in Jerusalem. Travelling into the desert of Eleutheropolis he sought a more ascetic way of life, but illness and the persuasion of his friends led him to enter the monastery of Romanus. He shared out his property among his brothers, gave his share to the poor and devoted himself to the monastic life near the town of Maiuma.

Severus was already committed to opposing the council of Chalcedon. Maiuma had been the episcopal seat of Peter the Iberian, one of the bishops who had consecrated Timothy Aelurus, and Severus was part of this tradition of opposition. He rejected the Henoticon of Zeno, which was an imperial attempt at conciliation between the pro and anti-Chalcedonian parties, because it dealt with the stumbling block of Chalcedon by ignoring it.

His criticism of Chalcedon was never based on the acceptance in any form of the heresy of Eutyches. Indeed in his work, Philalethes, or the Lover of Truth, he explained that,

Had it confessed hypostatic union, the Council would have confessed also 'one incarnate nature of God the Word', and would not have defined that the one Christ is 'in two natures' thereby dissolving the union.[68]

---

[68] Philalathes, p187 quoted in Handbook of Source Materials, p214, W.G. Young

Severus was sent to Constantinople and wrote his first major work there in 508 AD. While in the capital he became known to the Emperor Anastasius who had greater sympathy with the anti-Chalcedonians than with the pro-Chalcedonians led by Patriarch Macedonius. In 511 Patriarch Macedonius was replaced by Timothy, and then in 512, after a synod assembled by the Emperor in Sidon, the Patriarch Flavian was ejected because he would not anathematise Chalcedon and Severus was consecrated Patriarch in his place.

In his enthronement address Severus affirmed Nicaea, Constantinople and Ephesus. He also affirmed the Henoticon of Zeno as an Orthodox document, but he also explicity anathematised Chalcedon, the Tome of Leo, Nestorius and Eutyches, Diodore and Theodore of Tarsus. In 514 his Synod anathematised Chalcedon and the Tome while explaining the Henoticon as annulling Chalcedon.

All of this activity gives the lie to the prevalent opinion that in 451 AD the Oriental Orthodox went quietly into exile and schism. Here we see that the Church was alive with those who opposed Chalcedon, and it was those who supported it who found themselves on the defensive.

Severus continued his ascetic manner of life even as Patriarch. He sent away the many cooks from the episcopal residence and demolished the baths that previous bishops had built. In his homilies in the cathedral he constantly warned his people against attending the races and theatres.

But in 518 AD Emperor Anastasius died and the new emperor Justin immediately ordered the arrest and punishment of Patriarch Severus. He managed to escape to Egypt with some of his bishops while other anti-Chalcedonians were sent into a difficult exile. While in Egypt, moving from monastery to monastery, avoiding his enemies, he wrote some of his most important works and corresponded widely and continuously.

In 530 AD the emperor Justinian eased the persecution which the anti-Chalcedonians had been suffering. In 532 AD he even attempted to reconcile the two parties in the Church by calling a conference in Constantinople. Finally, in 534 AD Anthimus, an anti-Chalcedonian, became Patriarch of Constantinope and Theodosius, another anti-Chalcedonian and friend of Severus, became Patriarch of Alexandria. Once more it seemed that the anti-Chalcedonian movement might gain the ascendancy in the Church. This so alarmed the pro-Chalcedonians that they exercised all of their diplomatic skills to bring the opinion of Agapetus of Rome to bear on the emperor. The Emperor Justinian was engaged in efforts to recapture Rome and the West and sacrificed Anthimus for the pro-Chalcedonian Menas. In a synod held in Constantinople in 536 AD Severus and his colleagues were condemned. He was accused of being both a Nestorian and a Eutychian, his books were ordered to be burned and he was sentenced to be banished. He managed to escape from Constantinople with the help of the Empress Theodora and he returned to Egypt. There after a light illness he fell asleep. He was 73 years old.

In the period 518-520 AD Severus engaged in a correspondence with a certain Sergius. This Sergius had been attempting to expound the Orthodox teaching about the Incarnation of Christ, but had been criticised by his local synod because he had spoken without discretion. In three letters that were sent by Severus to Sergius we can find much of the Christology of Severus presented in just such an explanatory manner as may be useful today. These letters have been recently translated and published by Dr Iain Torrance, and are well worth study. Since they are so easily obtained they will now be used as the basis for this examination of the teaching of St Severus. This essay is only an introduction to the Christology of St Severus and deliberately restricts itself to this one work, published as *Christology After Chalcedon* (Iain Torrance, The Canterbury

Press, Norwich, 1988). It is not too difficult to acquire and in a small space describes much of the teaching of St Severus, both against the Nestorians and the Eutychians.

Sergius' problem was that in opposing the Nestorian position that in Christ the Divinity and humanity were naturally separate and united only in a personal manner, he strayed too far from the truth and failed to expound the Orthodox teaching. This Sergius taught that the opposite of a natural disunity was a simple unity in which there could only be one nature, which Sergius took in the sense of ousia or essence, and therefore created a new Christ nature which was neither essentially human or Divine. In most modern Christian's eyes this is the teaching of the Oriental Orthodox Churches. We are assumed to confess in one nature a simple and confused unity which destroys the distinction between humanity and Divinity. Severus' opposition of Sergius will clearly illustrate the fundamental difference between the 'one nature' of Sergius and the 'one incarnate nature' of Cyril and Severus.

Even a cursory glance at Severus' letters makes it abundantly clear that Severus was dependent on the thoughts and teachings of Cyril of Alexandria. In the three relatively short letters to Sergius we find more than 60 quotations from St Cyril. Many more than any other Father. Whenever Severus wants to make a point he will quote from Cyril. What does this tell us? Firstly, that Severus considered himself to be a disciple of Cyril of Alexandria. Thus we should not read into any of his teachings an anti-Cyrilline meaning which is not justified by his complete commitment to a Cyrilline Christology. Secondly, that the writings of Severus should be read in continuity with those of Cyril and not as though they taught something different. Any obscure points in the teaching of Severus should be explained by the teaching of Cyril and not assumed to be at odds with it.

There are a number of Christological points which need to be examined in the writings of Severus. It is important to consider the accusation that he taught both Nestorianism and Eutychianism. How could this be so? If Nestorianism teaches the separation of the natures in Christ and Eutychianism the confusion, then how could Severus possibly be guilty of teaching both heresies? Such an understanding, though unjustified, may have arisen among his opponents because of the phrase 'of two natures' which is key to the Oriental Orthodox Christology. Among the Oriental Orthodox it describes both the continuing distinction between the Divinity and humanity of Christ, whilst confessing the real and perfect union between them. In the hands of those who sought Severus punishment and exile it was twisted to stand for a pre-existent humanity and Divinity coming together in a confused unity, therefore a perceived Nestorianism and Eutychianism. Thus we need to examine carefully the teaching of Severus about the humanity and Divinity of Christ, as well as the union between them.

Let us first consider the accusation of Eutychianism. What can be found in these letters of Severus to refute such a charge? Almost immediately as the first letter begins, Severus writes to Sergius:

Know, therefore, that professing the natural particularity of the natures from which there is the One Christ is not just recently determined by us.[69]

Here Severus indicates that Sergius' error lay in supposing that union must mean the extinction of each natures particular existence. More than that, Severus places himself within the Orthodox tradition which had confessed the continuity of the natures in Christ. He continues this passage immediately with a substantial and important quotation from Cyril:

---

[69] I. Torrance, **Christology After Chalcedon**, Canterbury Press, 1988, p147

For even if the Only-Begotten Son of God, incarnate and inhominate, is said by us to be one, he is not confused because of this, as he seems to those people, nor has the nature of the Word passed over into the nature of the flesh, nor indeed has the nature of the flesh passed into that which is his, but while each one of them continues together in the particularity that belongs to the nature, and is thought of in accordance with the account which has just been given by us, the inexpressible and ineffable union shows us one nature of the son, but as I have said, incarnate.[70]

The quotation from Cyril explains the meaning of the sentence from Severus. This passage shows us that Severus is dependent on Cyril for his Christology and that when he speaks of the particularity of the natures in Christ he is summarising the quotation which he then provides from Cyril. This in turn teaches that the humanity of Christ continues to be humanity and the Divinity of Christ continues to be Divinity. Therefore the concept of 'one incarnate nature' cannot and should not, in Cyril or in Severus, be taken to stand for the extinction or confusion of either the humanity or Divinity.

Severus makes this absolutely explicit by stating:

When the Doctor has confessed one nature of God the Word, who is incarnate, he says that each of them continues together and is understood in the particularity that belongs to the nature.[71]

This makes clear that Severus teaches that the one nature of God the Word incarnate should be understood as allowing the two natures to continue to exist in the union of natures and to continue to preserve their distinctions and characteristics. There is no sense in which he teaches a Eutychian confusion of the humanity and Divinity.

---

[70] ibid, p148

[71] ibid, p148

Another quotation from Cyril is provided to illustrate what Severus means by the continuing distinctions of the humanity and Divinity of Christ:

Therefore let us recognise that even if the body which was born at Bethlehem is not the same, that is, as far as natural quality is concerned, as the Word which is from God and the Father, yet nevertheless it became his, and did not belong to another man beside the Son. But the Word incarnate is to be considered one Son and Christ and Lord.[72]

This is a key quotation because it expresses both Severus' confession of the continuing distinction and difference between the humanity born at Bethlehem and the eternal and divine Word, as well as his commitment to a union which makes one Christ without a confusion of these natures. The body born at Bethlehem was never the body of a man beside the Word or with the Word. From the moment of conception this humanity was the humanity of the Word, distinct from the divinity but never separated or divided, therefore, without suffering any change the humanity and the divinity are made one in the incarnation.

Severus, in his own words, writes to Sergius that:

..particularity implies the otherness of natures of those things which have come together in union, and the difference lies in natural quality. For the one is uncreated, but the other created....Nevertheless, while this difference and the particularity of the natures, from which comes the one Christ, still remains without confusion, it is said that the Word of Life was both seen and touched.[73]

How could it be expressed any clearer that Severus did not even conceive of the humanity and Divinity of Christ being confused in any way. The 'difference...remains without confusion', he confesses. Exactly the same teaching as steadfastly maintained by Cyril before him, and not at all to

---

[72] ibid, p148

[73] ibid, p148

be compared with the teaching of Eutyches, however that is described. The union is confessed with the teaching that the Divine Word was seen and touched by the Apostles, but it is clear that this union does not confuse the continuing distinction between the humanity and Divinity.

Indeed Severus is well aware of the heresy of those who confused the natures in Christ. He writes to Sergius of their madness and he refutes any sense in which his teaching of the union of the humanity and Divinity in Christ could be compared with the confusion of natures of the 'synousiasts'. Nor does he feel the need, as they have, to 'cure evil with evil', that is the evil of Nestorianism with the evil of Eutychianism.

To make this absolutely clear Severus quotes again from Cyril, who writes in his reply to a critic:

There is no share in any blame that one should recognise, for example, that the flesh is one thing in its own nature, apart from the Word which sprang from God and the Father, and that the Only-Begotten is another again, with respect to his own nature. Nevertheless to recognise these things is not to divide the natures after the union.[74]

These words should be taken as though written by Severus himself. He is quoting them with complete agreement. There is no blame, he says in Cyril's words, there is no blame associated with recognising that in Christ the humanity and Divinity are different things. The flesh is one thing, according to nature, the Divinity another, according to nature. Here is a clear expression of the Christology of the Oriental Orthodox. The recognition of the difference between the humanity and Divinity of Christ in no wise detracts from the confession of the true and perfect union of these natures. Both of these Christological facts are true. The humanity and Divinity retain their integrity, their

---

[74] ibid, p149

distinctions, but the union of them drives out division. There is no room for Nestorianism or Eutychianism.

Severus proceeds to explain rather more about how he conceives of the union taking place:

Let us make an enquiry of the divinity and humanity. They are not only different in everything but they are removed from each other and distinct as well. But when the union is professed from the two of them, the difference, again, in the quality of the natures from which there is the One Christ is not supressed, but in conjunction by hypostasis division is driven out.[75]

Here is the key to understanding Oriental Orthodox Christology: the difference remains, division is driven out and the union takes place hypostatically. No-one should allow any interpretation of the Christology of the Oriental Orthodox which mutilates this clear and straight-forward definition. If someone suggests that a confusion of natures is taught, then they are mistaken. It is clear that Severus, and all of us with him, confess the continuing difference of these natures. If someone suggests that we teach that these natures have their own independent existence then they are mistaken. It is clear that Severus, and all of us with him, confess a real and perfect union in which there is no division. And if others should suggest that we teach a mixture or confusion of essences or ousia then they are again mistaken, because Severus, and all of us with him confess a hypostatic union.

But this teaching should not be understood as something new, or something that originated after Chalcedon had confused the unity of the Church. Severus indicates his continuity and agreement with Cyril by quoting immediately from him:

I too allow that there is a great difference or distinction between humanity and Divinity. For these things which were named are seen to be other, according to the mode of how they are,

---

[75] ibid, p149

and they are not like each other in anything. But when the mystery which is in Christ has come for us into the middle, the principle of union does not ignore the difference but it removes the division; not because it confuses with each other or mixes the natures, but because the Word of God has shared in flesh and blood, thus again the Son too is understood and named as One.[76]

Oriental Orthodox should not be afraid to admit the real and absolute difference between humanity and Divinity. Not only is this the teaching of Severus, but it is the teaching of Cyril of Alexandria. The mystery of the incarnation is that in the union of humanity and Divinity the difference between these natures remains while division is driven out. Here in this quotation it is also clear that Severus and Cyril allow no confusion of these natures, or a mixture. The union is not like that. It is a real and perfect union that preserves the real difference between the humanity and Divinity.

So where does Severus dispute with Nestorius and those who divide Christ? It is certainly not in the recognition of the continuing difference between the humanity and Divinity. Rather, as Severus explains:

We confess the difference and the particularity and the otherness of the natures from which Christ is, for we do not quarrel about names, but we confess the particularity which lies in natural quality, and not that which will be set in parts, each one existing independently.[77]

So Severus makes clear that the argument with the supporters of Nestorius lies not in naming the natures of humanity and Divinity, nor in confessing their continuing difference and otherness. The argument lies in whether or not the union which is taught allows each nature to have its own seperate and independent existence, or whether, as Cyril of Alexandria teaches, we confess a union in which

---

[76] ibid, p150

[77] ibid, p150

these real and different natures are united such that Christ is One, even as the Nicene Creed professes.

It should be clear by now that the Oriental Orthodox, through the teaching of Severus and Cyril before him, and indeed through many other Fathers, teach as a fundamental Christological fact that the natures are different and retain this difference even in their perfect union.

Once again Severus is echoing Cyril's own words, since he had written years before:

It is not right that we should make a division into an independent diversity, so that they should become separate and apart from each other; rather we ought to bring them together to undivided union. For the Word became flesh, according to the words of John.[78]

This independent diversity is what we should reject. Not the fact of the diversity of the natures, the humanity and Divinity, which are completely other and different from each other. The heart of our Christology, indeed of our Orthodox Christology, is that these two distinct and different natures have been united in a union that has no division even whilst their is no confusion.

We do not refuse to confess the difference, God forbid! But we flee from this, that we should divide the one Christ in a duality of natures after the union. For if he is divided, the properties of each one of the natures are divided at the same time with him, and what is its own will cling to each one of them. But when a hypostatic union is professed, of which the fulfilment is that from two there is one Christ without confusion, one person, one hypostasis, one nature belonging to the Word incarnate.[79]

What Severus, and Cyril, strive so hard to prevent is a division of Christ such that there is a human and a God. This is the essence of Nestorianism. In this passage Severus

---

[78] ibid, p150

[79] ibid, p151

shows the strength of his feeling that we must absolutely confess that the humanity and Divinity of Christ are different things. There is no room for a Eutychian confusion of humanity and Divinity. This recognition of the difference of the nature is not what we object to. What we object to is creating a duality of natures, which does not mean the destruction of the difference between them, rather it means setting up two independent centres of existence, the humanity and the Divinity, and these independent centres of existence destroy the union. It is a hypostatic union that ensures the real union of these different natures. This passage makes clear that firstly, a hypostatic union does not introduce confusion between the humanity and the Divinity; secondly, that 'one nature belonging to the Word incarnate' does not mean either a confused divine/human nature nor does it mean that the humanity is swallowed up by the Divinity; thirdly, the passage makes plain that the union is one in which the different natures have their differences preserved but within one concrete existence, that of the Incarnate Christ, and not preserved independently as the Son of God and a man united in some external manner. The 'duality of natures' which is rejected is not the reality of the humanity and Divinity, but a division between them which destroys the union and which makes One Christ of the two without confusion.

It was Cyril, as Severus quotes, who had said that:

The properties of the Word became properties of manhood, and those of manhood, properties of the Word. For thus one Christ and Son and Lord is understood.[80]

This is Cyril speaking, Cyril the great Orthodox christologian. He can hardly be accused of confusing the natures of humanity and Divinity, nor of failing to confess the continuing distinction between them. Yet he describes here how in the union of natures in Christ there is a

---

[80] ibid, p151

communication of properties, without confusion, so that we may truly say that God was seen and heard and touched, that God suffered and died. Thus when Christ walked on the water this was neither a human action, since it is not human to walk on water, nor was it divine, since it is not of God to walk, but it is an evidence of the union of humanity and Divinity, without confusion such that we see always One Christ and not God and a man with him.

What could Severus object to in the teaching of those who supported Chalcedon? It was not that they confessed the reality and difference between the humanity and divinity. It was not that they refused to confuse the natures in Christ. But Severus did impress upon both Sergius in his letters to him, and to his own followers that:

When we anathematise those who say Emmanuel has two natures after the union, and speak of the activities and properties of these, we are not saying this as subjecting to anathema the fact of, or naming, natures, or activities, or properties, but speaking of two natures after the union, and because consequently those natures...are divided completely and in everything.[81]

We should object, then, with Severus, to those who divide Christ and not those who name the natures of which Christ is. There is no error in stating that Christ is of humanity and divinity, and that in union these differences persist. But there is error in setting up a humanity and a divinity with their own separate activities as though there were Christ the man and the Word of God, each perfect in a simple humanity or divinity and only united in some external manner. Following Severus' argument we see that it is not the saying that Emmanuel has two natures which is condemned, but saying that he has these two natures and then describing their activities separately, as though there was God the Word acting as God in heaven and Christ the man acting as man on earth. Severus allows the naming of

---

[81] ibid, p151

the natures. We can and must confess that Christ is human and divine, but we must not allow this Orthodox confession to be perverted such that we describe a man and the Word of God seperately. It is God the Word who is this man Jesus.

We also recognise a variety of utterances: for some are proper to God, while others are human, but one Word incarnate spoke both the former and the latter.[82]

This is a further explication of the Orthodox Christology of the Oriental Orthodox Churches. This simple sentence describes the continuing difference of the natures of which Christ is, whilst confessing that the union is such that the human and Divine utterances alike belong to God the Word. Not that the human utterances become mixed or confused, but they belong to God and are of God the Word even though they are uttered by His humanity. The divinity belongs to God the Word from eternity because it is his own nature. The humanity has become truly and completely his own in the incarnation and because of His love for us, and therefore we may truly say that God the Word was seen, and heard and touched. Yet without the confusion or mixture of the divinity which was his from eternity and the humanity which he united to himself in time.

This is what Severus means when he says:

For how will anyone divide walking upon the water? For to run upon the sea is foreign to the human nature, but it is not proper to the divine nature to use bodily feet. Therefore that action is of the incarnate Word, to whom belongs at the same time divine character and human, indivisibly.[83]

This is why Severus criticises those who try to divide up the activities of Christ as though they belonged to the different natures separately and not to the incarnate Word, who is of humanity and divinity unconfusedly. There is no

---

[82] ibid, p153

[83] ibid, p154

error in understanding that in his humanity Christ acts humanly, that speaking and eating and all such things are of humanity, and are not divine. But in the union of humanity and divinity in Christ, all of these things belong to God the Word who acts divinely in union with his humanity. The error that Severus opposes is the setting up of two seperate centres of activity such that there is a man with God rather than God incarnate.

He who confesses one nature incarnate of God the Word, and teaches an unconfused union, does not deny awareness of the difference and particularity which lies in natural quality of the the natures from which there is the one Christ.[84]

Surely Severus has shown clearly enough that there is not one iota of sympathy in his teaching for those who either deny the reality of the humanity and divinity in Christ. Nor is there any sense in which he allows these perfect, real and complete natures to suffer diminuition, confusion or mixture. Surely it is clear that it is the firm and decided teaching of the Oriental Orthodox Churches that the natures of humanity and divinity have a real, perfect, unconfused and continuing existence in union in the one hypostasis of the Word of God. That these natures in union mean that God the Word is truly incarnate, that he is really fully God and fully man.

It has often been presented as though opposition to the council of Chalcedon, and to the Tome of Leo, must of necessity be caused by some heretical impulse that confuses the natures of which Christ is, or dissolves the humanity in the Divinity, or teaches a heavenly humanity that is fundamentally not consubstantial with us. But the Fathers of the Oriental Orthodox Churches have never wandered from the faith of St Cyril or St Athanasius, and have always understood that if Christ were not fully God He would have no power to save us, and if He were not fully man then it

---

[84] ibid, p155

would not be man who was saved. When Severus opposed Chalcedon and Leo it was because he believed them to have failed to adequately safeguard the Orthodox Christology of St Cyril and St Athanasius, not at all because he wished to introduce some christological novelty.

For instance, Severus criticises the Tome of Leo, not because Leo of Rome had sought to counter the errors of Eutyches, but because he believed that it contained itself some christological defects. After discussing the union of Divinity and humanity in Christ he speaks thus:

It is possible to see that those things which are contained in the Tome of Leo go clearly against these things, and I quote them:

'For each one of the forms does what belongs to it. The Word doing what belongs to the Word, and the body fulfilling those things which belong to the body, and the one of them is radiant with wonders, but the other falls under insults.'[85]

Now it cannot be said that Severus failed to discern and distinguish the real difference between the humanity and Divinity of Christ. Neither did he ever fail to confess the reality and perfection of these natures in Christ. Therefore if he condemns this passage in the Tome it is not because he himself teaches heresy. In the eyes of Severus, his colleagues, his followers, and those before and after him this passage seemed to teach that the reality of the humanity and Divinity of Christ had their own centres of existence. The Word is set in parallel with the flesh, as though the Word was one centre and the flesh another. This passage seemed to be presenting a doctrine too much like the Nestorian Word and a man with Him.

Whether or not Leo meant to teach this is another question. But it is a fact that the Oriental Orthodox of the 5th and 6th centuries certainly believed that Leo was teaching exactly such a thing. Indeed the position was made more complicated by the agreement of Nestorius with the teaching

---

[85] ibid, p154

of the Tome, and later by the celebration of a feast of Nestorius by some of those bishops who had welcomed the Tome at Chalcedon. It looked to many people as though all of this was of a piece and was nothing more than the propagation of Nestorianism by other means, and under the pretence of a respect for St Cyril.

Severus described his opinion of this passage from Leo in the following words,

> *For if each form or nature does those things which are its own, those things are of a bastard partnership and of a relationship of friendship, such as a master's taking on himself the things which are performed by a servant, or vice-versa, a servant's being glorified with the outstanding possessions of a master, while those things which are not properties of human nature are ascribed to him out of a loving friendship. For he is a man clad with God, who in this way makes use of a power which is not his own.*[86]

The question in Severus' mind is not so much how may we divide the activities into human ones, Divine ones, and others which are of a mixed quality, since although he recognises the natural quality of humanity and Divinity he also confesses that all of the activities of Christ are always in reality both human and Divine. Not a mixture at all but the activities, whether human or Divine, belong always to the incarnate Word. He asks 'who' is doing these things?, 'who' do they belong to? and finds the categorisation of activities by Leo, and then even more the owning of each activity being described in the two centres of humanity and Divinity, to tend dangerously towards the division of Christ. The scriptures, and the Orthodox Fathers, taught that Christ, the Divine Word, *participated* in humanity. His humanity belongs to Him through His incarnation. The activities of His humanity, while being perfectly human, nevertheless belong to the Divine Word who has become incarnate. This sense of ownership, of participation, is missing in Leo's rather clinical and abstract division of activities, honour and insult. If the

---

[86] ibid, p154

humanity in isolation suffers the insult then it becomes harder to understand how, in Leo's thought, we may say that God suffers.

This is not a criticism of Leo's Tome, which has had many defenders over the last 1400 years, but in relation to the Orthodox Christology of Severus it is merely an attempt to show that in this point, as in many others that Severus made against Leo's Tome and Chalcedon, the desire was not to promote any Eutychian heresy, but rather to counter a perceived Nestorianism.

Severus not only taught against the Synousiast or Eutychian heresy and the perceived Nestorianism of Leo and the Chalcedonians. He taught positively about the union of natures in Christ, and this element of his Christology should also be briefly examined. Severus' teaching about the union of natures in Christ remains as firmly based on the Christology of St Cyril as the rest of his teaching. Thus he quotes Cyril,

'When the mystery of Christ is brought into the middle for us, the principle of the union on the one hand recognises difference, but on the other hand rejects division, while neither confusing nor mixing the natures with each other. But with the Word of God becoming a partaker of flesh and blood, one Son is understood and named in this way as well.'[87]

Once more we must understand that the union is of a type that recognises the difference between those elements of which it is constituted. But it is also a union that prohibits division. This rejection of division is not caused by a confusion or mixture of the natures, since this would be a failure to recognise the continuing difference. There is a continuing and dynamic interplay between these two features of the union. Continuing difference on the one hand and a rejection of division on the other. For many of the opponents of Severus and the Oriental Orthodox this first

---

[87] ibid, p171

aspect was as far as they read in St Cyril's own words. And in failing to read carefully they understood only that St Cyril taught a continuing difference, and thus claimed him as a champion of their own position. But they also exposed their teaching, as far as Severus was concerned, to the criticism that they fundamentally failed to understand the union and merely expressed the continuing perfection of humanity and Divinity without really teaching the union at all as St Cyril understood it. From Severus' point of view there was little difference between the avowed Nestorianism of Theodore, Diodore, Theodoret and Nestorius, and the neo-Nestorianism of those who rejected the Cyrilline theology of 'one incarnate nature of the Word'.

St Cyril continues, and Severus is also most insistent, that it is through the Word of God becoming a partaker of flesh and blood that we see the one Son. The humanity of Christ is thus shown to be not merely something that he has acquired or which he owns, but something in and through which the Divine Son of God participates in human existence. He has become man without change or diminuition of his Divinity, not merely associated himself with humanity in some way.

The means by which this real, complete and perfect union of humanity and Divinity has taken place, without change, confusion, separation or division, is, in the words of St Cyril, quoted once more by Severus:

'..completely inexpressible and not known by any man who lives, but to God who alone knows everything'.[88]

Nevertheless, Severus agrees with St Cyril that:

'The fact of union is accomplished in many ways. For example, when men are divided in affection and opinion and are thinking at variance with each other, they are said to be united through reconciliation of affection as they remove their differences out of the centre. Again for example, we say that those things

---

[88] ibid, p173

which cleave to each other or come together in different ways, whether by juxtaposition or mingling or mixture, are united. Therefore when we say that the Word of God was united to our nature, the mode of union is recognised to be above human comprehension for it is not like one of those ways which were mentioned.[189]

So we learn that Severus, and the Oriental Orthodox, do not teach that the union of humanity and Divinity in Christ are united in any of these ways. We find an explicit rejection of juxtaposition, mingling or mixture, but a confession of an incomprehensible to man union which removes division while preserving distinctions, such that the one Christ is both truly and perfectly man, truly and perfectly God, without confusion or change damaging either.

Severus writes thus against John the Grammarian,

Christ is known to be one from both, which came together into a natural union. He is one prosopon, one hypostasis and one nature (physis) of the Word incarnate, in the same way as man is one, who is made up of body and soul. He is one not by a harmonious association of two persons. That which operates is one, namely God the Word incarnate: He performs the things that befit God as well as the things that befit man, the flesh not being alien to the God-befitting operation. The Word did not work the Divine miracles without being incarnate, neither was the Word external to bodily and human operations and sufferings. For he was incarnate. He who in His nature was without body, became in the dispensation with body, having united to Himself in His Person flesh possessing a rational soul. Therefore in His flesh, which is subject to suffering, He is said to have suffered, ascribing to Himself the passions of the flesh which He united to Himself naturally.[90]

Severus is clear that the union is of two different elements, the pre-existent divinity and the humanity, and

---

[89] ibid, p172

[90] Against John the Grammarian, p286 quoted in H.S.M. p216

Christ is one reality from two real elements, neither of which is lost or confused in the union. But his stress is always that we see Christ as one incarnate Person, so that even though he suffers in His flesh, nevertheless it is God who suffers because it is the flesh of God. For Severus the reality of the incarnation is completely lost if the humanity and Divinity are not real, and are not really united. And if this quotation sound as though Severus might be allowing that the divinity suffers in some sense, then we should heed his message to Julian, who taught that the humanity of Christ was always impassible,

God the Word became incarnate and was made man by uniting to Himself in His Person flesh possessing a rational soul. Therefore, when He endured in reality undeserved suffering of body and soul in the body which was prone to suffer, He continued to be without suffering in the Godhead. So it was not like us who, without wanting to, suffer as men, that He endured passions, but of His own free choice. And again, it is not that He did not suffer, but that He accepted in a real way, without sin, the suffering of humanity.[91]

Severus is therefore absolutely committed to the reality of the humanity in Christ, united without division or confusion to the divinity, such that there is One Christ. Indeed Severus criticises the Eutychian Sergius, with whom he corresponded, for suggesting that allowing the reality of the humanity and Divinity is necessarily the same as confessing a Nestorian juxtaposition.

'How can you charge this inexpressible and truly divine union which the Word of God has miraculously accomplished, with being that union taught by Nestorius which is a conjunction by relationship, and believe that we are required to speak of two natures unless we confess, as you say, that at one time Christ had one ousia? But this is nothing other than a real confusion of ousia....For you think it is impossible to say that he is one unless he

---

[91] Against Julian, p34, quoted in H.S.M. p215

changes into one ousia, even when he is made up from two things of a different kind.[92]

Yet we find that Oriental Orthodox are continually being accused of reducing Christ to one ousia, either the Divine or some mixture of humanity and Divinity. But here Severus refuses to accept that his teaching requires or contains any such reduction. This is due, primarily to the failure of the Eastern Orthodox, and Western Christianity generally, to appreciate that oneness, or union, comes about in different ways, and that to speak of 'one incarnate nature' is not at all to confess one simple nature which must be either human, Divine, or a confusion. St Cyril is quoted by Severus, from his second letter to Succensus,

'For it is not the case that "one" is truly predicated only of things which are simple in nature, but it may also be predicated of those which have come together in composition, an example being the situation of man, composed from soul and body...Therefore those who say that, if the Word incarnate is one nature it follows in everything and in every respect that there will be confusion and mixture, as if the nature of man were decreased and stolen away, speak needlessly, for it is not decreased, nor as they say, stolen away. For it suffices for the complete demonstration of the fact that the Word became man to say that he was incarnate.'[93]

It is something of a mystery that were many Eastern Orthodox to be presented with the preceding paragraph, describing the union of natures in Christ as a 'composition', without attribution to St Cyril, it would be rejected as heretical and Eutychian. Indeed it has been the case that ordinary Eastern Orthodox, when presented by such texts, have declared St Cyril to be merely one father among many whose teachings have no particular weight. Yet this passage completely describes Oriental Orthodox Christology. The union is not a mixture, nor is it simply an external personal

---

[92] ibid, p173

[93] ibid, p174

union, but it is a composition such that the concrete reality of the incarnate Christ is human and Divine, even while the constituents of that reality remain perfect and different.

But it is not the Divine nature of the Word which is composite. The Divinity remains divinity and the Godhead has not become a quarternity with four hypostases. It is the hypostasis of the Word which is composite, composed in the incarnation of perfect and unconfused human and Divine reality and being. Thus we speak, with St Cyril and St Severus, not of 'one nature or hypostasis of the Word', as though it was made up of simple humanity, Divinity or a mixture, but of 'one incarnate hypostasis of the Word' since it is because of and in the incarnation that the one Christ is both human and Divine.

Thus St Cyril is quoted again and again from a variety of sources,

'It is not the case that in everything and from every respect only what is simple and of one type is called "one", but also those compounded from two or from many things of different types.'

'In his own will he became man, and without damage in any way he preserved the glory of his nature unchanged in himself, but took up manhood according to the economy. And he is understood one Son from two, a divine and human nature, which have run and come together to one, inexpressibly and in explicably composed to union, and in such a way that cannot be understood.'[94]

It is clear that when St Cyril speaks of one nature he is not speaking of one essence or ousia. Indeed in later times the Oriental Orthodox always used St Cyril's phrase 'one incarnate nature of the Word' with the addition 'or hypostasis' so that it was clear that they were describing one concrete reality, Christ who is both human and Divine by composition, rather than describing the underlying substance of humanity or divinity which remain what they always have been. 'One incarnate nature' says that this Christ

---

[94] ibid, p174

is both human and Divine, it does not say that humanity and Divinity have been confused so as to become some third 'Christ nature'.

Therefore St Severus rejects the teaching that Christ is two natures, not because he does not believe that Christ is perfectly human and perfectly Divine, indeed it must be clear that he believes in these perfections completely. But for him, and for the Oriental Orthodox, nature means, in many contexts, more than 'underlying substance or essence' and means a concrete and independent example of such an underlying essence. Indeed Oriental Orthodox are not happy with the idea that an ousia or essence can ever exist except as a nature, or concrete reality. It is not humanity that is harmed if I fall over, but this human, this concrete example of the human ousia. Thus Christ is 'one incarnate nature', one reality, but composite. He is 'of' or 'from' both humanity and Divinity, in the sense that these are the underlying substances of which the one reality is unconfusedly composed, but in the ears of St Cyril and St Severus, 'in two natures', without further explanation, sounds dangerously as though it confesses two independent realities, each existing separately, and is thus a variety of Nestorianism.

He explains,

'For the Word himself, who had existence before the ages and is forever together with the Father, and is seen in his own hypostasis and is simple in ousia, became composite in the economy, and that word "incarnate" ensures that it is understood that the flesh endowed with a reasonable soul existed in relationship to the Word himself, and was not independently completed in its own hypostasis.[95]

Thus, 'one incarnate nature' stands for the Divine Word with complete and perfect humanity united to him as his own humanity, and not for a new type of substance that is neither human nor Divine.

---

[95] ibid, p176

Since the Christology of the Oriental Orthodox is so manifestly Cyrilline and in accordance with the Fathers one wonders why there is such a failure to understand these things on the part of those who have separated themselves from us. Yet the Oriental Orthodox Churches have suffered centuries of misunderstanding and abuse. Even today there are many Christians whose aim is to highlight as widely as possible our supposed heresies. Publications have been produced with titles such as 'The Errors of the Monophysite Heretics', and websites exist to promote a false explanation of our Christology. Almost every encyclopaedia propogates such errors and includes throw away lines which suggest that we teach the humanity of Christ was dissolved or swallowed up in his divinity.

His Holiness Pope Shenouda III has been criticised by some Eastern Orthodox, who feel they have made some great discovery by reporting him as stating that the body of Christ is a Divine body. They fail completely to understand, firstly that His Holiness is not at all ignorant of theology, and does not speak what he does not mean. Secondly, and even more importantly, they show how far from the teaching and witness of St Cyril some have strayed, because St Cyril himself is quoted by St Severus as teaching,

'Therefore we say that the body of Christ is divine because it is the body of God, and is brilliant with inexpressible glory, incorruptible, holy and life-giving. But that it was changed into the nature of divinity, no-one of the holy Fathers thought or said, nor do we affirm this.' [96]

This failure illustrates the historic weakness of some Christologies, which fail to answer satisfactorily the question, 'whose is this flesh?', and satisfy themselves with a cataloguing and division of human and divine elements and behaviours. Yet the question is key to the Christology of St Cyril, St Severus, and the Oriental Orthodox.

---

[96] ibid, p180

St Cyril writes,

'Therefore let us acknowledge that the body which was born at Bethlehem, even if it is not the same - I mean in natural quality - with the Word which is from the Father, yet it became his, and not of some other son beside him. But one Son and Christ and Lord is understood even when the Word became incarnate.'[97]

This is the heart of Oriental Orthodox Christology. The humanity of Christ is not the same as his divinity, nor does it ever cease to be completely other than his divinity. But in the incarnation, and because of his love and the exercise of his will it has become truly his own humanity.

Again, in his writings against John the Grammarian, St Severus takes plain to make clear that while the humanity is not at any time apart from the divinity, nevertheless it is a real flesh, with the properties of humanity, and Christ is called Emmanuel because of the reality of His humanity, and because He is truly God with us, unchangeably, unconfusedly.

Before the union and the incarnation, the Word was simple, not incarnate, nor composite. But when he mercifully willed in the dispensation to become man unchangeably along with being what He was, then He was called Christ and Emmanuel – the name being taken from the act – and He became one with us, by reason of the fact that He united to Himself in His Person (hypostasis) flesh which was of the same substance with us and which was animated with a rational and intelligent soul.

The flesh did not come into being before, nor had it been formed already; but in the union with Him, it came into being inexplicably, so that conception, growth, gradual development and birth might be of the incarnate Word. On account of the essential union of the flesh, for which it is natural to be conceived and formed, to grow and be born, though He showed it to be beyond the laws of nature because it happened from the Virgin…and from the

---

[97] ibid, p214

Holy Spirit...he who calls Him Christ after the union most certainly signifies Him.[98]

In conclusion, the Christology of St Severus is in every respect in accord with that of St Cyril. It is truly, deeply and completely Orthodox in the sense that it expresses perfectly the Christology of the Fathers of the Holy Councils of Nicaea, Constantinople and Ephesus. There is not one iota of justification for the anathemas historically raised against him by the Byzantine Orthodox, and these anathemas can only have been issued by those who had hardly read anything of his teachings. The Christology of the Oriental Orthodox Churches stands with St Severus and St Cyril in utterly repudiating any teaching in which the distinctions of the natures of divinity and humanity cease to exist in the incarnation, or any teaching which damages the complete and perfect reality of the humanity and divinity of which Christ is. But neither should we cease to steadfastly confess that in the incarnation, and for our salvation, the Word of God has deigned to unite, in a manner past understanding, humanity with his divinity such that even as there is no confusion or mixture, equally there is no division or separation, but we see 'One Christ' and 'One Lord' as the creed confesses. This is the meaning of 'one incarnate nature of the Word', and this must continue to be the heart of our Orthodox Christology.

---

[98] Against John the Grammarian, p236, quoted in H.S.M p215

The Humanity of Christ

The Oriental Orthodox Churches have often been criticised for professing a faulty doctrine of the humanity of Christ. This criticism is heard as much in the 21st century as it was the 5th. We may respond with frustration that our actual doctrinal position is misunderstood, and misrepresented, but it is perhaps wiser to seek to explain and inform. Our Churches no longer face the pressure of Imperial opposition, and many of the Eastern Orthodox Churches, and indeed the Roman Catholic Church, have shown a willingness to listen and learn, rather than simply depend on age-old polemics in dealing with us.

The criticisms that are most often used against us are:

i. that we confess the humanity of Christ is dissolved or swallowed up by the humanity such that it has no real existence.
ii. that we confess that the humanity of Christ is not consubstantial with us but has come down from heaven and is merely a fantasy.
iii. that we confess that the humanity of Christ has been mixed or confused with his divinity such that a third nature, neither human nor divine, is created.
iv. that we confess that the humanity of Christ is defective in lacking a human will.

All of these criticisms may still be heard and read, in encyclopaedias and on websites, from clergy as well as lay people. The Columbia Encyclopaedia, Sixth edition 2001, states,

"Monophysitism was anticipated by Apollinarianism and was continuous with the principles of Eutyches, whose doctrine had been rejected in 451 at Chalcedon. Monophysitism challenged the orthodox definition of faith of Chalcedon and taught that in Jesus there were not two natures (divine and human) but one (divine)."[99]

If Eastern Orthodox Christians really believe this of us then it is not surprising that many remain hostile to the prospect of our reconciliation.

Of course the doctrine of the humanity of Christ is not the only issue which is a matter of dispute. But it is perhaps one of the most often used against us. We are accused of confessing a Christ whose humanity is not real, or is defective, or has been absorbed by his divinity. An investigation of the actual content of our faith will show plainly that we have never accepted any of these positions.

We should begin of course with St Cyril of Alexandria, who is the great champion of Orthodox Christology. There were many occasions when St Cyril himself faced much the same accusations that we bear. His position was misunderstood and misrepresented, so much so that Theodoret, whose writings were much later recognised as heretical by the Eastern Orthodox, wrote of St Cyril saying,

"In my opinion he appears to give heed to the truth, in order that, by concealing his unsound views by it, he may not be detected in asserting the same dogmas as the heretics. But nothing is stronger than truth, which by its own rays uncovers the darkness of falsehood. By the aid of its illumination we shall make his heterodox belief plain."[100]

---

[99] Columbia Encyclopaedia. Sixth Ed. 2001
[100] Nicene and Post-Nicene Fathers, Series II. Vol 3.

Now if St Cyril was misunderstood and accused of heresy, then perhaps we may take comfort in the situation we also face. Nevertheless we have a responsibility to do all we possibly can to clear up the confusion still experienced by those who condemn our Orthodox Churches as heretical.

It is clear from St Cyril that despite the conclusions of Theodoret, who also accused him of mixing the natures of humanity and divinity, he confessed a thoroughly Orthodox Christology. Indeed his Christology is the model for that of all the Oriental Orthodox Churches.

He writes in some of his letters,

"Our Lord Jesus Christ is, to be sure, the only begotten Son of God, his Word made man and made flesh, not to be divided into two sons, but that he was ineffably begotten from God before all time and in recent periods of time he was born according to the flesh from a woman, so that his person is one also. In this way we know that the Holy Virgin is the Mother of God, because he is God and man at the same time, that he who without change and without confusion is the only begotten, is incarnate and made man, and moreover that he was able to suffer according to the nature of his humanity. We know that it is impossible for him to suffer according to the nature of his divinity, and that he did suffer in his own flesh according to the scriptures."[101]

and,

"Accordingly we confess that the only begotten Son of God is perfect God, consubstantial to the Father according to divinity, and that the same Son is consubstantial to us according to humanity. For there was a union of two natures. Wherefore, we confess one Christ, one Son, one Lord.

---

[101] McEnerney, John. Trans. **St Cyril of Alexandria, Letters 51-110**. Letter 59. C.U.A. 1987

And, if it seems proper, let us point out as an example the composition in us ourselves according to which we are men. For we are composed of soul and body, and we see two natures, the one of the body and the other of the soul, but one man from both according to a union, and the composition of two natures does not make two men be considered as one, but one man.

For, if we shall give the answer that there is only one Christ from two different natures, those on the opposite side will say, if he is entirely one physis, how was he made man or of what kind of flesh was he made?

Those who say that there was a blending, or a mixture, or a confusion of God the Word according to the flesh, these the Catholic and Apostolic Church anathematizes."[102]

and yet again,

"I have never been of Apollinarius' persuasion (God forbid!) nor ever shall be. It is not my assertion that the holy body, which God the Word put on, lacked a soul. No, it contained a rational soul. Nor have I ever asserted or declared, as many report against us, mixture, confusion, or intermingling of natures."[103]

These passages teach us that the foundation of Oriental Orthodox Christology is rooted in a confession of the reality of the humanity of Christ. The first passage shows us that St Cyril teaches that the humanity of Christ derived from the humanity of Mary, his mother. It was not a fantasy, nor was it from heaven, but it was real humanity. A humanity that suffered in the flesh according to the scriptures. But it was a humanity that was united with his

---

[102] McEnerney, John. Trans. **St Cyril of Alexandria, Letters 51-110**. Letter 97. C.U.A. 1987

[103] McEnerney, John. Trans. **St Cyril of Alexandria, Letters 51-110**. Letter 100. C.U.A. 1987

divinity so that our Lord Jesus Christ remains one, not two. And it was a humanity that remained distinct but not separate from his divinity so that the nature of his divinity was not confused. Christ suffers in his humanity and is impassible in his divinity, but in all things he is one Lord, for it is his flesh which suffers and not another's.

The second passage makes quite clear that St Cyril, and those of us who follow his teachings, confess that the humanity of Christ is consubstantial with us. This was the point on which Eutychius faltered. He had read in the Creed that Christ was consubstantial with the Father but considered that speaking of Christ as being consubstantial with us, according to his humanity, was an innovation he could not accept. Of course St Cyril had already spoken in this way and therefore Eutychius was setting himself apart from the Orthodoxy of St Cyril.

If the humanity of Christ is consubstantial with us then it is like us in every way except sin. It is a humanity that hungers and thirsts, that aches and bleeds. More than that we find St Cyril teaching us that because the humanity is that of Christ, it belongs to him and is his, so we must say that it is the Word, the second person of the Holy and Consubstantial Trinity which is consubstantial with us according to his humanity, as he is consubstantial with the Father according to his divinity.

Because of this we confess that there is a union of two natures in our Lord, God and Saviour Jesus Christ. There is only 'One Lord', there is only one whose is both the humanity and the divinity. St Cyril points us to the example of our own human composition, both material and fleshly, and immaterial and spiritual. Yet these two completely different natures, or ways of being, are united without division or confusion to make us one man or woman.

Now St Cyril faced the same question that we do. If Christ is one physis or nature then of what sort is his humanity? But he explains that this union of natures is a composition, not a mixture. Christ is 'of' humanity and divinity, and just as the material and immaterial remain in us as human persons, so the reality of these natures remains in Christ, who continues to be 'of' two natures through the millennia after his incarnation.

Yet this is not a confusion, nor a mixture, nor a blending, and St Cyril anathematises those who teach thus. Humanity is humanity and in Christ is consubstantial with us. Divinity is divinity and in Christ is consubstantial with the Father.

Could St Cyril be much clearer? Yet in the third extract he goes as far as to condemn Apollinarius who taught that the humanity of Christ was without a soul. This humanity that St Cyril speaks of is entirely ours, yet without sin. It possesses all that is proper to humanity, including a human soul. It is a rational, that is a thinking and willing soul.

What can we learn from St Cyril? He teaches that the humanity of Christ is the same as ours. It is of the same substance, consubstantial with us. This is contrary to the teaching of Eutychius who confessed that Christ's humanity was from the Virgin Mary but was not consubstantial with us. He teaches that the humanity had a rational soul and was not merely a body being animated by the divine Word. But he is equally insistent that the humanity was united to the divinity, such that both the humanity and the divinity really belonged to the Word. It was his own humanity and not someone else's. And this humanity was united to the divinity according to his analogy as the immaterial component of our humanity is united to the material, without confusion, mixture or blending. Each remaining what it always is. Yet we are one man or woman, as Christ is one, both God and man. We do not exist in the nature of spirit and the nature of flesh, we are not two, but we exist as one in a union of spirit and flesh in our complete humanity. Neither, as St Cyril teaches, does Christ exist in the nature of divinity and in the nature of humanity, as though he were two, but he exists, after the incarnation, in the union of humanity and divinity, a union that preserves each but does not introduce division.

Perhaps it will be accepted that this is the teaching of St Cyril, and there are some in other churches who will even go so far as to disparage the teaching of St Cyril. But it may be suggested that this is no longer the teaching of the Oriental Orthodox Churches. A survey of the teaching of some of the Oriental Orthodox fathers should make it quite clear that in fact the Orthodox Christology of St Cyril remains the foundation of our own faith.

St Dioscorus is almost universally considered, outside of Oriental Orthodoxy, as an heretical and violent man who led many of the Eastern Christians into the heresy of Eutychus. Yet within our own Oriental Orthodox tradition we remember a very different man. Those writings which have come down to us show us a bishop who never failed to confess the complete humanity of Christ.

The proceedings of the Council of Chalcedon show us that St Dioscorus was not opposed to the phrase 'from two natures after the union'. He did not accept Eutychus' defective teaching of 'two natures before the union, one nature after the union'. His 'from two natures' is the same as St Cyril's 'of two natures'. Christ is always, after the incarnation, existing in the dynamic union of humanity and divinity. He does not exist in a static, parallel existence of humanity and divinity. Now if the Eastern Orthodox, as we believe, express this Orthodox conception of the continuing, dynamic union of humanity and divinity by using the term 'in two natures' this is acceptable, but if what is confessed is a static division of natures united only externally or notionally then this is not acceptable, and it is against this position that we have always stood firm.

If Christ is 'from two natures after the union' then these natures have to be real. How can Christ be 'from two natures', or 'of two natures' and yet one of these does not exist or is overwhelmed by the other?

St Dioscorus also wrote,

"God the Logos, consubstantial with the Father, at the end of the ages for our redemption became consubstantial with man in the flesh, remaining what he was before."[104]

This is entirely what has been found in the teaching of St Cyril. Christ is God the Word, or Logos. He is consubstantial with the Father according to his divinity, and consubstantial with us according to his flesh. This can in no sense at all be considered Eutychianism. As has been described before, Eutychius rejected the idea that Christ was consubstantial with us according to his humanity. Now if Christ is consubstantial with us then his humanity is real humanity, like us in every way except sin.

But St Dioscorus goes further and expresses that other Cyrilline teaching, that even when becoming man for us the Word never ceased to be what he was. If the Word 'remained what he was before' then his divinity suffered neither confusion, nor mixture nor any diminution at all. And if the Word is consubstantial with us according to the flesh then the flesh must be preserved as a reality. How can the Word be consubstantial with us if his humanity has no reality?

Another letter of St Dioscorus says,

"I know full well, having been brought up in the faith, that he has been begotten of the Father as God, and that the Same has been begotten of Mary as man. See Him walking on the sea as man, and Creator of the heavenly hosts as God; see him sleeping in the boat as man, and walking on

---

[104] Sellers, R.V. **The Council of Chalcedon** p31. n1. S.P.C.K. 1953

the seas as God; see Him hungry as man, and bestowing nourishment as God; see him thirsty as man, and giving drink as God; see him stoned by the Jews as man, and worshipped by angels as God; see him tempted as man, and driving away the demons as God; and similarly of many instances."[105]

Where does this passage show a failure to comprehend the continuing reality of humanity and divinity in Christ? It seems once more to be very similar to passages found in other writings of St Cyril, as indeed we would expect of St Cyril's disciple and successor. St Dioscorus teaches that in the earthly life of Christ we can see both the humanity and the divinity acting as is proper to each. Yet he does not act divinely and humanly on different occasions but in the union of humanity and divinity we see the unconfused natures acting as is appropriate.

How can it be thought that St Dioscorus denies the reality of the humanity, or confesses some sort of confusion? If Christ is described as 'sleeping in the boat as man' then how is he not perfectly and unconfusedly human? If Christ is described as walking, hungry and thirsty 'as a man' then how is the humanity of Christ not confessed? It seems rather that St Dioscorus is simply following the teaching of St Cyril.

Let us turn to St Timothy Aelurus, Pope of Alexandria after St Dioscorus. He wrote,

"For the Divine Logos, not yet incarnate, was conceived in the womb of the holy Virgin, and was then incarnate of the flesh of the holy Virgin, in a manner in which he alone knew, while remaining without change and without conversion as God."

This shows us that St Timothy taught that the flesh, that is the humanity, of Christ was taken from the Virgin Mary, but that in the union of humanity and divinity the nature of divinity did not suffer any change, nor was there a

---

[105] Sellers, R.V. **The Council of Chalcedon** p32. S.P.C.K. 1953

mixture or confusion. He states this more explicitly in a letter written from exile,

> "Since children partake of flesh and blood, he also participated in them, in order that he might, by his death, abrogate the power of death…..He did not receive the nature from the angels, but from the seed of Abraham. It was necessary that he should identify himself with his brethren in everything in order that he might be merciful…Since he endured suffering and temptation he is able to succour those who are being tempted."[106]

St Timothy reminds us that the humanity of Christ did not come from heaven, nor from angels, but is of the seed of Abraham. Taken from the flesh of his mother, Mary, it is of the same nature as our humanity. He writes elsewhere,

> "Let no-one, thinking to honour God, insult his mercy by refusing to abide by the teaching of our holy fathers, who have confessed that our Lord Jesus Christ became consubstantial with us in the flesh."[107]

We are not taught in these passages that Christ merely took flesh or humanity that was consubstantial with us, and then dissolved or overwhelmed it in his divinity such that it has no reality. On the contrary, he became, that is he remains, consubstantial with us. He bears still as his own flesh the humanity we bear. He says,

> "He who is of the same nature with the Father as to Godhead, the same became of the same nature with [Mary] and with us in the body."[108]

---

[106] Samuel, Fr V.C. **The Council of Chalcedon Re-examined**, p259. Xlibris2001

[107] Samuel, Fr V.C. **The Council of Chalcedon Re-examined**, p258. Xlibris2001

[108] Samuel, Fr V.C. **The Council of Chalcedon Re-examined**, p259. Xlibris2001

Now if the humanity of Christ has no reality, or is defective, then he has not become of the same nature with us. But St Timothy teaches us that we dishonour God if we fail to confess the reality and consubstantiality of the humanity of Christ. Seeing that St Timothy condemns those who do not make this confession it is a matter of some frustration that in fact he is accused, with us, of maintaining the position he rejects.

When he found that even among those who anathematised Chalcedon there were some who did indeed confuse the natures of divinity and humanity he took firm action. A certain Isaiah and Theophilus travelled to Constantinople and starting teaching a confusion of natures. St Timothy wrote letters against them and eventually excommunicated them. Why would he do this if in fact they were merely teaching a heresy that he himself believed?

In fact anyone reading the writings of St Timothy could not fail to be impressed by his Cyrilline Orthodoxy, if they approached such writings without prejudice. One last passage, found in his letters against the very people who taught a defective humanity of Christ, says conclusively,

"The Scriptures teach us of Christ that he identified himself with us in everything, and that he became perfectly of the same nature with us, but for the impulse of sin. He was born supernaturally apart from conjugal union. But he became perfect man, having been conceived in Mary the Virgin, and from her born by the Holy Spirit, and he himself continued to remain God incarnate without any change."[109]

What could be clearer? St Timothy Aelurus most definitely does not teach any diminution of the humanity of Christ. It is complete in everything that pertains to our humanity. He became man with no change at all to his divinity.

---

[109] Samuel, Fr V.C. **The Council of Chalcedon Re-examined**, p260. Xlibris 2001

We can find no denial of the humanity of Christ in the earliest non-Chalcedonian patriarchs. Without any difficulty we can also find the same constant witness to the reality of that humanity in the later, and even greater fathers. St Severus of Antioch, writing in the first part of the 6th century has much to say about the humanity of Christ.

He writes,

"When the Doctor [St Cyril] has confessed one nature of God the Word, who is incarnate, he says that each of them continues together and is understood in the particularity that belongs to the nature."[110]

Each nature continues together. Now if each nature continues then neither is dissolved or changed, nor is there any mixture or confusion. This is the teaching of St Cyril, and we find it repeated from the hand of St Severus. More than that, this passage, quoting from St Cyril, shows how the 'one incarnate nature of the Word incarnate', that famous saying, should be understood. It does not stand for the confusion or mixture of natures, neither does it stand for the dissolution of the humanity. For each 'continues together'.

In another passage St Severus quotes again from St Cyril saying,

"Therefore let us recognise that even if the body which was born at Bethlehem is not the same, that is, as far as natural quality is concerned, as the Word which is from God and the Father, yet nevertheless it became his, and did not belong to another man beside the Son. But the Word incarnate is to be considered one Son and Christ and Lord."[111]

---

[110] Torrance, Iain. **Christology After Chalcedon** p148. Canterbury Press. 1988

[111] Torrance, Iain. **Christology After Chalcedon** p148. Canterbury Press. 1988

Here it is clear that he understands and teaches that the humanity is completely other and different from the divinity. And nine months after the miraculous conception in the womb of the Virgin Mary, when the Word was born as a human baby, that humanity remained, as it always was, other than the divinity. But it had become his, that is the Word's, own humanity. Every action of the humanity of Christ was in fact the activity of the Word of God, there was no-one else whose activity it could be. Yet it was human activity, because the divine nature and the human nature are not the same.

It is clear that St Severus often quotes from St Cyril. Indeed in three letters written to a certain Sergius who had fallen into error he quotes over 60 times from St Cyril. One of these quotations, describing his own confession says,

"For even if the Only-Begotten Son of God, incarnate and inhominate, is said by us to be one, he is not confused because of this, as he seems to those people, nor has the nature of the Word passed over into the nature of the flesh, nor indeed has the nature of the flesh passed into that which is his, but while each one of them continues together in the particularity that belongs to the nature, and is thought of in accordance with the account which has just been given by us, the inexpressible and ineffable union shows us one nature of the son, but as I have said, incarnate."[112]

What could be clearer? We say of the Son of God that he is incarnate and has been made man, but we do not confuse the natures, or say that the humanity has become divinity or the divinity become humanity. Again we find the express teaching that each 'continues together'. And if we speak of 'one nature', it is in the sense that each of us as humans is 'one' and not two. So Christ is one individual not two, even though he is a union of humanity and divinity.

---

[112] Torrance, Iain. **Christology After Chalcedon** p148. Canterbury Press. 1988

A final passage from St Severus, since this is only a brief overview and his teachings could fill many volumes,

"There is no share in any blame that one should recognise, for example, that the flesh is one thing in its own nature, apart from the Word which sprang from God and the Father, and that the Only-Begotten is another again, with respect to his own nature. Nevertheless to recognise these things is not to divide the natures after the union."

Following St Severus the Oriental Orthodox Churches confess that the humanity is one thing and the divinity another. That is, they are not the same and do not become the same. Yet we do not divide the humanity from the divinity, nor make it act apart from the divinity as though it belonged to another.

St Severus is most strict in requiring that the confession of the integrity of the humanity and divinity in Christ be preserved. We know that he accepted the doctrinal content of the Henoticon of Zeno, a document designed by the Emperor Zeno to bring peace to the Church, but which was generally attacked by all sides for either failing to condemn Chalcedon, or failing to approve it.

This document says,

"And we confess as one and not two the only-begotten Son of God, even God, our Lord Jesus Christ who in truth was made man, consubstantial with the Father in divinity and the same consubstantial with us in humanity, who came down and was made flesh from the Holy Spirit and Mary the Virgin and Mother of God. For we declare to be of one being both the miracles and the sufferings which he endured voluntarily in the flesh. For those who divide or confound or introduce an illusion we utterly refuse to receive, since indeed the sinless incarnation, that was in truth from the Mother of God, did not create an additional entity of the Son. For the Trinity has remained a Trinity even after one of the Trinity, God the Word, was made flesh."[113]

This is not merely the confession of one man, but as a theological statement it was accepted by many of the non-Chalcedonian bishops. It shows that the fathers taught that Christ was 'in truth made man'. All possibility of a Eutychian fantasy incarnation is excluded. The consubstantiality of the humanity of Christ with us is re-iterated. It is not the case that he was consubstantial with us and then this humanity was somehow diminished, but as has already been shown from individual fathers, he remains consubstantial with us, a consubstantiality that demands the perfect and complete reality of his humanity.

What is positively taught is the union of humanity and divinity in Christ. What is condemned is the introduction of a division which separates the humanity and divinity such that they become two centres of activity; or a confounding of the natures such that they cease to preserve their integrity and reality; or even that the incarnation is an illusion in the manner of Eutychius who failed to confess the consubstantiality of the humanity of Christ with us.

All of these false understandings of the humanity of Christ are rejected by the Oriental Orthodox, and can be shown to have been rejected from the beginning. It can only be assumed in charity that the Eastern Orthodox lacked access to the writings of many of our fathers. Not one suggests in any place that the humanity of Christ is not consubstantial with us, or fails to preserve its integrity and reality in the incarnation.

If we advance to modern times we can find this same faith professed by all the Oriental Orthodox Churches. Archbishop Aram Keshishian, surely someone who would know what the Armenians believe, states:

---

[113] Whitby, Michael trans. **Ecclesiastical History of Evagrius Scholasticus** p149, Liverpool University Press. 2000

"The Christology of the Armenian Church is fundamentally in line with the Alexandrian Theological School. In fact, the Cyrillian formula of 'One Nature of the Incarnate Word' constitutes the foundation stone of her Christology. [It should be noted that] first, 'One Nature' is never interpreted in the Armenian Christology as a numerical one, but always a united one. This point is of crucial importance [for the Armenian Church] particularly in its anti-Eutychian and anti-Chalcedonian aspects. Second the term 'nature' (ousia, in Armenian bnut'iun) is used in Armenian theological literature in three different senses: (a) as essence, an abstract notion, (b) as substance, a concrete reality, (c) as person. In the context of anti-Chalcedonian Christology 'one nature' is used in a sense of 'one person' composed of two natures."[114]

Or Archbishop Aram Keshishian of the Armenians also says:

"We say, always in a formal way, that Nestorianism and Eutychianism have been rejected and anathematized by our churches and we adhere to that. In other words, we both anathematized, once again, Eutychian and Nestorian heresies."[115]

The Coptic Orthodox have also officially accepted a Christological statement which says:

"We confess that our Lord and God and Saviour and King of us all, Jesus Christ, is perfect God with respect to His divinity, perfect man with respect to His humanity. In Him His divinity is united with His humanity in a real, perfect union without mingling, without commixtion, without confusion, without alteration, without division, without separation. His divinity did not separate from His humanity

---

[114] Aram Keshishian, **The Witness of the Armenian Church in a Diaspora Situation** (New York: Prelacy of the Armenian Apostolic Church, 1978), p. 58-59
[115] Window Quarterly 4, 4 (1994); ACRAG c. 1994

for an instant, not for the twinkling of an eye. He who is God eternal and invisible became visible in the flesh, and took upon Himself the form of a servant. In Him are preserved all the properties of the divinity and all the properties of the humanity, together in a real, perfect, indivisible and inseparable union."

This is part of the official teaching of the Church, and it makes clear that there was no mixture or confusion of the humanity and Divinity in Christ which are preserved and remain unchanged and unconfused.

Or in a shorter form the statement was recast and equally authoritatively accepted as:

"We believe that our Lord, God and Saviour Jesus Christ, the Incarnate-Logos, is perfect in His Divinity and perfect in His Humanity. He made His Humanity One with His Divinity without Mixture, nor Mingling, nor Confusion. His Divinity was not separated from His Humanity even for a moment or twinkling of an eye. At the same time, we Anathematize the Doctrines of both Nestorius and Eutyches."

Again the unconfused distinction of humanity and Divinity is confessed, and also the doctrines of Eutyches are anathematised. This is the official teaching of the Coptic Orthodox Church, and since both these statements were written by Pope Shenouda and agreed by the Holy Synod of the Coptic Orthodox Patriarchate they are explicit statements of Christological teaching.

The Syrian Orthodox Church have made an official statement on Christology in the following words:

"In our turn we confess that He became incarnate for us, taking to himself a real body with a rational soul. He shared our humanity in all things but sin. We confess that our Lord and our God, our Saviour and the King of all, Jesus Christ, is perfect God as to His divinity and perfect man as to

His humanity. This Union is real, perfect, without blending or mingling, without confusion, without alteration, without division, without the least separation. He who is God eternal and invisible, became visible in the flesh and took the form of servant. In Him are united, in a real, perfect indivisible and inseparable way, divinity and humanity, and in Him all their properties are present and active."[116]

Christ is perfect God and perfect man. There doesn't seem to be a lack of distinction in this statement. Confusion or mingling is also explicitly rejected, and the humanity and Divinity are confessed to be present and active in Christ with all their properties undiminished in any way.

Or the Indian Orthodox have made a statement in the following words

"Our Lord Jesus Christ is one, perfect in his humanity and perfect in his divinity, at once consubstantial with the Father in his divinity, and consubstantial with us in his humanity. His humanity is one with his divinity — without change, without commingling, without division and without separation. In the Person of the Eternal Logos Incarnate are united and active in a real and perfect way the divine and human natures, with all their properties, faculties and operations."[117]

This statement confesses the dual consubstantiality of Christ, the perfection of each nature, and the union without confusion or change. And again the statement is careful to make clear that the divine and human natures are active in a real way. Active in a real way. Can this be much clearer?

The Oriental Orthodox Churches have never ceased to confess the real humanity of Christ. Consubstantial with

---

[116] Joint Statement Pope John Paul II and His Holiness Moran Mor Ignatius Zakka I Iwas. 1984

[117] Joint Statement between the Roman Catholic Church and the Malankara Orthodox Syrian Church. 1990

us, like us in every way except for sin. Preserving the integrity of both his humanity and divinity in the union of both. A union which is without confusion or mixture. More than ever, while the possibility of the reconciliation of the Orthodox Churches exists, we must ensure that we ourselves are confident in the content of our own faith and are able to explain this faith to others.

If we fail to communicate our faith then there are countless others, misunderstanding and misrepresenting our position, who are already filling the void. From St Cyril, through St Dioscorus to St Severus and up to the present day, our Christology is wholly Orthodox and without any stain of heresy.

Hypostasis in St Severus of Antioch

Severus of Antioch reveals the Non-Chalcedonian communion as being wholeheartedly Cyrilline in Christology. His teachings make clear that there is no substantial difference between the Christology of the present day Eastern Orthodox and that of the Oriental Orthodox, even while the nature of his objections to Chalcedon are given some justification.

An understanding of the Christology of any theologian of any period requires an appreciation of the manner in which theological terms are used, and the meaning being attached to them in a variety of contexts. Nowhere is this more important than when considering the writings of the church fathers of the Eastern and Oriental Orthodox communions. In the case of the Christological controversies of the 5th and 6th centuries it is especially important that the terms and phraseology be carefully described and explained. This paper considers especially the use of the term 'hypostasis' in St Severus.

The Second Agreed Statement of the Joint Dialogue between the Eastern and Oriental Orthodox states that:

"We have now clearly understood that both families have always loyally maintained the same authentic Orthodox Christological faith, and the unbroken continuity of the apostolic tradition, though they have used Christological terms in different ways." [118]

Of course if such an understanding had been possible in the past then Church history may well have developed differently. But in the controversial period the working out of the Christological issues was complicated by many other

---

[118] Second Agreed Statement of the Joint Commission, para 9. 1990.

political, social and theological factors. Not least that there were real Nestorians and real Eutychians active at that time.

Severus of Antioch is one of the most important fathers of the non-Chalcedonian Orthodox communion precisely because he brings the opposing view of Chalcedon and the Tome of Leo into focus. More than that, in writing against those who took a Eutychian view of the Incarnation he also clarifies the theological distance that exists between the non-Chaledonian Orthodox and those with whom they are generally, and erroneously, identified.

For Severus the term hypostasis is key to the understanding of a properly Orthodox Christology. He uses it in his theological letters, his controversial writings and even in his hymns. Yet the other Christological terms of ousia, physis, and prosopon should also be clearly defined from the point of view of Severus himself. In Christological controversy many of the problems of broken communion and the continued preservation of entrenched positions has been due to writers on one side of controversy assuming that they knew exactly what their opponents meant, or due to assuming that terms and phrases could only ever be used in one manner.[119]

This most important term, hypostasis, is usefully defined and explored in many of Severus' writings. It stands first and foremost for an individual. Writing to one of his correspondents he says,

"Do you call the flesh possessing an intelligent soul, which God the Word voluntarily united to himself hypostatically without any change, a specimen or a generality, that is one soul-possessing hypostasis, or the whole human generality? It is manifest that, if you wish to

---

[119] This is clear in the Tome of Leo addressed to Flavian of Constantinople where he cannot comprehend how Flavian can have failed to object to Eutyches speaking of 'one nature after the union'.

give a right-minded answer, you will say one soul-possessing body. Accordingly we say that from it and the hypostasis of God the Word the ineffable union was made: for the whole of the Godhead and the whole of humanity in general were not joined in a natural union, but special hypostases." [120]

It is clear from this question that Severus opposes the ideas of specimen and generality when he considers the term hypostasis. The soul-possessing hypostasis is a specimen, an individual, it is not the generality of humanity. Indeed this hypostasis is the soul-possessing body which is an individual instance of humanity in general.

For Severus the term hypostasis applies to the soul-possessing body of Christ, that is his complete humanity, such that he can speak of the incarnation being a union of hypostases. And indeed this concept is the centre of his Christology. This idea describes what it means for God the Word to have become flesh and dwelt among us.[121]

How can the Incarnation be considered a union of hypostases? Surely this demands a Nestorian existence of a human person before an assumption by the Word? This would of course be true if hypostasis were always taken in exactly the same manner. But Severus rejects this Nestorian perspective, referencing the writings of St Cyril. He says,

"And do not think that hypostases in all cases have a distinct person assigned to them, so that we should be thought, like the impious Nestorius, to speak of a union of persons, and to run counter to the God-inspired words of the holy Cyril, who in the second letter to the same Nestorius speaks thus: 'But that it should be so will in no way help the right principle of faith, even if some men spread about a union of persons. For the Scripture did not say that God the

---

[120] Brooks E. W. A Collection of Letters of Severus of Antioch. 1915. p16

[121] John 1:14

Word united to himself the person of a man, but that he became flesh'"[122]

Severus does not consider that it is necessary for every hypostasis to be a person, but it is necessary that even in the face of Nestorianism the hypostatic quality of the humanity united with God the Word should be insisted upon. He considers that there are two types of hypostasis. These are a self-subsisting and a non-self-subsisting hypostasis.

The self-subsisting hypostasis is illustrated by the examples of Peter and Paul. They are hypostases with an individual subsistence. They exist independently of each other, and all others, and the name of a person is given them, such that this hypostasis exists in and for itself and is called Peter, and this other independent hypostasis is called Paul. The criticism raised against the Nestorians and those of the Chalcedonians who seemed to support them was that they failed to make a distinction between self-subsistent and non-self-subsistent hypostases and therefore predicated a union of two independent individuals, God the Word, and a man.

Severus took the example of the union of soul and flesh in a man as a means of explaining his concept of a non-self-subsistent hypostasis. In a man, such as Peter, there is a union of a human soul and human flesh. The flesh is hypostatic, in that it is real and a genuine individual example of the generality of human flesh. But it is not independent, it does not exist in and for itself, but exists in union with the hypostatic human soul which animates it.

Peter is a self-subsistent hypostasis, his flesh is a non-self-subsistent hypostasis. In the union of his hypostatic soul and flesh there is composed a self-subsistent hypostasis which is given the name of person and called Peter.

---

[122] Brooks E. W. A Collection of Letters of Severus of Antioch. 1915. p17

Thus Severus is able to describe the union of Divinity and humanity in Christ in the same sense,

"Though the hypostasis of God the Word existed before, or rather was before all ages and times, being eternally with God both the Father and the Holy Spirit, yet still the flesh possessing an intelligent soul which he united to him did not exist before the union with him, nor was a distinct person assigned to it." [123]

The divine hypostasis of the Word is eternal and is a self-subsisting hypostasis, yet though the flesh possessing an intelligent soul is real and hypostatic, that is a complete instance and individual of the generality of humanity, nevertheless it is not a human person because it is not independent of the hypostasis of the Word. It belongs to the Word in a similar manner to the possession of the body by the soul of a man.

If the flesh or humanity which was united with God the Word had existed for even a moment before the incarnation then it would have been self-subsistent, and the doctrine propounded by the Nestorians would have been correct. Severus quotes St Gregory to refute this possibility,

"Whoever says that the man was formed, and God afterwards crept in is condemned: for this is not a birth of God, but an escape from birth." [124]

But Severus is always careful to preserve the integrity of these various hypostases of which Christ is composed. The flesh is true flesh, it is a real and complete individual of the generality of humanity. Yet it is not a union of a human person and the divine person of the Word. As Severus explains,

---

[123] Brooks E. W. A Collection of Letters of Severus of Antioch. 1915. p19

[124] Brooks E. W. A Collection of Letters of Severus of Antioch. 1915. p18. Where he is quoting Ep. 101 (*P. G.*, XXXVII, 177)

"But, when hypostases do not subsist in individual subsistence, as also in the case of the man among us, I mean him who is composed of soul and body, but are without confusion recognised in union and composition, being distinguished by the intellect only and displaying one hypostasis made out of two, such a union none will be so uninstructed as to call one of persons." [125]

Here the composition of a man is once more described as being made up of hypostatic elements, yet elements which do not self-subsist. And by analogy this is how Christ may be considered in the Incarnation. His person, his self-subsistence, is composed of his own eternal self-subsistent hypostasis, that is his individuated divinity which is a person and is named the Word, and the non-self-subsistent hypostatic humanity which he united with himself at the moment of the Incarnation, creating it entirely to be subsistent in the union of divinity and humanity. This humanity does not have a human person attached to it, but it is hypostatic and is a real human individual, yet the person who owns this human hypostasis is God the Word. The humanity subsists, but it is not self-subsistent, it is dependent on the union with the self-subsistent divine hypostasis and the divine person of the Word of God.

Severus quite naturally is able to draw our attention to the hypostases of which Christ is composed. He says,

"Following these God-inspired words of the holy fathers, and confessing our Lord Jesus Christ to be of two natures, regard the distinct hypostases themselves of which Emmanuel was composed, and the natural junction of these, and do not go up to generalities and essences, of the whole of the Godhead and humanity in general: for it is manifest that the whole of the Godhead is seen in the Trinity, and

---

[125] Brooks E. W. A Collection of Letters of Severus of Antioch. 1915. p18

humanity in general draws the mind to the whole human race." [126]

Here it is clear that he considers the hypostases to be distinct, that is, they are not confused, they do not produce some other type of hypostasis which is neither truly divine nor truly human. But rather the union of a real and self-subsistent divine hypostasis with a real and non-self-subsistent human hypostasis mean that the person of the Word, after the Incarnation, now subsists naturally in his divine hypostasis, and in the economy of our salvation he has chosen to subsist in a human hypostasis which he has made his own. There remains only one self-subsistent hypostasis which has now become incarnate, that is, has united to itself a human non-self-subsistent hypostasis.

What is not being proposed is that the generality of humanity and the generality of the divinity has been united. The term hypostasis excludes such generality by referring always to an individual instance of such a generality. But this is not to suggest that Severus ever fails to recognise the fact the hypostasis always belongs to an ousia and shares in the membership of the human genus by being a real and complete individuation of that ousia. He states in one of his sermons,

"In the same way hypostasis does not deny genus or ousia, or abolish it, but it sets apart and limits in particular icons the one who subsists." [127]

Severus also addresses the other Christological terms and phrases. He says,

---

[126] Brooks E. W. A Collection of Letters of Severus of Antioch. 1915. p19

[127] Chesnut Roberta C. Three Monophysite Christologies. 1976. p11. Translated by Chesnut from Hom CXXV (P. O. xxix.236)

"But now also we will come to what is required, and, we will again say, that 'ousia' signifies a generality, and 'hypostasis' a particularity, but 'being' and 'nature' introduce sometimes a general signification, sometimes a partial or particular one." [128]

Therefore, as far as Severus is concerned, ousia should be used to describe that which is general to all of a species. So all humans share in the human ousia which is individuated into human hypostases, which are unique and subsistent. He does not seem to think of ousia as some sort of philosophical model, rather it seems to be that which is really and practically shared among the members of a class or genus. Peter is a man, his ousia is that of humanity, not because there is a substance which exists somewhere out of which a man is made, or because there is a divine pattern or model, but because he manifestly belongs to that ousia.

Severus writes,

"The Word therefore who had become incarnate walked upon the sea, and after his death under the wound of the lance caused a stream of salvation to well forth from his side: again, after the Resurrection, he came in while the doors were shut, and appeared to the disciples in the house; whom he also allowed to touch him, showing that his flesh was tangible and solid, and of one ousia with us, and was also superior to corruption; and thereby he subverted the theory of phantasy." [129]

This explicitly teaches that the humanity of Christ is of the same ousia with us. He belongs, in his humanity, to

---

[128] Brooks E. W. A Collection of Letters of Severus of Antioch. 1915. p23

[129] Brooks E. W. A Collection of Letters of Severus of Antioch. 1915. p11

the same genus or class of being as all other humans. He could be touched, his flesh was solid. His was not a spiritual humanity, it was not a phantasy body. He was completely of the same humanity as us.

Indeed Severus quotes St Cyril to show that the term ousia defines that which characterises a class of being.

"And the wise Cyril in the second letter to Succensus calls the manhood which was hypostatically united to God the Word ousia, saying: 'For, if after saying 'one nature of the Word' we had stopped and not added 'incarnate', but set the dispensation as it were outside, they would perhaps in a way have a plausible argument when they pretend to ask, 'Where is the perfection in manhood? or how was the ousia after our model made up?' But, since the perfection in manhood and the characteristic of our ousia has been introduced by the fact that we said 'incarnate', let them be silent, since they have leaned upon the staff of a reed'" [130]

This quotation supports the contention of Severus that the humanity of Christ is of the same ousia as us. This is to say that Christ is consubstantial with us according to his humanity. By using the word incarnate we must understand, says St Cyril, and of course Severus together with him, that Christ is no longer simply the divine hypostasis of the Word of God, but is also perfect in his manhood and in every characteristic of humanity which is summed up in the concept of ousia.

Ousia is therefore the definition and the characteristics of a genus, and according to his humanity Christ is a perfect and complete example of a hypostasis of the human ousia, and according to his divinity is a perfect and complete example of a hypostasis of the divine ousia.

---

[130] Brooks E. W. A Collection of Letters of Severus of Antioch. 1915. p21

Now Eutyches hesitated to say that Christ was consubstantial with us, although he did confess that Christ was human, and there were those who taught that because Christ had been conceived in a miraculous manner this set him apart from the human ousia. Severus answers them and criticises them for attacking the whole basis of our salvation. He writes,

"Therefore when you hear that the conception of Emmanuel took place in a divine way and at the same time in a human way, how do you completely remove him from human properties, which the incarnate Word receives willingly? For unless we say the flesh was capable of receiving the things which belonged to it, with the exception of sin – for this is not part of the ousia, but a sickness which, as I have said, occurs as a result of inattention – he was able neither to suffer the cross on our behalf nor to endure death." [131]

Therefore the human ousia which the Word shares, in the Incarnation, with all humanity does not include sin. This means that sin is not a essential component of the human ousia. But in everything else the human ousia out of which the non-self-subsistent human hypostasis of Christ has been individuated is complete and lacks nothing which goes to make up a human being. If Christ had not drawn his human hypostasis from the human ousia which we share then his suffering and death and resurrection would mean nothing, and our salvation would not have been accomplished.

Indeed, as Severus states, it is important that no aspect of the human ousia be removed from the humanity of Christ. If it fails to maintain its integrity in the union with the divine hypostasis of the Word then again our salvation is rendered void. If the humanity loses some of its properties

---

[131] Torrance Iain R. Christology After Chalcedon. 1988. p157.
Where Torrance is translating the first letter of Severus to Sergius, a Eutychian leaning theologian.

then it is no longer the human ousia which is individuated in Christ. But of course Severus rejects the possibility that the humanity of Christ is defective in any way.

What then of the miracles, the Transfiguration, the walking on Galilee? How are these to be understood if the integrity of the humanity of Christ, his consubstantiality with us, is to be preserved? Severus answers,

"For his face was radiant like the sun on the mountain, as we hear the Gospel, and his garments were white like light. But these things do not indicate a change of ousia, far from it, but the brilliance and the multitude of the glory which is proper to God." [132]

Severus could not be much clearer. Even when shining with the glory of the divinity the humanity remains what it is. Yet it is glorified by being the own humanity of God the Word. Just as Moses' face shone with the glory of God when he had been in the divine presence as far as was possible for any created being. He had not ceased to be a member of the ousia or genus of humanity. His humanity had not changed what it was, but it shone with a reflected glory, as the moon shines with the reflected light of the sun, but is not changed into a star and always remains what it is.

If we consider prosopon or person we may note that Severus teaches that not all hypostases bear a person and a name. He quotes St Cyril who says,

"And do not think that hypostases in all cases have a distinct person assigned to them, so that we should be thought, like the impious Nestorius, to speak of a union of persons……. For the Scripture did not say that God the Word united to himself the person of a man, but that he became flesh" [133]

---

[132] Torrance Iain R. Christology After Chalcedon. 1988. p180.

[133] Brooks E. W. A Collection of Letters of Severus of Antioch. 1915. p17

It is already clear that Severus considers the humanity of Christ to be hypostatic, yet non-self-subsistent, and such non-self-subsistent hypostases are those which do not have a person assigned to them. If the humanity of Christ were personal in its own right then, as Severus means to indicate by this quotation, we would be forced to confess a Nestorian union of persons.

St Cyril is clear that the humanity which Christ united to himself was not personal, or rather it did not bear the imprint of a human person. Rather the person of the divine Word is the person who owns that particular human hypostasis and gives it a name. Severus considers that only a self-subsistent hypostasis can bear a person and a name. He says,

"From what has been stated the doctor teaches that the peculiarity of the natural union is that the hypostases are in composition and are perfect without diminution, but refuse to continue an individual existence so as to be numbered as two, and to have its own person impressed upon each of them, which a conjunction in honour cannot possibly do." [134]

It is individual existence then which determines if a hypostasis has a person impressed upon it. In Severus' terms this is the self-subsistent hypostasis. In the Incarnation this means that the divinity of Christ, the self-subsistent divine hypostasis of the Word, is that which bears a person, and that person is God the Word himself. The humanity cannot bear another person because it is not-self-subsistent. It does not have the necessary 'individual existence'.

The fact that Severus is willing to speak even of a union of hypostases shows clearly that for him, and for the non-Chalcedonian communion, the integrity of the humanity and Divinity of Christ is always preserved. This is almost the

---

[134] Brooks E. W. A Collection of Letters of Severus of Antioch. 1915. p39

opposite of the position often attributed to him by uhis opponents and shows the necessity for allowing historical thinkers, especially from the controversial period of the 4th to 7th centuries, to speak for themselves.

St Timothy Aelurus of Alexandria

There are few of the Fathers of the Oriental Orthodox communion who escape uncritical censure on the part of the Eastern Orthodox. Uncritical because based on a few polemical comments deriving from the period of the Christological controversies and failing entirely to take into account any of the writings and historical records deriving from the Oriental Orthodox communities in which they were active.

Timothy falls into this category of unreasonably maligned figures. Condemned as both a murderer and Eutychian, he has passed into the Roman Catholic and Eastern Orthodox histories as a figure entirely without any redeeming features.

Yet, as is often the case, the truth is very different. Timothy reveals himself, in his letters and theological writings, and in the historical record, as a kind and eirienic figure, struggling with more effort than even the Chalcedonians against the heresy of Eutyches, while also seeking to reverse the Chalcedonian settlement.

It must be recognised that his efforts ended in failure. Nevertheless a study of his life and writings provides an important insight into not only the theological environment in which he found himself, but also into the thought of Dioscorus who preceded him. It is quite clear that Timothy considered himself in every respect to be following in the footsteps of both Cyril and Dioscorus. He quotes with approval from both in his letters and theological works, treating them as authoritative sources for his anti-Eutychian and anti-Nestorian polemics. In a real sense, therefore, a study of Timothy is a study of Dioscorus, from whom much less has been preserved by the way of documentary record.

The sources used for this study of Timothy of Alexandria may be categorised as being of three different types. There are his letters, such as have survived; his polemical writings against the Tome of Leo and the council of Chalcedon; and the ecclesiastical histories which refer to him and contain some further examples of his writings.

The major features of his life and episcopate can be usefully divided into the historical periods of the controversy surrounding the murder of Proterius, his extended period of exile, his return and influence upon the Emperor Basiliscus, and theologically into his activities against the Eutychians, his writings against the Chalcedonian settlement and his eirienic approach to the reconciliation of members of the Proterian party.

The Consecration of Timothy

St Timothy had been a monk in the desert monasteries when St Cyril had him brought, against his own inclination, to Alexandria and ordained a priest. He was, therefore, a priest during some of the patriarchate of Cyril of Alexandria, and all of the patriarchate of Dioscorus, both before and during that bishop's exile. Zachariah of Mitylene, in his Chronicle, describes Timothy as 'of the same faith as Dioscorus' and 'well versed in all the truth of the faith of the doctors of the Church'[135]. If this is so then we may confidently study the writings of Timothy as a source for both the teaching of Dioscorus, and the Christological perspectives of the Alexandrian Church in the 5th century.

During the council of Chalcedon in 451 AD, Dioscorus was exiled to Gangra. After several years of exile in that place he died on September 11th, 454 AD. Gangra was the Metropolitan See of Paphlagonia, in Asia-Minor, and a place associated with salt extraction from the earliest times

---

[135] Hamilton F.J. & Brooks E.W. trans. **Zachariah of Mitylene, Syriac Chronicle**, Book 4. Ch 1. p64, 1899

to even the present. This can hardly have been a pleasant place since in 523 AD it is recorded that Philoxenus of Mabbogh was sent to exile in Gangra, from Philippopolis in Thrace, his previous place of exile, and, as a life of Philoxenus describes,

"Having filled the Church with divine doctrines, and expounded the Scriptures, and laid open to disgrace the faith of the Nestorians by means of his writings against them, they cast him forth into exile in the city of Gangra, and they suffocated him with smoke. Now they shut him up in an upper chamber, and made smoke in the room below it, and they shut the doors: in this way was he crowned, and he was suffocated by them in the true faith."[136]

Timothy was fortunate that he did not share the same fate as both Dioscorus and Philoxenus during his exile in Gangra. Though it can surely have not been intended as a pleasant experience. Other political opponents of the empire were often sent to the salt mines, both in Gangra and elsewhere, and few of them can have returned. The prayers of the Coptic Orthodox Church still intercede for 'those who are held in prisons, those in exile or captivity, or in bitter bondage'.[137]

Of course the Alexandrian Church continued to consider Dioscorus as its rightful archbishop, even though he had been deposed and exiled at the council of Chalcedon in 451 AD. The acts of that council were considered null and void in Alexandria, indeed it was viewed as an anti-council in much the same manner that the council of Ephesus in 449 AD came to be rejected by most of those who had gathered at Chalcedon. Therefore no legitimate ecclesiastical authority

---

[136] Budge Wallis E.A. **Philoxenus, Ascetic Discourses (1894) pp.xviii-xxxi. The Life of Philoxenus**, xxvi.

[137] Offering of Incense, British Orthodox Church. Metropolitical Press. 1995. p12

had deposed Dioscorus and he continued to be de jure archbishop and patriarch of Alexandria.

The imperial authorities and Roman legates had not been content to seek the deposition of Dioscorus. It was necessary that a strong successor be provided who could be guaranteed to be both loyal to the Chalcedonian settlement and to eradicate opposition in Egypt. The man chosen was Proterius. This Proterius had himself been a priest of Alexandria, according to Zachariah.[138] Yet, seeing an opportunity for advancement, he changed his allegiance and became a thoroughgoing advocate for Chalcedon. He hardly endeared himself to his putative flock. It is recorded that he used force to try and gain acceptance for himself and Chalcedon, and banished his opponents and used the civil powers to seize their property. He certainly failed to gain acceptance by the majority of the Alexandrian and Egyptian people. Indeed the Coptic Orthodox Synaxarium still contains accounts of some of the depredations inflicted on the people during his rule.

It would seem that Timothy, together with other priests and bishops, had been deposed by a synod formed by Proterius and those few who supported him.[139] Nevertheless this deposition had no more weight in Alexandria and Egypt than that of Dioscorus. In fact those who resisted Proterius are accounted martyrs and confessors in the Coptic Orthodox Church, while of course in the Eastern Orthodox tradition the documentary evidence for Proterius' violence is suppressed and he is, himself, considered a saint. This can only be achieved by ignoring much of the historical material relevant to this period. Even the Chalcedonian historian Evagrius Scholasticus describes some of the violence perpetrated against the Alexandrian people by Proterius'

---

[138] Hamilton F.J. & Brooks E.W. trans. **Zachariah of Mitylene, Syriac Chronicle**, Book 4. Ch 1. p48, 1899

[139] Walford E. **Evagrius Scholasticus, Ecclesiastical History**, p72 Bagster, 1846

military forces, which included widespread rape, and denial of provisions in an attempt to starve the populace into submission.[140] Zachariah is more explicit in his description of the events,

"Proterius was very indignant, and he gave gifts into the hand of the Romans, and he armed them against the people, and he filled their hands with the blood of believers, who were slain; for they also strengthened themselves, and made war. And many died at the very Altar, and in the Baptistery, who had fled and taken refuge there."[141]

Not surprisingly, when the Alexandrians heard that the Emperor Marcian had died, in 457 AD, they were able to take advantage of the absence of Dionysius, the general whose forces had propped up the usurping patriarchate of Proterius, and consult among themselves to elect a true successor of Dioscorus.[142]

The Alexandrian Church agreed upon Timothy. He was considered as having the same faith as Dioscorus, being well versed in the Fathers, a man of ascetic lifestyle but with the ability to pastor the Church. The monks and people carried him to one of the major Churches in the city where he was consecrated by two Egyptian bishops and St Peter the Iberian, who had left his monastic home in Palestine and was staying in Alexandria at that time. According to Zachariah's Chronicle, while he was being carried to his consecration the people, priests and monks heard a spiritual voice saying 'Consecrate him by force, even though he be unwilling, and set him on the throne of Saint Mark'.[143]

---

[140] Walford E. **Evagrius Scholasticus, Ecclesiastical History**, p64 Bagster, 1846

[141] Hamilton F.J. & Brooks E.W. trans. **Zachariah of Mitylene, Syriac Chronicle**, Book 4. Ch 1. p48, 1899

[142] Hamilton F.J. & Brooks E.W. trans. **Zachariah of Mitylene, Syriac Chronicle**, Book 4. Ch 1. p64, 1899

[143] Hamilton F.J. & Brooks E.W. trans. **Zachariah of Mitylene,**

Grillmeier rather confusingly states[144] that Timothy was only consecrated by two bishops, Peter the Iberian and Eusebius of Pelusium. He can only come to this judgement by ignoring the account of Zacharias and following solely the account of the Chalcedonian historian Evagrius Scholasticus[145]. Evagrius notes that Peter and Eusebius was present at the consecration, but he does not say that only Peter and Eusebius were present, this is stated only in the partisan account provided by the Proterian clergy after their expulsion. In fact the Chronicle of Zachariah mentions two Egyptian bishops, one of whom must have been Eusebius of Pelusium, who were in Alexandria and consecrated Timothy, together with Peter the Iberian. Unfortunately, Grillmeier repeatedly shows a marked bias against Timothy and often appears to present historical material in an unfair manner.

Grillmeier says that St Timothy was secretly consecrated after the death of St Dioscorus, but this also appears not to reflect either Zacharias or Evagrius, since both state that the consecration of St Timothy took place during the period after the death of Emperor Marcian in 457 AD, while St Dioscorus died in exile at Gangra in 454 AD. Neither was the consecration in secret. In fact it was well known that there were now two rival bishops of Alexandria in the city, and the general Dionysius hurriedly returned with his army, took St Timothy prisoner and caused the slaughter of many Christians in the city. In fact things became so difficult in the city that eventually St Timothy had to be restored[146].

Syriac Chronicle, Book 4. Ch 1. p65, 1899

[144] Grillmeier A. **Christ in Christian Tradition** Vol 2. Part 4. p10 Mowbray, 1996

[145] Walford E. **Evagrius Scholasticus, Ecclesiastical History**, p70 Bagster, 1846

[146] Hamilton F.J. & Brooks E.W. trans. **Zachariah of Mitylene,**

On the death of Dioscorus there was such great love felt towards him by the ordinary people that his name remained in the diptychs among the living, as if he were still their own archbishop and patriarch. Apparently Marcian, while still alive, had become aware that the Alexandrians wished to elect an archbishop of their own, in place of the intruding Proterius. He sent an official to meet with the Alexandrians and convince them to unite with Proterius. This official, John the Silentiarii, seems to have been impressed with the principled stand that the populace, with their priests and bishops, were taking.

"When he came and saw the crowd, the numbers of monks arrayed in chastity, and possessing readiness of speech in defence of the faith, and also the strong body of the common people who were believers, with whom he had to deal, he was astounded, and said, "I am ready, if the Lord will, to inform the king and to plead with him on your behalf." And he received from them a petition— which gave information concerning their faith; and concerning all that happened to them at the hands of Proterius; and concerning the impious conduct of the man, and his wickedness, and the Church property which he expended upon vanity—written at length in words which I omit to reproduce here, lest I should be tedious to the reader.

And when John returned to the king and told him about these matters, he said to him, "We sent you, indeed, to persuade and exhort the Egyptians to obey our will: but you have returned to us, not according as we wished, since we find you an Egyptian." However, when he perceived the things that were written about Proterius, in the petition which the monks sent, he blamed the pride and the craftiness of the man. And while he was occupied with this matter, he died, having reigned six years and a half".[147]

Syriac Chronicle, Book 4. Ch 1. p65, 1899

[147] Hamilton F.J. & Brooks E.W. trans. **Zachariah of Mitylene,**

Zachariah also comments on the relative strength of the two churches in Alexandria. At the recording of names for enrolment as catechumens and baptismal candidates at the beginning of Great Lent, those reading out and recording the names of the candidates being presented to Timothy grew weary with the great number. Only five candidates were presented at this time to Proterius. In fact the people of the city rose up and chased Proterius out of the church he had made his own.

The Murder of Proterius

It was during this tumult that the death of Proterius occurred. Zacharias says,

"When Proterius continued to threaten the Romans, and to display his rage against them; because they took his gold, but did not fill their hands with the blood of his enemies : then, indeed, a certain Roman was stirred to anger in his heart, and was boiling over with rage ; and he invited Proterius to look round and he would show him the corpses of the slain as they lay. And suddenly and secretly, he drew his sword and stabbed Proterius in the ribs along with his Roman comrades, and they despatched him, and dragged him to the Tetrapylum, calling out respecting him as they went along, "This is Proterius." And others suspected that it was some crafty plot. But the Romans left the body, and went away. Then the people, perceiving this, became also greatly excited, and they dragged off the corpse, and burnt it with fire in the Hippodrome."[148]

So Zachariah is clear that one of the Roman mercenary troops killed Proterius, not from any theological

---

Syriac Chronicle, Book 4. Ch 1. p59, 1899

[148] Hamilton F.J. & Brooks E.W. trans. **Zachariah of Mitylene, Syriac Chronicle**, Book 4. Ch 1. p66, 1899

impulse but out of irritation at his constant demands for force to be applied to those who opposed him.

If we turn to Evagrius, who is a Chalcedonian, we find that he also notes,

"....the account given of the transaction by the writer of the life of Peter, also says that Proterius was not killed by the populace, but by one of the soldiers."[149]

And Grillmeier also notes that the Chronicle of Michael the Syrian also writes of Proterius being killed by a Roman soldier.[150]

But then, rather perversely, he states that these references are unconvincing. He chooses instead to rely entirely on the naturally partisan statements of the Proterian clergy who had fled Alexandria after Proterius' death. Their description of the events in Alexandria are rather different.

"When Dionysius, on account of the urgency of these disorders, had occupied the city with the utmost dispatch, and was taking prompt measures to quench the towering conflagration of the sedition, some of the Alexandrians, at the instigation of Timotheus, according to the written report made to Leo, despatched Proterius when he appeared, by thrusting a sword through his bowels, after he had fled for refuge to the holy baptistery. Suspending the body by a cord, they displayed it to the public in the quarter called Tetrapylum, jeering and vociferating that the victim was Proterius; and, after dragging it through the whole city, committed it to the flames; not even refraining themselves from tasting his intestines, like beasts of prey."[151]

---

[149] Walford E. **Evagrius Scholasticus, Ecclesiastical History**, p70 Bagster, 1846

[150] Grillmeier A. **Christ in Christian Tradition** Vol 2. Part 4. p11, n23 Mowbray, 1996

[151] Walford E. **Evagrius Scholasticus, Ecclesiastical History**, p71 Bagster, 1846

Now this passage seems most unlikely? Do we really imagine that Christians, of which ever party, would resort to cannibalism? This account, despatched to Leo of Rome, continues,

"And while undisturbed peace was prevailing among the orthodox people of our country and Alexandria, Timotheus, immediately after the holy synod at Chalcedon, being at that time a presbyter, severed himself from the Catholic church and faith, together with only four or five bishops and a few monks, of those who, as well as himself, were infected with the heretical errors of Apollinaris and his followers; on account of which opinions they were then deposed by Proterius, of divine memory, and the general synod of Egypt, and duly experienced the motion of the imperial will, in the sentence of banishment."

Now this passage is clearly misleading and mischievous. We know already that almost the entire population of Alexandria supported St Timothy, and the fact that the escaping Proterians numbered only a handful shows that in fact it was they who were in the minority? What was this 'general Synod of Egypt' that banished St Timothy? It is a fabrication since in fact St Timothy was restored to Alexandria specifically because he was so much loved and respected by the Church.

Even Grillmeier has to note that Leo of Rome was misled as to the following of St Timothy in Alexandria and thought that only four bishops supported him. This could not be further from the truth.

The letter to Leo of Rome continues,

"And after the interval of only one day, while Proterius, beloved of God, was occupying, as usual, the episcopal residence, Timotheus, taking with him the two bishops who had been justly deposed, and the clergy who, as we have said, were condemned to banishment with them, as if he had received rightful ordination at the hands of the two, though not one of the orthodox bishops of the whole

Egyptian diocese was present, as is customary on occasion of the ordinations of the bishop of the church of Alexandria — he possesses himself, as he presumed, of the archiepiscopal see, though manifestly guilty of an adulterous outrage on the church, as already having her rightful spouse in one who was performing the divine offices in her, and canonically occupied his proper throne."

Clearly this also is a partisan statement. Even if Proterius were not guilty of the violent excesses which he seems to have urged against the Alexandrians, and the evidence suggests he was, nevertheless he remained a promoter of Chalcedon and was an agent of the Imperial power. A heretic cannot 'canonically occupy' any episcopal throne, and by this light alone was reasonably considered a false bishop by the Alexandrians. He had been intruded while their own dearly beloved St Dioscorus was still alive.

"The blessed man could do nothing else than give place to wrath, according to what is written, and take refuge in the venerable baptistery from the assault of those who were pursuing him to death, a place which especially inspires awe even into barbarians and savages, though ignorant of its dignity, and the grace which flows from it. Notwithstanding, however, those who were eager to carry into execution the design which Timotheus had from the first conceived, and who could not endure that his life should be protected by those undefiled precincts, neither reverenced the dignity of the place, nor yet the season (for it was the solemnity of the saving paschal feast), nor were awe-struck at the priestly office which mediates between God and man; but put the blameless man to death, cruelly butchering him with six others.

They then drew forth his body, covered with wounds, and having dragged it in horrid procession with unfeeling mockery through almost every part of the city, ruthlessly loaded the senseless corpse with indignity, so far as to tear it limb from limb, and not even abstain from tasting, like beasts of prey, the flesh of him whom but just before they were supposed to have as a mediator between God and man. They then committed what remained of the body to the flames, and scattered the ashes to the winds, exceeding the utmost ferocity of wild beasts."

No wonder that Leo of Rome was filled with such indignation against St Timothy when he read this account. Yet the evidence is entirely found only in this letter. Evagrius cannot believe it himself and has to record that,

"Zacharias, however, while treating at length of these events, is of opinion that the greater part of the circumstances thus detailed actually occurred, but through the fault of Proterius, by his instigation of serious disturbances in the city, and that these outrages were committed, not by the populace, but by some of the soldiery; grounding his opinion on a letter addressed by Timotheus to Leo."[152]

How can we believe these unseemly accusations against a bishop? Even more how can we believe them when the record of Zachariah shows what sort of man St Timothy was. Immediately on becoming sole bishop of Alexandria we find,

"But Timothy, when he appeared before them as the only chief priest of Alexandria, showed that he was really what a priest should be. For the silver and the gold that were given to the Romans in the days of Proterius, he expended upon the poor, and the widows, and the entertaining of strangers, and upon the needy in the city. So that, in a short time, the rich men, perceiving his honourable conduct, lovingly and devotedly supplied him with funds, both gold and silver."

How like St Severus this is. For in his case, when he succeeded to the throne of the See of Antioch he closed the

---

[152] Walford E. **Evagrius Scholasticus, Ecclesiastical History**, p74 Bagster, 1846

episcopal baths, and dismissed the chefs who had prepared fine foods for his Chalcedonian predecessor and lived simply as a monk. We may reasonably ask why St Timothy is remembered as someone worthy of such affection if in fact he was the prime agent in an episcopal murder. Zachariah provides the reason behind this campaign of vilification.

"The presbyters and all the clergy belonging to the Proterian party, since they knew all his virtues and his angelic mode of life, and the devotion of the citizens to him, joined themselves together and made libels in which they entreated him that they might be received. They also promised that they would go to Rome to Leo, and admonish him concerning the novelties which he had written in the Tome.

But the jealousy and hatred of the citizens against these persons were great, on account of the events which had occurred in the days of Proterius, and the various sufferings which they had endured. So they would not consent to their reception."

St Timothy is well attested as an eirienic patriarch. He insisted that those who came over to the Orthodox from the Proterian party should be received on the provision of a signed statement of faith and a rejection of Chalcedon and the Tome, being received even in their clerical rank after one years probation. But on this occasion his peaceable intent could not prevail over the anger of the people, who had seen so many killed on the streets of Alexandria at Proterius' instigation. As Zachariah records, the outcome provoked the false accounts of events which were then sent to Leo of Rome, the Emperor and many other bishops. Zachariah says,

"This was the reason why matters were disturbed and thrown into confusion. For when these men were ignominiously refused, they betook themselves to Rome, and there they told about the contempt of the canons, and about the dreadful death of Proterius; and they said that he died for the sake of the Synod and for the honour of Leo; and that they themselves, also, had endured many indignities; and further, that Timothy had come forward in a lawless manner and taken the priesthood."[153]

So in fact we have three sources, and even Evagrius, a fourth, contradicting or at least questioning the account proposed by the Proterian party. Yet Grillmeier still chooses to assume that the contradicted account is the true one. He notes that "there is no word of regret about this outrage from any anti-Chalcedonian". But why should there be if in fact the records are clear that it had nothing to do with St Timothy at all.

Unfortunately Leo of Rome chose to listen to the Proterian account and took it as the truth. He wrote to the Proterian bishops now seeking support in Constantinople and informed them that he had already urged the Emperor to intervene. He consoled them by the thought that the anti-Chalcedonians in Alexandria would receive no mercy from the Emperor when he acted, because he had already been stirred by Leo to,

"….not allow murderous spirits whom no reverence for place or time could deter from shedding their ruler's blood, to gain anything from his clemency, more particularly when they desire to reconsider the council of Chalcedon to the overthrow of the Faith."[154]

Indeed in his letter to the Emperor he had already refused to allow the Emperor to call a council to try and reconcile the parties, and had described the Christians in Alexandria as 'blasphemous parricides', because they had, as he supposed, murdered their spiritual father. He warns the Emperor that the mere presence of those who should be cut off from the name of Christian 'dim your own splendour,

---

[153] Hamilton F.J. & Brooks E.W. trans. **Zachariah of Mitylene, Syriac Chronicle**, Book 4. Ch 1. p66, 1899

[154] Leo of Rome, Letter CLVIII Nicene and Post-Nicene Fathers, Series II, Vol XII.

most glorious Emperor'. He dismisses the petition of the Orthodox in Alexandria, describing it as 'the fiction of heretics'. One wonders if Leo of Rome truly believed that cannibalism took place in Alexandria. Nevertheless he urges the Emperor to act, and has nothing but opprobrium to heap upon St Timothy.

Yet this is all based only on hearsay and the word of a small group of embittered men who had lost much and had everything to gain by spinning as gross a libel as possible. Leo was already mistaken in thinking that only a handful of people supported St Timothy in Alexandria and Egypt, even Chalcedonian historians suggest that in fact Proterius had been murdered by his own mercenaries, and the Emperor Leo, when writing to Anatolius of Constantinople records what must be convincing since he is not an anti-Chalcedonian, and describes,

"the before-mentioned Timotheus, whom the people of Alexandria and their dignitaries, senators, and shipmasters request for their bishop, and what relates to the other transactions, as intimated by the tenor of the petitions, as well as regarding the synod at Chalcedon, to which these parties by no means assent."[155]

So it is clear that even the Emperor knew that Leo of Rome was misled and misleading when he claimed that hardly anyone supported St Timothy. In fact the people, their leaders and the merchants in the city all demanded St Timothy for their bishop. If the Proterian account was deceitful in this respect then it is legitimate to consider it an unreliable witness in any other respect.

The Exile of St Timothy

---

[155] Walford E. **Evagrius Scholasticus, Ecclesiastical History**, p76 Bagster, 1846

Of course none of these considerations bore any weight with the Emperor, or those bishops who responded to the Imperial request for opinions about the consecration of St Timothy. And indeed anyone receiving what was presented by Leo of Rome as a reliable and lurid account of episcopal murder could hardly fail to find against St Timothy. Anatolius of Constantinople, agreeing with Leo of Rome, counselled the Emperor not to call a council, but to rather send out letters to bishops in every place. Zachariah suggests that the reason Anatolius did not wish a council to be held was that he was concerned that his own prerogatives might suffer if the 28th canon of Chalcedon should be repealed.

Fortunately Zachariah has preserved the letter which St Timothy wrote to the Emperor Leo defending his faith against the accusations of the Proterians and Leo of Rome. In it he presents his own faith in the incarnation, saying,

"For thus also the three hundred and eighteen blessed fathers taught concerning the true Incarnation of our Lord and Saviour Jesus Christ, that He became man, according to His dispensation, which He Himself knows. And with them I agree and believe, as do all others who prosper in the true faith. For in it there is nothing difficult, neither does the definition of the faith which the fathers proclaimed require addition. And all (whoever they be) holding other opinions and corrupted by heresy, are rejected by me. And I also myself flee from them. For this is a disease which destroys the soul, namely, the doctrine of Apollinaris, and the blasphemies of Nestorius, both those who hold erroneous views about the Incarnation of Jesus Christ, Who became flesh from us; and introduce into Him the cleavage in two, and divide asunder even the dispensation of the only-begotten Son of God: and those, on the other hand, who say with respect to His Body that it was taken from Heaven, or that God the Word was changed, or that He suffered in His own Nature; and who do not confess that to a human body what pertains to the soul derived from us was united.

"And I say to any who have fallen into one or other of these heresies, 'You are in grievous error, and you do not know the Scriptures.' And with such I do not hold communion, nor do I love them as believers. But I am joined, and united, and truly agreeing with the faith which was defined at Nicea; and it is my care to live in accordance with it."

Now when Leo of Rome wrote to the Emperor Leo he dealt with the issue of the possibility of St Timothy being reconciled. He says,

"Nor need we now state all that makes Timothy accursed, since what has been done through him and on his account, has abundantly and conspicuously come to the knowledge of the whole world, and whatever has been perpetrated by an unruly mob against justice, all rests on his head, whose wishes were served by its mad hands. And hence, even if in his profession of faith he neglects nothing, and deceives us in nothing, it best consorts with your glory absolutely to exclude him from this design of his because in the bishop of so great a city the universal Church ought to rejoice with holy exultation, so that the true peace of the LORD may be glorified not only by the preaching of the Faith, but also by the example of men's conduct."

And

"But you see, venerable Emperor, and clearly understand, that in the person, whose excommunication is contemplated, it is not only the integrity of his faith that must be considered; for even, if that could be purged by any punishments and confessions, and completely restored by any conditions, yet the wicked and bloody deeds that have been committed can never be done away by the protestations of plausible words."

This makes it clear that there was nothing objectionable in St Timothy's confession, and that whatever he said could never be acceptable in Leo of Rome's eyes, because he had chosen to believe the report of a handful of

Proterians. It was in the matter of his supposed conduct that St Timothy was considered irredeemable.

Thus it came about that St Timothy found himself banished to Gangra. Not on account of any heresy but because it was claimed that he had acted uncanonically and was implicated in the murder of Proterius.

Gangra is in Northern Turkey, and on his journey into exile he was taken into Palestine and up the coast. Throughout his journey crowds came out to seek his blessing,

"But when the cities and the inhabitants of Palestine and the seacoast heard it, they came to him to be sanctified, and that the sick among them gain healing for their diseases through the grace of God which was attached to his person; and they snatched torn pieces of stuff from his garments, that they might have them to protect them from evil."[156]

It is clear that the people and clergy of Alexandria had a great affection for St Timothy, and that this respect and veneration extended outside of Alexandria and Egypt, and was held by many faithful Orthodox throughout the region. Even in his exile it seems that St Timothy was able to continue his good works. We read,

"…the believing, virtuous, and miracle-working Timothy, was the friend of the poor; because he used to receive gifts from the believers of Alexandria and Egypt and other places, and to make liberal distribution for the relief of the needy."[157]

Now even here in Gangra St Timothy was not able to find relief from those who wished him ill. Gennadius, who had become the patriarch of Constantinople after Anatolius,

---

[156] Hamilton F.J. & Brooks E.W. trans. **Zachariah of Mitylene, Syriac Chronicle**, Book 4. Ch 1. p77, 1899

[157] Hamilton F.J. & Brooks E.W. trans. **Zachariah of Mitylene, Syriac Chronicle**, Book 4. Ch 1. p79, 1899

moved the Emperor to have St Timothy sent even further from any civilised place, and so he found himself sent by boat, even in the middle of winter, to Cherson, a region far away and north of the Crimea. Much of the animosity felt against him was due to the correspondence which he maintained with the Orthodox, both against the Eutychians and the Chalcedonians.

St Timothy continued to win supporters in high places. His writings were studied even in Constantinople.

"In consequence of these writings, those persons who understood the matter left Gennadius of Constantinople and joined in communion with Acacius the presbyter and Master of the Orphans, the brother of Timocletus the composer, who joined the believers, and strenuously opposed the Nestorians; and he also set verses to music, and they used to sing them. And the people were delighted with them, and they flocked in crowds to the Orphan Hospital."[158]

The Return of St Timothy from Exile

Just as the death of Marcian had allowed the election and consecration of St Timothy, so the death of Emperor Leo in 474 AD allowed an opportunity for St Timothy to be restored to Alexandria after eighteen years of exile. Zeno, who had risen to become the commander of the army, the *magister militum*, succeeded to the imperial throne, and immediately the clergy and people of Alexandria sent representatives to Constantinople requesting the return of St Timothy from his exile in far off Cherson. Zeno was of Isaurian origin however, and had taken the Greek name of Zeno on his marriage to the Emperor Leo's daughter, Ariadne. He was not popular among many of the Greek court, who especially resented the presence of Isaurian soldiers and officers in the city.

---

[158] Hamilton F.J. & Brooks E.W. trans. **Zachariah of Mitylene, Syriac Chronicle**, Book 4. Ch 1. p80, 1899

As a result, even before the Alexandrians reached Constantinople, there was a coup in January 474 AD and Leo's brother-in-law Basiliscus was placed on the throne by Verina, Leo's widow.

When the deputation from Alexandria arrived in the Imperial city they found themselves presented to Basiliscus, who was much impressed by them, as indeed were the queen, the court, and Acacius, Patriarch of Constantinople at the time.

Emperor Basiliscus gave orders that St Timothy should be restored from his long, but fruitful, exile, and while he was on his way to Constantinople the bishop Acacius prepared the church of Irene for his use, and set aside some of his own retinue and priests to serve him. He began to waver, however, and started to believe that one of the Alexandrian deputation, Theopompus the monk, was being prepared for the episcopacy in his place. In this state of mind he tried to oppose the pending arrival of St Timothy.

Nevertheless the exiled Patriarch of Alexandria finally entered the city in great state. Crowds of Alexandrian sailors and curious citizens of the Constantinople turned out to welcome him. He was taken to the royal palace and large numbers of people came to him to be blessed and receive healing at his hands.[159] St Timothy seems to have impressed many of those whom he met, including the Emperor and Acacius of Constantinople. Zachariah records,

"And becoming intimate both with Basiliscus and his wife, Timothy, along with those who happened to be there with him and on his behalf, persuaded the king, so that he consented to write encyclical letters, in which he would anathematise the Tome and the addition which was made at Chalcedon. For Paul the monk, who was a rhetorician and a sophist, drew them up. And it was he who, in a discussion

---

[159] Hamilton F.J. & Brooks E.W. trans. **Zachariah of Mitylene, Syriac Chronicle**, Book 4. Ch 1. p104, 1899

with Acacius the patriarch, was able to show that the heresies of Nestorius and Eutyches are one and the same; though they are generally thought to be diametrically opposed to each other. For the one, indeed, making objection declares that it would be a degradation to God to be born of a woman, and to be made in all points like as we are, by becoming partaker of flesh and blood; whereas He was only partaker by identity of name, and by power and indwelling, and by operation. But the other, indeed, for the purpose of liberating and exalting God, so that He should not suffer degradation and contempt by association with a human body, publishes the doctrine that He became incarnate from His own essence, and that He assumed a heavenly body; and that just as there is no part of the seal left upon the wax, nor of the golden signet upon the clay, so neither did there cleave to Christ any portion of humanity whatsoever."[160]

It is clear that St Timothy was no Eutychian. Indeed he understood entirely the defects of the Eutychian and Apollinarian Christology, both of which denied the full humanity of Christ, consubstantial with us. It is also clear that both the Emperor and the Patriarch were convinced by theological argument rather than mere political consideration. With this in mind Basiliscus restored Peter of Antioch and Paul of Ephesus to their own sees and promulgated his famous Encyclical.

"….And earnestly desiring to honour the fear of God more than any affair of man, through zeal for the Lord Jesus Christ our God, to Whom we owe our creation, exaltation, and glory; moreover also, being fully persuaded that the unity of His flock is the salvation of ourselves and our people, and is the sure and immovable foundation, and the lofty bulwark of our kingdom ; we now, moved by a wise impulse, are bringing union and unity to the Church of Christ in every part of our dominion, namely, the faith of the

---

[160] Hamilton F.J. & Brooks E.W. trans. **Zachariah of Mitylene, Syriac Chronicle**, Book 4. Ch 1. p105, 1899

three hundred and eighteen bishops, who being previously prepared by the Holy Ghost, assembled at Nicea, the security and well-being of human life, the faith which we hold, like all who have been before us, and in which we believe and are baptized, that it may hold and rule all the Churches with their chosen canons: the faith which is complete and perfect in all piety and true belief, and which rejects and exposes all heresies, and thrusts them out of the Church: the faith which the one hundred and fifty bishops, being assembled here to oppose and condemn the fighters against the Spirit, the Holy Lord confirmed, and with which they concurred and agreed : the faith which was also confirmed by the transactions of the two Councils at Ephesus, along with the chief priests of Rome and Alexandria, Celestine and Cyril, and Dioscorus, in condemnation of the heretic Nestorius, and all who after him have held similar opinions, and have confounded the order of the Church, and disturbed the peace of the world, and cleft asunder the unity; we mean the Tome of Leo, and the decrees of Chalcedon, whether by way of definition of the faith, or doctrine, or interpretation, or addition, or whatsoever other innovation was said or done contrary to the faith and the definition of the three hundred and eighteen.

"And therefore we command that wherever, here or elsewhere, such written doctrine be found, it shall be anathematised and burnt in the fire. For in accordance with this order, our blessed predecessors in the kingdom, Constantine the Great and Theodosius, in like manner, commanded and ordained. And also, the three subsequent Synods, that of the one hundred and fifty bishops here, and the two of Ephesus, ratified only the faith of Nicea, and agreed to the true definition there made.

"Moreover, we anathematise everyone who does not confess that the only-begotten Son of God truly became incarnate by the Holy Ghost from the Virgin Mary; not taking a body from heaven, in mere semblance or phantasy.

And also we anathematise all the false teaching of all those heresies which are contrary to the true faith of the fathers…..."[161].

This document is notable for its recognition of the second council of Ephesus in 449 AD, which is described as condemning the heresy of Nestorius, and for its categorisation of the Tome of Leo and the decrees of Chalcedon as breaking the unity of the Church and perpetuating that same heresy. The Encyclical orders the destruction of any written materials containing such doctrines and anathematises those who fail to confess the reality of the incarnation, and all the false teachings which are contrary to the fathers.

All in all the document is rather restrained. The Tome and Chalcedon are criticised as being of the same opinion as Nestorius, but the anathema is reserved for those who fail to confess the incarnation and have a Eutychian Christology, and it falls equally upon the false teachings of any who set themselves against the fathers. Practically speaking it sets aside the Tome and Chalcedon, restores the authority of the second council of Ephesus and anathematises those who truly hold to Eutychian ideas.

The Encyclical was sent out throughout the Empire and was signed by St Timothy, Peter of Antioch, Paul of Ephesus, the bishops of Asia and the East, and Anastasius of Jerusalem and his Synod. Altogether about 700 bishops signed their agreement with the document. The bishops of the province of Asia Minor gathered at Ephesus and sent the following statement to the Emperor.

"But now that the light of the true faith has arisen upon us, and the dark cloud of error been rolled away from us, we make known by this declaration our true faith to your Majesties and to all the world. And we say that freely and

---

[161] Hamilton F.J. & Brooks E.W. trans. **Zachariah of Mitylene, Syriac Chronicle**, Book 4. Ch 1. p106, 1899

with willing consent, by the aid of John the Evangelist as our teacher, we have signed this Encyclical; and we agree to it and to everything in it, without compulsion, or fear, or favour of man. And if at any future time violence shall meet us from man, we are prepared to despise fire and sword and banishment and the spoiling of our goods, and to treat all bodily suffering with contempt; so that we may adhere to the true faith. We have anathematised and we do anathematise the Tome of Leo and the decrees of Chalcedon; which have been the cause of much blood-shedding, and confusion, and tumult, and trouble, and divisions, and strifes in all the world. For we are satisfied with the doctrine and faith of the apostles and of the holy fathers, the three hundred and eighteen bishops; to which also the illustrious Council of the one hundred and fifty in the Royal City, and the two other holy Synods at Ephesus adhered, and which they confirmed. And we join with them in anathematising Nestorius, and everyone who does not confess that the only-begotten Son of God was incarnate by the Holy Ghost, of the Virgin Mary; He becoming perfect man, while yet He remained, without change and the same, perfect God; and that He was not incarnate from Heaven in semblance or phantasy. And we further anathematise all other heresies." [162]

It is necessary to note that the bishops of Asia Minor state that they have agreed to and signed the Encyclical without compulsion, and without political considerations. They even state that if they are threatened with violence or exile in the future they are willing to despise such persecution for the sake of the true faith which the Encyclical promotes. The bishops gathered at Ephesus also give authority to the second council at Ephesus in 449 AD under Pope Dioscorus. This second council, and the Encyclical of Basiliscus, is understood as anathematising Nestorius, and rejecting Eutychianism. The bishops agree with the Emperor

---

[162] Hamilton F.J. & Brooks E.W. trans. **Zachariah of Mitylene, Syriac Chronicle**, Book 4. Ch 1. p108, 1899

Basiliscus and explicitly anathematise the Tome of Leo and the decrees of Chalcedon.

Zachariah mentions that the bishops of the other regions wrote similar letters, some even considering, in an honorific sense, the Emperor Basiliscus as a 319th bishop among the fathers of Nicaea. The intent of the Encyclical, St Timothy who had influenced the Emperor to issue it, and that of the bishops who signed it, seems to have been to ensure that both Nestorianism and Eutychianism were condemned while the Chalcedonian Christological settlement was rolled back to that of the second council of Ephesus in 449 AD. It was to be no longer acceptable to speak of Christ as being 'in two natures', once more the Cyrilline terminology 'of two natures' was to be solely authorised. The Encyclical and the bishops agreeing to it were careful to ensure that the doctrine of the real incarnation of Christ, as perfect God and perfect man, without change, was confessed.

In fact the purpose of the Encyclical was to gain support from the bishops of the whole Empire for the imperial objective, which was to suppress all mention of Chalcedon and the Tome, as being the root of disunity in the Church at that time, while also ensuring that both Nestorianism and Eutychianism were anathematised.

It is something of a surprise to find so many bishops subscribing to the Encyclical only 23 years after the council of Chalcedon. A great many of the bishops must have been signatories of Chalcedon itself, and certainly to have been monks and priests at that time.

There was opposition to St Timothy in Constantinople. Not from the Chalcedonians so much as from the Eutychianists, who had hoped that St Timothy would support them. Far from it. He continued to oppose them in person as he had by his letters from exile. As a result of his public statements the Eutychianists seperated themselves from him, while many others joined themselves to him. Nevertheless the Eutychianists had some influence at court and Theoctistus, the Master of the Offices, urged St Timothy to leave Constantinople for Alexandria, where he would be safe.

St Timothy therefore travelled to Ephesus, en route for Alexandria, where the bishop Paul was restored to his see by a synod convened there, and Ephesus was able to regain many of the canonical privileges which had been taken from it at Chalcedon and given to Constantinople. For a moment it was as if Chalcedon had never taken place.

On his arrival in Alexandria he was greeted by crowds of people speaking all the different languages represented in the city, with torches and songs of praise, and they conducted him to the great church chanting, 'Blessed is he who comes in the name of the Lord'.[163]

There is a difference of opinion between Zachariah and Evagrius in respect of the welcome which St Timothy received in Alexandria. This seems to be due to Evagrius simply misreading Zachariah's account. Zachariah mentions that a number of people withdrew from him when he arrived in Alexandria,

"And inasmuch as he was a peaceable and kind man, and also gentle in his words, and by no means passionate, he remitted to the members of the Proterian party the term of repentance, which he had written and appointed for the penitents when he was in banishment.......

But certain persons, who were ignorant of the rights of divine love, severed themselves from him on account of his gentleness and mildness towards the penitents, in that he required nothing else from them except that they should anathematise the Synod and the Tome, and confess the true faith; and because he did not hold them aloof, even for a

---

[163] Hamilton F.J. & Brooks E.W. trans. **Zachariah of Mitylene, Syriac Chronicle**, Book 4. Ch 1. p110, 1899

little while, from the communion which they had made desolate.

But at the head of these persons was Theodoret the bishop of Joppa, who had been consecrated by Theodosius some time before. And he was then filled with envy because he had not also been received back again to his see. And, lo! the illustrious Peter the Iberian did not return to Gaza; and he did not at all agree with this faction, but he was warmly attached to Timothy, and he proved that his conduct and actions were in conformity with the will of God. But the Separatists who sided with Theodotus fell into such error that they even practised reanointing, and they were called Anachristo-Novatians." [164]

From this passage it is clear that St Timothy maintained his eirenic and reconciliatory approach, which was that those who had supported Chalcedon and the Tome could be received into communion if they simply anathematised the Tome and the Council and, in the case of clergy, remained constant for the course of a year. It is also clear that a small group of rigourists existed which rejected this approach and wished to consider the Chalcedonian party as being without sacramental grace, so that they chrismated those that came over to them.

Now Evagrius Scholasticus takes this passage and misinterprets it completely. He writes,

"Proceeding thence, he arrives at Alexandria, and uniformly required all who approached him to anathematise the synod at Chalcedon. Accordingly, there abandon him, as has been recorded by the same Zacharius, many of his party, and among them Theodotus, one of the bishops ordained at Joppa by Theodosius, who had, by means of certain persons, become bishop of Jerusalem, at the time when Juvenalis betook himself to Byzantium." [165]

---

[164] Hamilton F.J. & Brooks E.W. trans. **Zachariah of Mitylene, Syriac Chronicle**, Book 4. Ch 1. p111, 1899

Now of course it is true that St Timothy required those in his communion to anthematise the council of Chalcedon, but Evagrius represents the seperation of Theodotus as being caused by this requirement. As though St Timothy were the strict enforcer of the anti-Chalcedonian position offending even his supporters by his severity. Nothing could be further from the truth, as Zachariah, the author of Evagrius' information actually makes very clear. St Timothy was the gentle and peaceable bishop while Theodotus was the Novatian, going beyond what Orthodoxy required for the reconciliation of seperated believers.

This shows just how difficult it is to gain a fair appreciation of St Timothy from any Chalcedonian sources since even where the primary sources of information are plainly in St Timothy's favour the Chalcedonian histories manage to paint something entirely negative.

Zachariah gives a few glimpses of the spirit of St Timothy when he had been restored to Alexandria. The Proterian Patriarch, Timothy Salophaciolus, a quiet man himself, had retired to his monastery and supported himself, as a simple monk, by the weaving of baskets. St Timothy arranged that he should receive a pension of a denarius a day for his own use.

He insisted on giving as gifts to the Emperor, the nobles and the tax-gatherers, merely a few pennies, reasoning that it was the duty of the Church to expend itself on the widows and orphans. And the people of Alexandria especially loved him because he had brought back from exile the remains of St Dioscorus and his brother Anatolius, which were laid among the other bishops of Alexandria in great state.

Unfortunately, Acacius of Constantinople was not willing to lose any of the powers which Chalcedon had given

---

[165] Walford E. **Evagrius Scholasticus, Ecclesiastical History**, p129 Bagster, 1846

to the Imperial city, and he stirred up those who remained in opposition to the Emperor and his Encyclical, even calling on Daniel the Stylite to come and add his authority. The Emperor was proclaimed a heretic and fearful for his security within the city, and even more fearful of Zeno, the Emperor he had himself usurped, and who was now approaching with an army, he issued an Anti-Encyclical, reversing his previous position.

Zeno entered the city and regained his throne, cancelling all the actions which had taken place under Basiliscus. He deposed Peter of Antioch and Paul of Ephesus, but St Timothy passed away in 476 AD while threats were being raised against him. He was buried with great honour by Peter Mongus who succeeded him.

As a footnote to the historical context of St Timothy's life it should be noted with some disappointment and even shame that many of the bishops who had signed the Encyclical, stating that they were not acting under compulsion, now wrote to the new Emperor claiming that their agreement had been entirely due to necessity. Even Evagrius sounds rather ashamed of these wavering supporters of Chalcedon and writes,

"The bishops of Asia, to sooth Acacius, address to him a deprecatory plea, and implore his pardon in a repentant memorial, wherein they alleged, that they had subscribed the circular by compulsion and not voluntarily; and they affirmed with an oath that the case was really thus, and that they had settled their faith, and still maintained it in accordance with the synod at Chalcedon. The purport of the document is as follows.

An epistle or petition sent from the bishops of Asia, to Acacius, bishop of Constantinople. "To Acacius, the most holy and pious patriarch of the church in the imperial city of Constantine, the New Rome." And it afterwards proceeds: "We have been duly visited by the person who will also act as our representative." And shortly after: "By these letters we acquaint you that we subscribed, not designedly but of necessity, having agreed to these matters with letters and words, not with the heart. For, by your acceptable prayers and the will of the higher Power, we hold the faith as we have received it from the three hundred and eighteen lights of the world, and the hundred and fifty holy fathers; and, moreover, we assent to the terms which were piously and rightly framed at Chalcedon by the holy fathers there assembled."

Whether Zacharias has slandered these persons, or they themselves lied in asserting that they were unwilling to subscribe, I am not able to say." [166]

Whether they had signed the Encyclical out of fear and lied when they said they had faced no compulsion, or later lied when they said that they had faced compulsion, either way they come out of the episode shamefully. While St Timothy had spent 18 years in exile rather than sacrifice his principles and faith to save his position many of these bishops seem to have blown this way and that with whatever theological position had Imperial support.

Nevertheless Zachariah records that Anastasius of Jerusalem remained faithful to the position of the Encyclical, as did the provinces in his Synod. And Epiphanius of Magdolum departed to Alexandria rather than deny what he had agreed to.

The Christology of St Timothy of Alexandria

We are fortunate that we have a number of sources of theological materials from the pen of St Timothy. Some of these are found in the histories of Zachariah and Evagrius, others are letters recently translated into English, while others remain available only in other European languages.

---

[166] Walford E. **Evagrius Scholasticus, Ecclesiastical History**, p132 Bagster, 1846

Much of the material concerns St Timothy's struggle against Eutychians in Alexandria and especially in Constantinople.

There was a community of these heretics in Constantinople who were claiming that St Timothy believed as they did. He wrote a lengthy letter against them, containing many proofs from the fathers that Christ should be confessed as consubstantial in His Godhead with the Father, and consubstantial in flesh with us. He writes,

"For we believe, in accordance with the tradition of the fathers, that our Lord Jesus Christ was consubstantial in flesh with us, and one with his own flesh. For we hear the holy Apostle declaring: 'Since therefore the children share in flesh and blood, he himself partook of it like them, ….Therefore he had to be made like his brethren in every respect, so that he might become a merciful and faithful high priest in what pertains to God…..' This expression, 'like us in everything' counsels all of us, who wish to live and enjoy eternal benefits, to confess that our Lord Jesus Christ's flesh is derived from Mary the holy Virgin and Mother of God, because he was consubstantial in the flesh with her and with us, he who is consubstantial in his Godhead with the Father".[167]

St Timothy then goes on to quote from St Athanasius, St Basil, St Gregory, St Ambrose, St Theophilus, St Cyril and St John Chrysostom. He uses all of these passages to stress that Christ is really consubstantial with us according to his humanity, while remaining consubstantial with the Father according to his Divinity.

The Eutychian party in Constantinople failed to heed his rebuke and St Timothy was finally forced to send a letter excommunicating two prominent members of the heretical community, Isaiah, who had been a bishop, and Theophilus

---

[167] Ebied R.Y. and Wickham L.R. **Syriac Letters of Timothy Aelurus** Journal of Theological Studies XXI pt 2, p352.

who was a priest. They had professed the heresy of Eutyches for some time privately, and after having failed to reform their opinions St Timothy now addressed himself to the Church of Alexandria warning all the faithful about them. He wrote, saying,

"I promised that if they refrained from heterodoxy and confessed that our Lord was consubstantial in flesh with us and that he was not of a different nature, I would maintain them in their former honour and would grasp them with the same love…..I then saw that they persisted for about four years in not repenting, in being disobedient to the doctrine of the holy fathers and bishops and in refusing to accept that our Lord took flesh from the holy Virgin, and in asserting that he did not truly partake of her blood or flesh at all." [168]

It is clear that St Timothy had no time for proponents of the heresy of Eutyches, and he considered that it was merely a companion heresy of Nestorianism, both of which refused to confess that God the Word had become truly incarnate. St Timothy cannot be considered a Eutychian. He confesses that 'our Lord was consubstantial in the flesh with us'. This was Eutyches' sticking point. He believed that Christ was man, but not of the same humanity as us.

St Timothy was so hostile to the Eutychian poison that he had no choice but to write,

"It seemed to me to be necessary, for the sake of those simple folk who are falling victim to them, to inform everyone, naming the above mentioned Isaiah and Theophilus as persons who, by asserting that our Lord and God Jesus Christ is of an alien nature from us and that he was not consubstantial in flesh with men and that he was not really human, have alienated themselves from communion

---

[168] Ebied R.Y. and Wickham L.R. **Syriac Letters of Timothy Aelurus** Journal of Theological Studies XXI pt 2, p358.

with the holy fathers and with me, and give warning that no man henceforth should hold communion with them". [169]

This must surely prove that St Timothy believed that our Lord Jesus Christ was consubstantial with us, and really human. Christ would not be 'really human' if his humanity was swallowed up in his Divinity, or if his humanity came from heaven, or if he was of some third Christ essence, neither human nor Divine. He shows himself to be a consistent follower of the teaching of his predecessors, indeed he quotes from a letter of St Dioscorus which shows clearly that both of them confessed the real and complete humanity of Christ, which was not an 'unreal appearance' in any sense, but was the true flesh of the Word of God, who 'became man, without abandoning his being Son of God, in order that we might, through the grace of God, become sons of God'.[170]

A few excerpts from this letter show how both St Timothy and St Dioscorus thought about the humanity of Christ, in opposition to the Eutychians. He writes,

"My declaration is that no man shall assert that the flesh, which our Lord took from holy Mary, through the Holy Spirit, in a manner known only to himself, is different from or alien to our body……'It was right that in everything he should be made like his brethren'. The phrase is 'in everything'. It does not exclude any part of our nature at all. It includes nerves, hair, bones, veins, belly, heart, kidneys, liver, and lung. That flesh of our Saviour, which was born of Mary, and which was ensouled with a rational soul, was constituted of every element of which we are composed….For he was with us, like us, for us. He was not, God forbid, an unreal appearance, as the heresy of the evil

---

[169] Ebied R.Y. and Wickham L.R. **Syriac Letters of Timothy Aelurus** Journal of Theological Studies XXI pt 2, p359.

[170] Ebied R.Y. and Wickham L.R. **Syriac Letters of Timothy Aelurus** Journal of Theological Studies XXI pt 2, p360.

Manichees has it. But he truly issued from Mary, Mother of God, according to his will, thus restoring, by his present advent to us, the shattered vessel...These are the views we hold and confess." [171]

How could anyone, reading these words, believe that either St Timothy or St Dioscorus were Eutychians, teaching a fantasy incarnation in which Christ was actually not 'made flesh' at all? It is surely excluded in every sentence and phrase and by the explicit rejection of an incarnation in appearance only.

Elsewhere he writes,

"These anti-Christs neither acknowledge that Jesus Christ has come into the world in human flesh, nor believe that God the Word became man whilst remaining God unchanged.... Some of them say that our Lord's incarnation was illusion, imagination and unreal..They are now preaching the evil doctrines of the Phantasiast heresy by saying that the body of our Lord and God Jesus Christ is uncreated, that body which was constituted of created manhood." [172]

And he writes much more in the same vein. Now if it is anti-Christ to deny the real humanity of Christ, his complete consubstantiality with us, save sin, and his unchanged Divinity, then how can St Timothy be accused of these same things? He says that 'our Lord was truly man for our sake and for the sake of our salvation', and these are thoughts which no Eutychian could ever share.

But St Timothy also wrote against Chalcedon and the settlement which had been imposed by Imperial force. There is no doubt that he considered the Tome of Leo and

---

[171] Ebied R.Y. and Wickham L.R. **Syriac Letters of Timothy Aelurus** Journal of Theological Studies XXI pt 2, p360.

[172] Ebied R.Y. and Wickham L.R. **Syriac Letters of Timothy Aelurus** Journal of Theological Studies XXI pt 2, p367.

Chalcedon to have been compromised by Nestorianism. Thus he writes to his people in Egypt,

"On the question you wrote to me about, of the unknown and foreign religious who come to you, first acquaint them with the harm, of which they may be unconscious, of the heresy of the Diphysites. If they agree to take our side, let them anathematise those who hold such views, namely the Council of Chalcedon, the Tome of Leo of Rome, and the whole heresy." [173]

Now the heresy of the Diphysites is not the confession of the perfect and complete humanity and Divinity of Christ, hypostatically united without confusion, mixture, division or separation. It is the confession of a Christ in whom the humanity and Divinity stand in a relationship of independent realities, united only externally and in honour and name. This passage, and others like it from the letters of St Timothy, show that he was not rejecting Chalcedon and the Tome as a result of politics, or out of wilfuillness, but because he was convinced that it had facilitated 'those two wolves which have leaped forwardly over the wall and entered into the divine fold of Christ's flock'. It was as a matter of spiritual necessity that he objected to Chalcedon and the Tome.

The error St Timothy found in Chalcedon and the Tome was exactly that of allowing Christ to be separated and divided into two. Two persons, two self-subsistent hypostases, two independent realities. And it is a fact that there were plenty of supporters of the Tome and Chalcedon who did divide Christ in such a way and provided plenty of cause for concern among the anti-Chalcedonian party.

It is well known that Nestorius himself had written that the Tome of Leo expressed his own Christology. And there were monks even in Constantinople keeping a feast of

---

[173] Ebied R.Y. and Wickham L.R. **Syriac Letters of Timothy Aelurus** Journal of Theological Studies XXI pt 2, p362.

Nestorius after he died in exile. And in the West, the provinces under the authority of Rome and in North Africa considered that Chalcedon had in fact defended the teaching of Theodoret and Ibas. There were plenty of real Nestorians, as there were real Eutychians. But whereas St Timothy fought vigourously against the Eutychians, it seemed to him that the Tome and Chalcedon had quite simply accepted a Nestorian Christology and had failed to struggle against it at all.

It cannot be asserted that St Timothy rejected the Tome and Chalcedon because they taught the reality of the humanity and Divinity in Christ. It is already clear that this was entirely his own confession. If he objected to them it was because he considered that they had failed to exclude the Nestorian heresy from the Church.

The Encyclical of Basiliscus was perhaps the high point in his efforts to reverse what he saw as a Nestorian settlement after Chalcedon. It is clear from the Encyclical, written under the influence of St Timothy, who had been recalled from exile, that Eutychianism and Nestorianism were to be excluded,

"We anathematise everyone who does not confess that the only-begotten Son of God truly became incarnate by the Holy Ghost from the Virgin Mary; not taking a body from heaven, in mere semblance or phantasy....... We ordain that the basis and settlement of human felicity, namely, the symbol of the three hundred and eighteen holy fathers who were assembled, in concert with the Holy Spirit, at Nicaea, into which both ourselves and all our believing predecessors were baptised; that this alone should have reception and authority with the orthodox people in all the most holy churches of God, as the only formulary of the right faith, and sufficient for the utter destruction of every heresy, and for the complete unity of the holy churches of God; without prejudice, notwithstanding, to the force of the acts of the hundred and fifty holy fathers assembled in this imperial city, in confirmation of the sacred symbol itself, and in condemnation of those who blasphemed against the Holy Ghost; as well as of all that were passed in the metropolitan city of the Ephesians against the impious Nestorius and those who subsequently favoured his opinions." [174]

So as far as St Timothy was required, the solution to the divisions introduced by the Tome and Chalcedon, both Christologically and Ecclesiologically, was to base the rejection of Nestorianism on the first council of Ephesus, with the anathemas of St Cyril, and the rejection of Eutychianism on an explicit anathema in the Encyclical. The Tome and Chalcedon had no place in this alternative settlement, indeed they were considered as part of the problem. Yet it must be insisted over and over again that St Timothy did not reject the Tome and Chalcedon because he was a Eutychian, but because he was vehemently opposed to any failure to confess the true and real incarnation of Christ, which he considered both Nestorianism and Eutychianism were guilty of.

But St Timothy should not be considered a harsh and aggressive polemicist. On the contrary he was a gentle man and filled with concern for those he thought had been deceived by error. We can note the manner in which he dealt with different categories of believers.

If we consider the ordinary believer, perhaps a little confused by ecclesiological events over the previous years, St Timothy has the following instructions,

"If, therefore, an ordinary, simple person comes to you, confessing the holy faith of the consubstantial Trinity, and desirous of being in communion with you who acknowledge our Lord's fleshly consubstantiality with us – I entreat you, not to constrain those who hold such views as these at all with other words, nor require from them

---

[174] Walford E. **Evagrius Scholasticus, Ecclesiastical History**, p123 Bagster, 1846

additional verbal subtleties, but leave such people to praise God and bless the Lord in the simplicity and innocence of their hearts....Anyone who does not abuse the saints touching this declaration: 'I confess that our Lord is our brother and that he was of the same fleshly stock as us for the sake of our salvation', accept such an one in our Lord." [175]

St Timothy is not overly concerned about words and formulas. He seeks a right content to a person's faith. If a simple soul, not particularly theologically literate, confesses that Christ is consubstantial with us according to his humanity, then such a one is Orthodox. No chrismation, no period of probation. The simple believer is received into communion on the basis of his simple confession in the reality of the incarnation.

Other believers were simply required to anathematise those who held heretical views, both Nestorian and Eutychian. The aim was to restore separated Christians to commune as easily as possible with due regard to the necessity for making a clean break with Nestorianism and Eutychianism.

Finally, in regard to clergy, whether ordained bishop, priest or deacon, St Timothy was equally considerate rather than committed to an violent approach. His instructions were,

"Let such an one repair to the bishops, clergy of ours or orthodox religious, in his vicinity, so that they may be trustworthy witnesses of his present repentance. Let him anathematise in writing, before the orthodox who belong to the whole place, the Council of Chalcedon and the Tome by wicked Leo of Rome....Then let him thus be granted the burden of penance in God, in such a case as his is limited to one year." [176]

---

[175] Ebied R.Y. and Wickham L.R. **Syriac Letters of Timothy Aelurus** Journal of Theological Studies XXI pt 2, p365.

[176] Ebied R.Y. and Wickham L.R. **Syriac Letters of Timothy**

Thus even in the case of clergy coming over to the anti-Chalcedonian communion it was necessary only for an anathema to be pronounced upon the Tome and Chalcedon, and for a period of penance to prove the stability of such repentance.

St Timothy was certainly a gentle and peaceable bishop, even his long exile had not embittered him. His letters are filled with pastoral concern, even for those bound up in what were considered the errors of the Tome and Chalcedon. He took a moderate but vigourous stand against the conjoined errors of Nestorianism and Eutychianism, both of which failed to confess the real incarnation of Christ.

St Timothy clearly confesses that the humanity of Christ is entirely consubstantial with us, save sin, and that the Divinity of Christ remained without change when Christ became incarnate. He is no Eutychian, but a faithful disciple of St Cyril, as St Dioscorus, his predecessor equally was. The whole tenor of his letters, and the content of the ecclesiastical histories of the period, strongly resist the partisan and unreliable account of St Timothy's involvement in the death of Proterius, the intruding Patriarch of Alexandria.

St Timothy has been unfairly treated by history. He is perhaps too little known even by members of the Oriental Orthodox communion of Churches. The evidence shows that he was a genuinely eirenic bishop, with a pastoral spirit deserving the honour that the Church has accorded him as St Timothy the Great of Alexandria.

Aelurus Journal of Theological Studies XXI pt 2, p363.

After Chalcedon - Orthodoxy in the 5th/6th Centuries

It seems to be received as an historical fact that after the Council of Chalcedon those Christians who refused to accept its decisions and doctrinal statements were immediately isolated and rapidly withdrew into their own communion. This opinion is far from reflecting historical reality, and yet it is often presumed to be true by Oriental Orthodox as much as Chalcedonian Orthodox.

It fails to take full account of the truth that for a Council to be Ecumenical it must be received by the whole Church, and ignores the reality that large numbers of Orthodox Christians rejected it, and continued to oppose it. This opinion assumes that because one group of Orthodox defined the Faith in a particular way any who disagreed with that definition must of necessity have separated themselves from the Faith and therefore from the Church. Yet in the years after Chalcedon, and throughout the 6th century, those who rejected Chalcedon continued to play a significant, and at times dominant, role in the Orthodox Church.

Even before the Council of Chalcedon there had been tensions between those who followed the teaching and terminology of St. Cyril and those who favoured the teaching and terminology of the Antiochean School. The Council of Ephesus in 431 AD had not resolved these tensions even though it had firmly stated the Orthodox position. The Council had left the Church divided and there were large numbers of Orthodox who were out of communion with one another. St. Cyril understood that it was the substance of Christological teaching which was at stake and allowed the use of certain Antiochean terminology, such as speaking of two natures after the union, where it could be unequivocally seen that those using such terminology were fully Orthodox in their understanding of Christ. Thus he was able to restore communion with the Antiocheans under John of Antioch.

Though communion was restored there were still many tensions between these two theological expressions. Yet there was no sense in which either party was viewed as having been a separate Church. Nor was there seen to be a need for any of the episcopal acts of those who had objected to the Council of Ephesus to be repeated, nor were they viewed as invalid. Indeed some Antiocheans continued to be supporters of Nestorius and other heretics such as Theodoret and Diodore even while being in communion with St. Cyril and those who believed according to the Council of Ephesus. These differing attitudes towards Nestorius and his teachings undoubtedly caused problems, and towards the end of his life St. Cyril considered that the Antiocheans had failed to be really converted to Ephesine Orthodoxy. But there was never any sense that once out of communion there could never be the possibility of being back in communion, or that once in error and un-Orthodox there was no prospect of correction and being Orthodox again. When St. Cyril considered that the Antiocheans had substantially accepted an Orthodox Christology then all the other difficulties that remained were passed over to be dealt with later.

Thus at Chalcedon the fact that from the Alexandrian perspective most of the Orthodox world had fallen into error was not something that could not be remedied. And indeed the followers of Chalcedon hoped that those who rejected the Council could be persuaded to accept it. Neither side understood either the acceptance or rejection of the Council to be irrevocable and the end for all time of any prospect of the other side being Orthodox.

The period of a century and a half following Chalcedon is not the story of a small group of malcontents slipping into obscurity. It is in fact a period during which the Non-Chalcedonians fought hard to restore the whole Church to Cyrilline Orthodoxy, and on several occasions seemed on the verge of doing so. In some respects the situation was similar to the current difficulties in the Anglican Church. There were Non-Chalcedonian congregations trying to cope with Chalcedonian bishops, and bishops faced with opposition from their Patriarchs. It was a period of some confusion but the theological conflict was played out within the Orthodox Church not between two completely separate Churches each claiming to be Orthodox.

There were three main factors complicating the theological debate that took place after Chalcedon. Rome had been lost to the barbarians, there was a growing sense of national identity in the various parts of the Empire, and the great Sees were continually in competition with each other. The Emperors had to balance the desire to regain Rome with the need to try and preserve unity within the Empire of the East. Theological divisions were no help and a uniform Christology was always one of the Emperors underlying ambitions. At times this meant that political policies impinged on theological and ecclesiastical affairs.

Thus Marcian supported Chalcedon and it must have appeared to him that there was the prospect of unity in the Church based on its Christological statement. But if that was indeed his opinion then he was quickly proved wrong. Pope St. Dioscorus may well have withstood his enemies alone, but the people of Alexandria were as staunch defenders of Cyrilline Orthodoxy as any of their bishops, and they were the first to make plain that the See of Alexandria was united in opposition to Chalcedon. When Proterius was appointed Patriarch in place of the exiled Pope Dioscorus he was greeted by a rioting crowd of Alexandrians. Opposition was not limited to Egypt. In Jerusalem the monks rejected Juvenal who had submitted to Chalcedon and appointed Theodosius in his place. The Emperor acted to replace Juvenal with another bishop who accepted Chalcedon but Theodosius had already consecrated several bishops who maintained opposition to Chalcedon.

In 457.AD the Emperor Marcian died. Those who had opposed Chalcedon were able to return to Alexandria and the people elected Timothy Aelurus as their bishop. Proterius was simply ignored, as far as the people of Egypt were concerned, he was merely an Imperial appointee. The Patriarchate of Alexandria was the only Church in Egypt. Those few who supported Proterius were not a different Church, and neither were the followers of Timothy a separate non-Orthodox sect. Thus when Timothy Aelurus was deposed and exiled by the command of the Emperor it was possible for another Timothy, nicknamed Salophaciolus or Trembling Cap, to be the Patriarch of both the Chalcedonian and Non-Chalcedonians in Egypt.

In 474.AD Zeno became Emperor, but he was the subject of a palace coup and Basiliscus became Emperor for just 20 months. During this time Timothy Aelurus was recalled from exile and became once more the head of the Church of Alexandria. He travelled to Constantinople where he was joined by the exiled Patriarch of Antioch, Peter the Fuller. The emperor was persuaded by these Patriarchs to send an encyclical to all the bishops throughout the empire calling upon them to anathematise the Tome of Leo and all the things said and done at Chalcedon which were innovations beyond the Faith of the three hundred and eighteen holy Fathers. Over 500 bishops subscribed to this letter, including the Patriarchs of Alexandria, Jerusalem and Antioch. The whole ecclesiastical situation seemed to have changed. It was now the Chalcedonians who were on the defensive.

A council was called at Ephesus and a large number of bishops gathered under Patriarchs Timothy and Peter to anathematise Chalcedon, recognise the autonomy of Ephesus and restore the former rights of the see to its bishop. When the council had concluded its business a letter was written to the emperor which said,

"We have anathematised and do anathematise the Tome of Leo and the decrees of Chalcedon, which have been the cause of much blood shedding and confusion, and tumult, and division and strifes in all the world. For we are satisfied with the doctrine and faith of the Apostles and the holy Fathers, the Three Hundred and Eighteen; to which also the illustrious Council of the One Hundred and Fifty in the royal city, and the two other holy Synods at Ephesus adhered, and which they confirmed."

Patriarch Timothy returned to Alexandria and the whole city came out to greet him. The compromise replacement who had held the Patriarchate while Timothy was in exile agreed to retire on a Church pension, and the holy relics of Pope St. Dioscorus were brought from Gangra, his place of exile, to be buried with the other Alexandrian bishops. It seemed for a while that the followers of St. Cyril would see the true faith established throughout the empire once more. A stand was made against those who leant towards the Eutychian heresy and Timothy disciplined several of his bishops. Yet Timothy always took a moderate line with Christians who came over to the Oriental position from having supported Chalcedon, and only insisted that they reject the dyophysite doctrine in writing. Those who had supported Chalcedon were never re-baptised or even anointed, clearly a sign that Timothy, and those with him, saw the followers of Chalcedon as fellow Christians even though they might be in error.

But Zeno returned from his exile and Basiliscus quickly issued another encyclical trying to gain support from the Chalcedonians. Patriarchs Timothy of Alexandria and Anastasius of Jerusalem refused to have anything to do with this new letter, but Zeno, when he had driven Basiliscus into exile, left them in peace since they were both elderly. This is another indication that though both sides opposed each other theologically they were nevertheless able to see a substantial measure of common ground between themselves. If the Chalcedonians had believed Timothy and Anastasius to be heretical in Christological substance then they would surely have not suffered them to retain their positions and influence under any circumstances.

Zeno realised that he could not force Chalcedon upon the empire. He was supported by Acacius, the Chalcedonian Patriarch of Constantinople, who also realised that concessions would need to be made to the opponents of Chalcedon. Acacius drew up the Henoticon as a document that could unite the divided Christians of the East. The text makes no use of the phrase 'two natures' and stresses the pre-eminence of the Nicene faith. It anathematises both Nestorius and Eutyches and all who think contrary to the teachings of Niceae. The Twelve Chapters of St. Cyril are received and while the reality of Christ's Godhead and manhood are upheld, any idea of 'two Sons' is most emphatically rejected. The Cyrilline teaching that 'both the miracles and the sufferings are those of one Person', the Second Person of the Trinity who became Incarnate.

Acacius addressed his letter to 'the bishops, clergy, monks and laity of Alexandria, Egypt, Libya and Pentapolis'. This is again evidence that he believed his theological opponents to be fully part of the Orthodox Church rather than a non-Orthodox sect. It is his fellow Christians he is trying to conciliate and not those who have lost any claim to Christian faith.

The Henoticon was understood to be an Imperial statement of faith which abrogated Chalcedon and the Tome of Leo. It seemed as though things could go back to the situation before Chalcedon had been called. Both Zeno and Acacius had been freed from the need to placate Western opinion by the establishment of a Vandal kingdom centred on Ravenna. The Henoticon caused a schism between the East and West which lasted 35 years but at the time the opinion of the Pope of Rome carried little weight in Constantinople.

Even though Zeno had expelled Basiliscus things were still going well for the opponents of Chalcedon. For the first time the great Sees of Constantinople, Antioch, Jerusalem and Alexandria were united and Zeno was praised as 'the triumphant star of Christ from the East'. Even the more extreme opponents of Chalcedon accepted that the Henoticon contained a right confession of faith.

Emperor Zeno died in 491 AD and was succeeded by Anastasius, a supporter of the anti-Chalcedonian position. The new emperor was determined to maintain the unity that prevailed in the East, and as a result of his policies 'the Council of Chalcedon was neither openly proclaimed, nor yet repudiated by all'. This is again evidence that the Orthodox Church at that time was able to cope with a certain plurality of opinion within the bounds agreed in the Henoticon. It was not that Christology no longer mattered, but with both the Nestorian and Eutychian positions being explicitly anathematised there was some scope for a variety of opinion about terminology.

In Egypt, however, there remained a large minority who insisted that the Henoticon didn't go far enough, and together with that Orthodox statement it was necessary to anathematise the Council of Chalcedon and the Tome of Leo. Thus the Patriarchs of Alexandria all anathematised the

Council, indeed as described previously this was the method used to reconcile those who had been supporters of the Chalcedon. As the opponents of Chalcedon again gained influence in the empire the requirement to anathematise the Council became more insistent. By 512 AD the unity based on the Henoticon was still holding, but in the See of Antioch the Patriarch was now Flavian who was in sympathy with the doctrine of the two natures. He gathered together his bishops and most of them made it clear that they objected to the more rigorous policy being pursued by the opponents of Chalcedon. They supported the Henoticon but were unwilling to wholeheartedly anathematise the Council.

Flavian had left himself exposed and an edict of deposition was issued. The emperor fully supported all these moves and St. Severus, perhaps the greatest of Oriental Orthodox theologians, was brought to Antioch and made Patriarch. When he entered the cathedral and ascended the throne of St Ignatius all the people cried out,

"Set our city free from the Council of Chalcedon! Anathematise now this council which has turned the world upside down! Anathematise now the council of the distorters of faith! Let all the bishops anathematise it now!"

The supremacy of the opponents of Chalcedon was almost complete. At a synod held at Tyre the Henoticon was explained as abrogating the Council and the doctrinal statements which it issued, and which were viewed as additions to the faith, were anathematised. By 516 AD even the supporters of Chalcedon were willing to accept the Council and the Tome, 'not as a definition of faith, nor as a symbol, nor as an interpretation, but only as an anathema against Nestorius and Eutyches.'

Even at this high point of non-Chalcedonian influence and power there was no sense of their being two

Churches in the empire. The struggle was for theological truth within the Church not between two different Churches. Both supporters and opponents of Chalcedon could co-exist in a compromise position based on the Henoticon but as the position of the opponents was increasingly established in the empire the requirement to explicitly anathematise Chalcedon meant that in all the great Sees it was the non-Chalcedonians who held the most important positions.

On July 1st, 518 AD, Anastasius died and almost overnight the situation changed. The opponents of Chalcedon now found themselves the opponents of the emperor. The new emperor, Justin, demanded strict uniformity throughout his empire, and he had determined that as far as the Church was concerned that would be a Chalcedonian uniformity. He entered into discussions with Rome about a re-union of East and West and within a year Rome had gained everything it asked for, Acacius was condemned and most of the non-Chalcedonian bishops had been deposed and exiled. Severus fled into Egypt where he spent the rest of his life supporting the non-Chalcedonian faithful and moving from monastery to monastery. Many other resisting bishops also found sanctuary in Egypt and it was at this time and under an increasingly severe persecution that the opponents of Chalcedon and its supporters found themselves becoming distinct Churches, though both still described themselves as Orthodox.

By 525 AD the imperial policy was that all resisting monks should be driven out of their monasteries. All over Arabia and Palestine the monks had to leave their monasteries, were robbed, put in irons and subjected to various tortures. Those faithful who gave them shelter were treated in the same way, and it seemed as if a great wave of persecution swept over all those who opposed Chalcedon. The monasteries of Syria broke off communion with the Chalcedonian bishops and all of them signed an anathema against Chalcedon and the Tome of Leo. In response the Imperial soldiers were sent to expel the monks. It was Winter, just two days before Christmas, and many of the faithful went out into the wilderness with the monks to accompany them some of the way in their journey. The old and sick were forced out and were borne along by the healthy on litters. These persecutions continued for many years until the godly empress Theodora was able to prevail on her husband to allow the monks to return to their monasteries.

In Egypt the Popes found themselves persecuted and imperial appointees imposed on the throne of St Mark. One such was Paul of Tinnis who arrived in Alexandria at the head of a body of soldiers. During his year in Alexandria no-one would communicate with him except the Imperial troops and provincial government. The emperor responded to these actions, which he viewed as a personal insult, by closing the Egyptian churches and setting a guard on them. Yet through this, and worse persecution, the people of Egypt refused to submit to the imperial policy of Chalcedonianism and felt themselves growing further apart from their Byzantine brethren.

Yet despite all of these difficulties there was still the possibility of a real union between the supporters and opponents of Chalcedon. In 530 AD the emperor relaxed his persecution of the resisting Christians and in 532 AD summoned the leaders of the non-Chalcedonians to Constantinople for a conference with the Chalcedonians. Severus did not attend this first meeting, but in 534 AD he made the long journey and was able to meet Anthimus who was made Patriarch of Constantinople and who refused to receive Chalcedon. In this year Theodosius, a friend of Severus, became Patriarch of Alexandria. Thus for a short time there were three opponents of Chalcedon in important positions.

The Emperor Justinian was never really committed to conciliating the non-Chalcedonians. He was more interested in union with Rome and the West. Thus in 536 AD Anthimus was deposed and Severus was condemned as a Nestorian and a Eutychian. The Empress Theodora, ever a supporter of Severus and the non-Chalcedonians helped him to escape back to Egypt where he died a few years later. But it was the last opportunity for any real chance at union. The persecution of non-Chalcedonians started again and the non-Chalcedonian's position increasingly became confused with national resistance to Byzantine oppression.

There were still contacts between the non-Chalcedonians and the Chalcedonians. There were further conferences between 550 and 564 AD, and when the Empress Theodora died a large body of Egyptian monks went up to Constantinople. On each occasion the non-Chalcedonians presented the Cyrilline doctrines about Christ and the reasons for their resistance to Chalcedon, but on each occasion they went home having achieved nothing. At the Second Council of Constantinople the writings of the Nestorians Ibas, Theodore and Theodoret were condemned, and the statements issued by the Chalcedonian bishops gathered there were still broadly in line with those of the Henoticon. The Council tried to express its opposition to the teachings of both Nestorius and Eutyches and spoke in its decrees came close to the non-Chalcedonian position. One such decree states,

"If anyone using the expression, "in two natures," does not confess that our one Lord Jesus Christ has been revealed in the divinity and in the humanity, so as to designate by that expression a difference of the natures of which an ineffable union is unconfusedly made, a union in which neither the nature of the Word was changed into that of the flesh, nor that of the flesh into that of the Word, for each remained that it was by nature, the union being hypostatic; but shall take the expression with regard to the mystery of Christ in a sense so as to divide the parties, or recognising the two natures in the only Lord Jesus, God the Word made man, does not content himself with taking in a theoretical manner the difference of the natures which compose him, which difference is not destroyed by the union between them, for one is composed of the two and the two are in one, but shall make use of the number two to divide the natures or to make of them Persons properly so called: let him be anathema."

There had certainly been a shift over time from the strictly Chalcedonian expressions about Christ, and at this Council it seemed that some non-Chalcedonian concerns had been given due weight. But Chalcedonian attitudes were hardening rather than softening and with the succession of Councils held by the Chalcedonians the non-Chalcedonians found themselves increasingly the subject of anathema and excluded from positions of influence within the empire.

Nevertheless, it can been seen that until the accession of Justin in 532 AD the opponents of Chalcedon had more influence and greater opportunity to further their theological position than had the supporters of Chalcedon. It was only with the reigns of the Emperors Justin and Justinian that the non-Chalcedonians found themselves facing the full weight of imperial aggression. Until that time the differences between the opponents and supporters of Chalcedon were predominantly theological and the Henoticon showed that the two sides could be reconciled. But such was the force of the persecution under Justin and Justinian that national feelings were aroused against the Byzantine empire and the theological position of non-Chalcedonianism became mixed with the political position of anti-Byzantinianism.

If a date should be placed on the separation of these two bodies of Christians it would be better to place it at 532

AD rather than 451 AD. The non-Chalcedonians had yet to reach the zenith of their influence in 451 AD and in 532 AD they were to suddenly find themselves at their lowest. Yet it is interesting that the two sides were still able to talk to each other, with some measure of equality, even up to 564 AD. This suggests that in the modern discussions between the Chalcedonians and non-Chalcedonians there is the possibility of dialogue as equals even while recognising the distinctives in each position. And it also suggests that Orthodoxy can accomodate such differences as exist between Chalcedonians and non-Chalcedonians as long as the heresies of Nestorius and Eutyches are explicitly condemned. An attitude of outright hostility between the two families of Orthodox is not a neccessity, and nor is there a requirement for either side to give up all distinctives in an imposed uniformity.

The history of theological tension after Chalcedon provides some hope for modern times. The ecclesiastical position of extreme Chalcedonians is not 'traditional', rather it represents a fear of any difference and a concentration on secondary issues while agreement in substantial matters is ignored. The conciliatory efforts of moderate Chalcedonians and non-Chalcedonians better represents the 'traditional' attitudes of the fathers of these years, and indeed of St Cyril himself. Following in their footsteps with humility and compassion there is once more the possibility of a real theological unity that respects difference and is able to cope with it.

The Oriental Orthodox Rejection of Chalcedon – An Introduction

The Oriental Orthodox are routinely accused of holding an heretical and Eutychianist Christology, and on that basis rejecting the Council of Chalcedon. Yet the evidence, from the time of Chalcedon, through the following centuries, and even to the present day, shows clearly that this is not the case.

Chalcedon was rejected for wholly Orthodox concerns, and though it might be the case that the text of the Chalcedonian Definition is liable to an Orthodox interpretation, it is nevertheless also the case that these concerns were not properly addressed at the time, or at any time following the council. They remain legitimate issues which the Chalcedonian Orthodox should at least make some effort to comprehend and understand.

These concerns, couched in anathemas issued after the council had taken place, show clearly that it was not because of Eutychianism that the rejection of Chalcedon was so principled and long lasting. Rather it was because of legitimate objections to the events which took place there, and the theological documents which the council produced.

The first explicit response to Chalcedon is found in the biography of Dioscorus of Alexandria, preserved as the 'Histoire de Dioscore, patriarche d'Alexandrie, écrite par son disciple Théopiste'[177]. This is a document, composed by an eyewitness to the events of Dioscorus' life, written in Greek, preserved in a Syriac copy, and translated into French at the beginning of the 20th century. Théopiste describes how Dioscorus had written a number of anathemas concerning the causes for which the Orthodox had separated from the Chalcedonians.

---

[177] F.Nau, *Journal Asiatique, X ser.*, t .I (1903) p 1-108

The content of these anathemas is found in another document, 'The Confession of Faith of Jacob Baradeus'[178], which has been preserved in two versions, an Arabic and an Ethiopian[179], In both of them Jacob approves and admits the 'six anathemas which Dioscorus pronounced against the Fourth Council'. The confession of faith then proceeds to provide the substance of these six anathemas, which follow:

i. Chalcedon is anathematised because the members of the council contradicted the faith of Nicaea, introducing a different nature into the Trinity by proposing a fourth hypostasis.

ii. Chalcedon is anathematised because it has trampled under foot the canons and prescriptions of the Fathers.

iii. Chalcedon is anathematised because the teachings which were established there have overturned the teachings of the council of Ephesus, and in making a new definition of the faith the council has fallen under the anathemas issued at Ephesus.

iv. Chalcedon is anathematised because it has corrupted the patristic doctrine and has received the Tome of Leo.

v. Chalcedon is anathematised because it has accepted the communion of the partisans of Nestorius, such as Ibas.

vi. Chalcedon is anathematised because in conformity with the doctrine of Nestorius the members of the council have distinguished two natures in Christ, separated into their proprieties; and they have offered Christ two adorations, calling one God and the other man.

It is clear that these anathemas of Dioscorus had a wider authority since they appear in a document associated with the missionary bishop Jacob Baradeus, and were thus

---

[178] Kleyn, *Jacobus Baradeus*, p121

[179] Cornill, *Zeitschrift der deut. Morg Gesellschaft*, t. XXX, 1876

distributed throughout the anti-Chalcedonian Orthodox communion well over a century after the martyrdom of Dioscorus at the hands of the Chalcedonians.

More than that, an almost identical list appears in the writings of Philoxenus of Mabbogh[180]. A comparison of these two lists shows that the same concerns prompted the ongoing rejection of Chalcedon.

The first anathema in these lists concerns the contention that Chalcedon had itself rejected the Nicene faith. This is based on the understanding of Chalcedon as teaching 'two sons', a Divine and a human. The creed of Niceae states, 'I believe in …One Lord Jesus Christ', and this phrase was understood as safeguarding the unity of subject in Jesus Christ, the Incarnate Word. Jesus Christ is not God the Word, and another. But Chalcedon was interpreted by the followers of St Cyril of Alexandria, after that council, as having taught exactly that.

Indeed if it is remembered that the term 'nature' was often used in the sense of 'individual' then it is clear that the Alexandrians and other opponents of Chalcedon were at least reasonable in finding such terms as 'in two natures' difficult to reconcile with Niceae. Christ the Incarnate Word is not 'two individuals', He is One Divine Person who is incarnate, that is, who is fully man whilst remaining what He is by nature, Divine. He had become man by an act of grace and loving condescension. He is not a human person, even though He is fully and perfectly human.

Therefore, in the context of a Christological crisis that had been raging for decades before Nestorius became archbishop of Constantinople, it was, and is, reasonable that the language of duality used at Chalcedon could have been

---

[180] Budge, *Addit. 14529 (f.68a) Brit. Mus* in *The Discourses*, II p. XCVIII-XCIX

understood as 'Nestorian'. The tradition of the heretical theologians Theodore and Diodore used such terms, and therefore they were bound to be difficult, or even impossible, for a Cyrilline Christology to interpret in any manner other than as perpetuating such an heretical Christology.

It must be said that the anathema is entirely justified against anyone who interprets Chalcedon as allowing the teaching of such a duality of subject in Christ, the Incarnate Word. This weakness in Chalcedon was dealt with comprehensively at the Fifth Council held by the Chalcedonians at Constantinople in 553 AD. This clearly shows that the Chalcedonians did indeed have a problem with Chalcedon being interpreted, among their own party, as being consistent with the heretical Christologies of Theodore and Diodore.

The Fifth Council includes in one of its canons the following passage:

If anyone understands the expression "one only Person of our Lord Jesus Christ" in this sense, that it is the union of many hypostases, and if he attempts thus to introduce into the mystery of Christ two hypostases, or two Persons, and, after having introduced two persons, speaks of one Person only out of dignity, honour or worship, as both Theodorus and Nestorius insanely have written; if anyone shall calumniate the holy Council of Chalcedon, pretending that it made use of this expression [one hypostasis] in this impious sense, and if he will not recognize rather that the Word of God is united with the flesh hypostatically, and that therefore there is but one hypostasis or one only Person, and that the holy Council of Chalcedon has professed in this sense the one Person of our Lord Jesus Christ: let him be anathema. [181]

Who were these Chalcedonians who were using the Council of Chalcedon as a means of supporting their heretical Christology? They must have included the large

---

[181] Nicene and Post-Nicene Fathers, Series II, Vol XIV

numbers of Chalcedonians who refused to accept this Fifth Council because it was seen as damaging Chalcedon which they interpreted as receiving the Christology of Theodore, Ibas and Theodoret, the authors of the so called Three Chapters.

After this Fifth Council all of the North African Church refused to communion with Rome over this issue, and the homeward bound Pope elect could only find two bishops who would consecrate him, all the rest of the West went into schism. In fact there was such a strong commitment to the idea that Chalcedon had approved the teachings of Theodore, Ibas and Theodoret that some parts of the West remained in schism from the mainstream Chalcedonians until 700 AD.

There was every reason for Chalcedonianism to wish to close the Christological loop-holes that Chalcedon had preserved for such heretical ideas to flourish, and the fact that this canon was required shows that the first anathema of Dioscorus was also entirely justified and reasonable.

The second anathema which appears in the lists of Dioscorus, Jacob and Philoxenus is due to the Council of Chalcedon because it had overturned the canons and prescriptions of the Fathers even while suggesting that it was respecting them and granting them authority.

The Definitio of Chalcedon insists that it is,

...renewing the unerring faith of the Fathers, publishing to all men the Creed of the Three Hundred and Eighteen, and to their number adding, as their peers, the Fathers who have received the same summary of religion. Such are the One Hundred and Fifty holy Fathers who afterwards assembled in the great Constantinople and ratified the same faith. Moreover, observing the order and every form relating to the faith, which was observed by the holy synod formerly held in Ephesus, of which Celestine of Rome and Cyril of Alexandria, of holy memory, were the leaders, we do

declare that the exposition of the right and blameless faith made by the Three Hundred and Eighteen holy and blessed Fathers, assembled at Nice in the reign of Constantine of pious memory, shall be pre-eminent: and that those things shall be of force also.[182]

Yet it seemed to those who could not accept Chalcedon that far from accepting the previous canons and councils the Chalcedonians were ignoring them. Nor was this only the opinion of the anti-Chalcedonians since after the Chalcedonians had promulgated their canons the Latin legate, Lucentius, opposed the council, saying,

The Apostolic See gave orders that all things should be done in our presence and therefore whatever yesterday was done to the prejudice of the canons during our absence, we beseech your highness to command to be rescinded. But if not, let our opposition be placed in the minutes, and pray let us know clearly what we are to report to that most apostolic bishop who is the ruler of the whole church, so that he may be able to take action with regard to the indignity done to his See and to the setting at naught of the canons.

This has particular regard to Canon XXVIII of Chalcedon which established Constantinople as being next to Rome in primacy and rather than giving a merely honorary consideration gave Constantinople authority over three provinces for the first time.

Tillemont, in his commentary on the council says that,

Leo also complains that the Council of Chalcedon broke the decrees of the Council of Nice, the practice of antiquity, and the rights of Metropolitans. Certainly it was an odious innovation to see a Bishop made the chief, not of one department but of three; for which no example could be found save in the authority which the

---

[182] Nicene and Post-Nicene Fathers, Series II, Vol XIV

Popes took over Illyricum, where, however, they did not claim the power to ordain any Bishop.[183]

This issue shows that it was not only anti-Chalcedonians who believed that Chalcedon had acted uncanonically and contrary to the tradition and practice of the Church. It is clear that the Romans also thought this to be the case.

It might be argued that Leo of Rome, and the anti-Chalcedonians were and are wrong, but it cannot be argued that the anti-Chalcedonian objection was frivolous and without cause.

The third anathema has particular relation to the Cyrilline council at Ephesus. This anathema has in mind particularly that canon of Ephesus which says,

When these things had been read, the holy Synod decreed that it is unlawful for any man to bring forward, or to write, or to compose a different Faith as a rival to that established by the holy Fathers assembled with the Holy Ghost in Nicaea.

But those who shall dare to compose a different faith, or to introduce or offer it to persons desiring to turn to the acknowledgment of the truth, whether from Heathenism or from Judaism, or from any heresy whatsoever, shall be deposed, if they be bishops or clergymen; bishops from the episcopate and clergymen from the clergy; and if they be laymen, they shall be anathematized.[184]

Of course the Chalcedonian Definitio had exactly the appearance of a 'new' Faith. It defines the content of the faith and is not content to simply refer back to the Nicean-Constantinopolitan Creed. Indeed a committee, which provokingly included the heretic Theodoret, was tasked to develop a statement of faith, and the Definitio certainly has authority within Chalcedonianism as a statement of Faith, and therefore a creed.

---

[183] Nicene and Post-Nicene Fathers, Series II, Vol XIV

[184] Nicene and Post-Nicene Fathers, Series II, Vol XIV

Where had any previous council defined Christ as being 'in two natures'? None had done so. Therefore the definition of Christ as being 'in two natures' must be considered a new statement of faith, even if it might be justified by modern Chalcedonians. Yet Chalcedon itself insisted,

> When these things had been read, the holy Synod decreed that it is unlawful for any man to bring forward, or to write, or to compose a different Faith as a rival to that established by the holy Fathers assembled with the Holy Ghost in Nicaea.
>
> But those who shall dare to compose a different faith, or to introduce or offer it to persons desiring to turn to the acknowledgment of the truth, whether from Heathenism or from Judaism, or from any heresy whatsoever, shall be deposed, if they be bishops or clergymen; bishops from the episcopate and clergymen from the clergy; and if they be laymen, they shall be anathematized.[185]

The irony is that while the council insisted that it was doing nothing new, it condemned those who refused to accept a new definition of the faith, and a new Christological terminology.

Once again, there may be those who will justify the Chalcedonian definition and the Chalcedonian terminology, but it cannot be said that the anti-Chalcedonian objection on this point was without reason, and justification.

The fourth anathema particularly concerns the reception of the Tome of Leo, and the contention that it had corrupted Faith rather than maintained it. This is not the place to analyse the anti-Chalcedonian rejection of the Tome in detail. But it is clear that the Tome was not rejected because of any Eutychianism.

Just a single illustration will show that the objections to the Tome were at least reasonable, even if Chalcedonians

---

[185] Nicene and Post-Nicene Fathers, Series II, Vol XIV

might consider them unjustified. One such problem passage in the Tome says,

> *For each "form" does the acts which belong to it, in communion with the other; the Word, that is, performing what belongs to the Word, and the flesh carrying out what belongs to the flesh; the one of these shines out in miracles, the other succumbs to injuries.*[186]

What are these 'forms' that are acting separately? How is it that the Word performs some acts and the flesh performs some others? Do not all the acts belong to the Word whose flesh it is? It can hardly be surprising that the anti-Chalcedonians found this passage so objectionable.

Indeed Nestorius himself opposes St Cyril and writes in a similar vein to the Tome of Leo, saying,

> *If any one, in confessing the sufferings of the flesh, ascribes these also to the Word of God as to the flesh in which he appeared, and thus does not distinguish the dignity of the natures; let him be anathema.*[187]

Now this sounds remarkably similar to the Tome of Leo, since it proposes that the sufferings of the flesh should not be ascribed to the Word. Of course this does not mean that the Tome of Leo was Nestorian, though Nestorius is on record as saying that it was consistent with his Christology. But the important point is that it could very easily *sound* Nestorian, and it certainly did to the anti-Chalcedon followers of St Cyril.

It was St Cyril who had insisted,

> *Whosoever shall not recognize that the Word of God suffered in the flesh, that he was crucified in the flesh, and that likewise in that same flesh he tasted death and that he is become the first-begotten of the dead, for, as he is God, he is the life and it is he that giveth life: let him be anathema.*[188]

---

[186] Nicene and Post-Nicene Fathers, Series II, Vol XIV

[187] Nicene and Post-Nicene Fathers, Series II, Vol XIV

Now it is not easy to take the passage from the Tome, 'the one of these, the Word, shines in miracles, the other succumbs to injuries', with the anathema of St Cyril which says, 'the Word of God suffered in the flesh'.

Once again it seems entirely reasonable that the council of Chalcedon should have been rejected on this point. The council can be explained and interpreted in an Orthodox manner, but taking into account the context in which the council took place it is justified that this issue be raised as a stumbling block to agreement in the historical period.

The fifth anathema concerns the reception of those who were considered partisans of Nestorius, such as Ibas. He is an interesting case. A committed disciple of the Antiochean heretics, Theodore, Diodore and Theodoret. He had written a letter to Maris, a Persian, in which he charges St Cyril with heresy and rejects his Twelve Anathemas.

At the council of Chalcedon the letter of Ibas was studied and pronounced to be Orthodox. The Acts of the council state,

At the Council of Chalcedon the Patriarch Maximus of Antioch and the Roman legates declared: "Having read his letter again, we declare that he is orthodox."[189]

Yet at the 5th Council when the letter was read the Fathers there responded by saying,

In the third place the letter which is said to have been written by Ibas to Maris the Persian, was brought forward for examination, and we found that it, too, should be read. When it was read immediately its impiety was manifest to all. And it was right to make the condemnation and anathematism of the aforesaid Three Chapters, as even to this time there had been some question on the subject. But because the defenders of these impious ones,

---

[188] Nicene and Post-Nicene Fathers, Series II, Vol XIV

[189] Catholic Encyclopaedia, Vol VII, *Ibas*. 1910

Theodore and Nestorius, were scheming in some way or other to confirm these persons and their impiety, and were saving that this impious letter, which praised and defended Theodore and Nestorius and their impiety, had been received by the holy Council of Chalcedon we thought it necessary to shew that the holy synod was free of the impiety which was contained in that letter, that it might be clear that they who say such things do not do so with the favour of this holy council, but that through its name they may confirm their own impiety.[190]

The council states that the impiety of the letter was immediately apparent, yet Chalcedon determined that it was orthodox. Indeed the 5th council attempts to show that Chalcedon had not received the letter of Ibas. But even the Catholic Encyclopaedia repeats the passage from the Acts, that the letter was received as orthodox.

Now if the 5th council found the letter heretical how much more must the anti-Chalcedonians have found it impossible to accept Chalcedon when it approved Ibas. As described previously most of the Western Church and North African Church received Ibas, Theodore and Theodoret as entirely Orthodox, and as having been approved by Chalcedon.

These facts show that it is perfectly and completely reasonable that the council of Chalcedon should have been rejected on this basis. Explanations which seek to excuse the reception of Theodoret and Ibas are possible, but these do not detract from the justification which lies behind the objection to Chalcedon on this point.

Finally, the sixth anathema addresses explicitly the use of the 'in two natures' terminology by the council. It could hardly avoid being considered Nestorian. If the phrase 'one incarnate nature' was the watchword of St Cyril, then 'in two natures' described the tradition of Diodore and Theodore, as received by Nestorius.

---

[190] Nicene and Post-Nicene Fathers, Series II, Vol XIV

Ibas had used the phrase in his letter to Maris, the letter which the 5th council found to be filled with impiety. Nestorius himself had repeatedly spoken of Christ as being two natures. He had written,

If any one says that Christ, who is also Emmanuel, is One, not [merely] in consequence of connection, but [also] in nature, and does not acknowledge the connection of the two natures, that of the Logos and of the assumed manhood, in one Son, as still continuing without mingling; let him be anathema.[191]

And

If any one assigns the expressions of the Gospels and Apostolic letters, which refer to the two natures of Christ, to one only of those natures, and even ascribes suffering to the divine Word, both in the flesh and in the Godhead; let him be anathema.[192]

Of course the issue here is not whether the council of Chalcedon intended to be Nestorianising but whether or not the outcome of the council had the appearance of being Nestorianising.

At Chalcedon the terminology of St Cyril was abandoned, and the phrase 'one incarnate nature of the Word' was not used. Theodoret, the opponent of St Cyril, and a constant supporter of Nestorius since 431 AD, was not only received at the council but was asked to draft a statement of faith. The anti-Cyrilline letter of Ibas was received as Orthodox. The Tome was accepted, though it seemed in direct contradiction of the Twelve Anathemas which were received at Ephesus some twenty years previous.

Subsequent history also supported the negative view of the anti-Chalcedonians. There were supporters of Ibas, Theodore and Theodoret throughout the Chalcedonian communion. They loudly complained in 553 AD that the 5th

---

[191] Nicene and Post-Nicene Fathers, Series II, Vol XIV

[192] Nicene and Post-Nicene Fathers, Series II, Vol XIV

Council was abandoning the decision of Chalcedon respecting these men and their teachings.

The 5th council is also a record of the various groups sheltering within the Chalcedonian settlement who had not been extinguished. Groups who still held a fundamentally Nestorian Christology.

In conclusion, this brief introduction to the rejection of Chalcedon shows that from the earliest period after Chalcedon there was a consistent and reasoned rejection of Chalcedon, based on the anathemas of St Dioscorus, but being taken up widely throughout the anti-Chalcedonian communion.

This rejection was based on particular issues of concern which were and remain reasonable points of view. Though it may be possible for each one to be explained away by the Chalcedonians, nevertheless this does not appear to have happened in any coherent manner during the controversial period.

At no point was Chalcedon rejected because of any support for a Eutychian Christology. Neither does it seem that the ill treatment of St Dioscorus himself was a major stumbling block. The issues were always those of principle and theology, not politics and personalities.

These issues remain important, and a reconciliation of the Chalcedonian and anti-Chalcedonian communions still demands that they are treated seriously and eirenically by the Chalcedonians. They are often brushed aside as irrelevant, but a proper understanding of our own tradition requires that they answered.

The Intercession of the Archangel Michael in St Severus of Antioch

The Encomium of St Severus upon the Archangel Michael contains some interesting material which is well worth study. An encomium, in this context, is essentially a form of homily which praises a particular saint or angelic being. In this case St Severus is concerned with the Archangel Michael, and his encomium was preached on the occasion of the feast of the Archangel. An encomium on the Archangel Michael was also preached by St Theodosius of Alexandria, and he used the account of St Michael helping the god-fearing Dorothea and Theopista, which features in the Coptic Synaxarium for Hatour 12, the feast of the Archangel Michael. St Severus bases his encomium on a different story altogether, but he also uses it to show how St Michael could be relied upon to come to the aid of faithful Christians.

The encomium of St Severus is interesting not so much for the story he uses, which may perhaps be a pious fiction, but for the substance of the teaching which he offers his congregation both at the beginning and end of his sermon. St Severus reminds his hearers of the occasion in the Gospels when the Archangel appeared in the tomb when he gave the news of the resurrection to the women. Then he introduces his story by explaining how it will show that St Michael is truly the great supporter of all faithful Christians.

St Severus describes several aspects of the ministry of St Michael. He says that he 'entreats God to forgive the whole race of men their sins'. That he delivers the saints out of all their afflictions, and strengthens the martyrs. That he is present with 'those who walk after God with all their hearts', and that 'he prays to God that he may be their helper'.

Then St Severus proceeds to provide an account of the conversion of a pagan to the Christian faith, and the various trials which he and his family successfully face with the help of St Michael. On every occasion when the converted family faced persecution and even death, St Michael appeared in a visible manner as a nobleman or a general and acted in a manner which saved them.

St Severus rounds up his encomium by describing how the farmers entreat St Michael to pray for the seeds of the field, and by his prayers they grow and bear fruit. That the sailors in the ships entreat him and are kept safe. That the hermits in the mountainous places entreat him, and by his prayers they are strengthened in their ascesis. That the monks entreat him, and he becomes a peacemaker in their midst. He describes how the bishops, priests and deacons entreat St Michael at the altar, and how the sick find healing when they entreat him. St Severus sums up his teaching by saying,

To those who live he gives strength in their time of need, and for those who are dead he prays to God to show mercy on them.

St Severus chooses to speak in terms of a contract which the Christian needs to make with St Michael. Not in any sort of superstitious or mechanical manner, but a spiritual contract which will provide spiritual benefit. He speaks of St Michael praying to God that He might have mercy on all men, of whom he has become an ambassador. He says,

Let us give him the things he desires, so that he may stir himself for us on account of them, and that he may love us exceedingly, and may pray to God for us.

Perhaps this sounds a little suspicious? What would St Michael desire of us? Does he seek praise and worship for himself? What are these things that St Severus believes St Michael desires of us? They are that we should love one another in the love of God. That we should live in the unity of brotherly love, and that we should avoid the sins of slander and lust. According to St Severus the sin of fornication is one which is greatly hated by both God and his angels.

St Severus teaches his audience that it is only with an upright heart that we may entreat St Michael and ask him to pray for us before God. In the final passage of his encomium he insists that it is through the prayers of St Michael and the Holy Mother of God that the world is preserved, St Michael as the head of the Angelic hosts, and the Blessed Virgin as the Mother of the Church.

It seems clear that in the pastoral witness of St Severus the figure of the Archangel Michael is most important, even as important as the Mother of God. He can be relied upon as a faithful and powerful intercessor for all faithful Christians, indeed for all men, since he asks for the salvation of all. Yet we may not take his intercession for granted. If we are to benefit from his prayers then we must seek to be men and women of upright hearts and lives, especially in regard to being in a state of peace and unity with our Christian brethren.

Some Brief Thoughts on the Eucharist from St Jacob of Serugh

St Jacob of Serugh is most well known for the collection of more than seven hundred metrical homilies, many of which remain unpublished. He is second in only to St Ephrem the Syrian, the Harp of the Spirit, and is himself known as the Flute of the Spirit. He was born in the middle of the 5th century, and became a bishop only in the last years of his life, although he had been a chor-episcopus for many years, serving the rural churches in the area of Serugh, which now lies on the Turkish side of the border with Syria. In his memra or verse homily to St Simeon the Stylite he speaks of himself, saying,

I am your flute, breathe into me Your Spirit, O Son of God. Let me give forth melodies filled with wonder about this beautiful one.

Among the great many verse homilies which he composed, several deal with the Eucharist, and portions of these have been translated into European languages. While later commentators tend to concentrate on drawing out various spiritual interpretations of the rites and actions of the Liturgy, St Jacob says little directly about the rites themselves and prefers a mystical and scriptural commentary on the sacrament.

This brief article will consider portions of two homilies which touch on the Eucharist and which are available in English (Jacob of Serugh, Homily extracts, tr. R.H. Connolly. The Downside Review 27 (1908)). The first homily deals directly with the situation of Christians leaving the Church at the point when the Catechumens are dismissed. St Jacob describes in passing some of the aspects of the liturgy as he celebrated it, referring to 'the sound of Psalms', 'the Prophets', and 'the Apostles', which must describe the Lections of the Church. Then he speaks of the priest saying, 'Him who is not baptised let him go forth', which must describe the dismissal of the Catechumens. St Jacob urges those who have been born with the second birth to remain and cry out, 'Our Father', which must refer to the Lord's Prayer, which only those who have been baptised and born again may truly pray.

Having warned those worldly Christians who leave the Church before the consecration so as to be about their business, he describes what they will be missing, and describes in some detail his own understanding of the meaning of the Eucharist.

In the first place he describes the priest and the people *'beseeching the Father that he will send his Son, that he may come down and dwell upon the oblation. And the Holy Spirit, his Power, lights down in the bread and wine and sanctifies it, yea, makes it the Body and the Blood'*.

He then speaks of the means by which Christ is received by the faithful, saying, *'by his brooding he mingles them in a holy manner, and they become one with him, as it is written, mystically....But he who goes out...has cut himself off from the brooding... these mysteries full of life are administered'*.

These passages teach us several things about St Jacob's understanding. Firstly the invocation of God is a matter of the people and the priest and is not simply a clerical function. It is neither the people alone who beseech God, nor the priest alone, but the whole Church united together beseeches God. The gathered community asks that God will send his Son, and the Holy Spirit upon the bread and wine. This distinguishes the teaching of St Jacob from those Protestant interpretations of the Eucharist, in which it becomes a memorial and a reminder of the sacrifice of Christ. Within the Syrian Orthodox context of St Jacob it is clearly understood as a ritual act in which the Divine presence of the Son and the Holy Spirit was earnestly sought. It is not simply a human response to the events of the Passion.

Indeed we see from these passages that in the Eucharist St Jacob understands that the Holy Spirit descends, and enters into the bread and wine in some manner and *'sanctifies it and makes it the Body and Blood'*. There is therefore a divine action in the Eucharist, a divine ownership and a divine transformation. The Holy Spirit descends, the Holy Spirit sets this particular offering of bread and wine apart for the use of God, and the Holy Spirit makes this particular offering of bread and wine which has been taken by God for his use into the Body and Blood of our Lord.

We see that St Jacob wants to use the Hebraic sense of the Holy Spirit brooding when he contemplates the Eucharist. This word 'brooding' is found in the account of Creation in Genesis 1:2 where the Spirit of God brooded over the face of the waters. In both the sense of Genesis and of St Jacob we may consider the Holy Spirit bringing forth life. He broods over the Eucharistic elements, but he broods over those who receive these elements and brings forth life in them. Indeed the mysteries are full of life, being full of the Holy Spirit who is the Divine life.

Those who leave the Church before the consecration and communion do not experience this creative brooding of the Spirit of God, and do not find life being renewed within them. It is clear from the words of St Jacob that he understands these elements of bread and wine, which become the Body and Blood of our Lord, to have life within them, and to produce life in those who receive them. They are life and life-giving as being filled with the power of God.

St Jacob then addresses those Christians who decide not to attend the Liturgy until after the consecration so that they can quickly attend and receive, and then return to their business affairs. He turns to a series of metaphors and illustrations to describe the blessings he believes are present in the Liturgy for those who faithfully commit themselves to prayer and praise at this time. These are designed to shame the distracted Christian who does not think he has enough time to worship God.

St Jacob speaks of the Great Physician, who will not charge anything for his services and who will *'apply mercy to your disease'*. He speaks of entreating the Creditor, asking him *'to cancel the note of hand that is terrifying you'*. He speaks of *'the Son of God sacrificed and set forth upon the table for sinners to pardon them'*. He says that, *'the Bridegroom has come down and given you his body and sealed you with his blood'*.

It is clear that St Jacob does not consider the Eucharist to have simply one aspect. We can see from these examples that he wishes us to consider that in the Eucharist we receive healing; we find that the debt owed by our sins is cancelled; that the Son pardons us by his sacrifice of himself; and that we receive the body of the Bridegroom and are sealed by his blood. There is a personal element to many of these aspects. We do not receive these blessings in a notional and legalistic sense, but by participating earnestly in the mystery of the Eucharist we find that the Holy Spirit broods upon us and works these out in our own life.

St Jacob urges us to *'bring in before him all your petitions earnestly'*, and *'pour out tears before the table of the Godhead'*. It is not possible, as far as St Jacob is concerned, for a person to turn up late to the Liturgy, with his mind full of worldly affairs, receive communion and then quickly leave the Church while expecting any blessing. Though the life-giving quality of the Eucharist does not depend on the worthiness of those who receive, and who should *'reveal your plagues, O sick soul, and show your diseases'*, nevertheless if the Eucharist is not approached with earnestness and with repentance then we should not expect that the Holy Spirit will remain upon us to renew us.

St Jacob elaborates when he says, *'In that hour when the priest sacrifices the Son before the Father, gird yourself, enter, O soul, and ask for pardon with a loud voice. Say to the Father, "Behold thy Son, a sacrifice to reconcile Thee. Pardon me in Him who died for me was buried. Behold Thy Oblation. Accept from my hands Him who is from Thee'*.

It is clear that in some sense we must consider the Eucharist as a sacrifice on our behalf, or rather perhaps a participation in that one eternal sacrifice which was offered once and for all on the cross. It is because we have been baptised into Christ that we are able to remain in the Church during the consecration. Having been baptised we are able to stand before the Father in the worthiness that is in Christ, and not in our own unworthiness. This is not a mechanical view of the atonement, but it requires a continuing participation in Christ, and a continuing sense of repentance. St Jacob does not allow a casual approach to the mysteries, as if Christ had done all that was necessary. On the contrary, it is because we are in Christ that we are able to receive the Holy Spirit brooding in the Eucharist elements, but we must make every effort to be 'in Christ', through earnestness, tears, repentance and a committed participation in the Liturgy.

Again it is clear that St Jacob allows no room for a Protestant view of the Eucharist, but is entirely Orthodox in his understanding. The Eucharist is a sacrifice and an oblation, but it is an offering to God of that which he has already provided, just as Abraham sacrificed to God the ram which God himself provided.

This sacrifice is not a purely spiritual one, in the sense that the elements of bread and wine are purely symbolic. Rather the bread and wine are transformed into the true body and blood of our Lord so that St Jacob can speak of *'brides eating their betrothed'*, and *'his Body and his Blood he has set forth at the feast before them that sit at table, that they may eat of him, and live with him without end. Meat and drink is our Lord at his marriage supper'*. Clearly we receive divine life by consuming the Eucharist elements which are become Christ. This is both a spiritual and a physical communication. The Holy Spirit is spirit and bodiless, but he broods within us and upon us by our physical eating and drinking of the Body and Blood of Christ. But this physical eating of the Body and Blood of our Lord also has a physical effect and unites us with Christ in his renewed humanity. Indeed it may be understood that the union of our material humanity with that of the new humanity of Christ is facilitated by the divine presence of the Holy Spirit in the same Body and Blood. This does not mean that we physically consume the divine nature of the Holy Spirit, but it does mean that the Holy Spirit is present, as he wills and knows, in the elements as we consume them, and therefore the effects are both physical and spiritual.

The same edition of the Downside Review contains excerpts from a second homily which is concerned with the Holy Week, and also refers to the teaching of St Jacob about the Eucharist. It begins with St Jacob discusses the case of Melchizedek. He says that Melchizedek offered the Eucharist in a mystical sense, but only *'sacrificed bread and wine to God, and nothing besides'*. But the bread and wine of the Eucharist *'our Lord made Body and Blood'*. It is clear that St Jacob wants us to contrast the sacrifice of Melchizedek, which was only bread and wine, with that of Christ himself, which was more than bread and wine, but was truly Body and Blood.

Yet perhaps some will say that though this sacrifice of the Eucharist is not simply bread and wine it is only in a figurative sense the Body and Blood of our Lord, indeed many Protestants have insisted on such a view in modern Christian history. But St Jacob is very clear. He says, *'who will dare to say now that it was not his Body?'*, and *'the Apostles...while he was still alive and reclining with them, ate him'*. If this is not clear enough, and if it still allows some figurative understanding then St Jacob is even clearer.

He says, *'from when he took it and called it Body it was not bread, but his Body, and they ate him while they marvelled'*. The Apostles did not question what the Lord said, and it can be understood that St Jacob is addressing this same sentiment to his congregation. At the moment of communion we do not question, but we receive what we have been taught. As St Jacob says, *'faith stoops not to questioning; she knows to affirm'*.

According to St Jacob we affirm the reality of the Eucharist because it would never have crossed the minds of the Apostles to consider that the one who was alive with them at the table should be understood as dead, and sacrificed as the bread and wine they were consuming. Therefore the institution of the Eucharist is a matter of revelation by Christ himself. St Jacob says, *'He stood as Priest and performed the priest's function upon himself among his disciples, that he might depict a type to the priesthood for it to imitate, he taught them... he made known to them...he gave an example'*.

Therefore the Eucharist is not rooted in the exercise of man's religious and spiritual imagination, but it is part of the Apostolic deposit, received from Christ himself. Indeed we pray in our ancient Orthodox and Catholic Liturgies, 'in the night when he was betrayed, he took the bread into his holy, undefiled, blameless and immortal hands...'. This is the teaching of St Jacob; that the most shocking aspect of the Eucharist, that in the mysteries we truly receive the Body and Blood of Christ for the renewal of our lives and for forgiveness of sins, is not an invention of later generations of Christians, but is at the very core of our Faith, having been received from the very mouth of Christ himself.

The language of Eucharistic sacrifice, of Body and Blood, or priest and oblation, are inseparable from our Faith, as far as St Jacob is concerned. We are not gathered to make a human commemoration of an historic act, or to worship a God who is not present. But equally the Eucharist is not a human response to God, but is God's offering of himself. To receive such a gift, the gift of life in the Holy Spirit, demands our wholehearted and complete devotion. Upon those who approach the altar and commune with repentance and a sense of their own unworthiness the Holy Spirit descends and broods creatively, bringing life and forgiveness of sins.

A Syrian monk as educator – a brief consideration of Abbot Simeon in the Lives of the Eastern Saints by John of Ephesus.

John of Ephesus is an important source for information about the non-Chalcedonian communion during the 6th century. He was born in about 507 AD in the area which is now the eastern border area of Turkey, and was at the time under the ecclesiastical jurisdiction of Amida in Mesopotamia, the present day Diyarbakir. As a young boy he was placed in the monastery of the Maro the Stylite, who saved his life as an infant. He joined the community in due course and entered into a period of exile with the other brothers as they were driven from place to place by the Imperial authorities.

In 529 AD he was ordained a deacon by the non-Chalcedonian leader John of Tella, and eventually settled in Constantinople among the refugees sheltered there by the Empress Theodora. In 558 AD, while acting on behalf of the Emperor Justinian, he was consecrated titular bishop of Ephesus by Jacob Burd'aya. In the last decades of his life he faced constant persecution, exile and imprisonment, and had to smuggle his *Ecclesiastical History* out of prison, where he died in about 589 AD.

In the late 560's he published his narrative account of fifty-eight Mesopotamian and Syrian ascetics whom he had personally known or met. It is with this work that the present notes are concerned. In particular we turn our attention to the chapter concerned with Simeon the Recluse and his disciple Sergius. They lived outside a village in the area where John of Ephesus had been brought up, and were obviously well known to him.

There are several passages in the account of this ascetic which allow us to reconstruct the appearance of his monastic retreat. In the first place John of Ephesus writes,

This man, because of the great hospitality that existed in him, used not to shut himself up in a hut like all the others, because as I have said, he would not endure to do so, since he used to perform the ministration to the brothers who resorted to him... On this account he made himself some small huts, and a little enclosed court and garden without a gate; and thus he was shut up within them with one disciple or two; and at one place he made for himself a way of ascending and descending the wall, on account of the strange brothers who resorted to him; and thus therefore he fulfilled in himself two purposes, both that of seclusion and that of the entertainment of strangers.

This passage shows us that whereas many of the hermits in the area appear to have secluded themselves within a small hut, Simeon, because he offered hospitality to those monks who came to visit him, had constructed a compound, surrounded by a wall. Within this compound were several huts and a garden for growing food. The only means of entry and exit was by some sort of staircase or ladder which allowed access over the wall.

In another passage John of Ephesus says,

That garden measured about ten cubits one way, and about twenty the other, and (and heavenly blessing rested upon the place to such an extent that what was sown in it was enough for forty men.

A Roman cubit was about 17.5 inches, therefore the garden area within Simeon's compound was approximately 14.5 feet by 22 feet. If we allow space for 2 or 3 small huts as well, then the compound itself cannot have been much bigger than 22 feet by 22 feet.

When John of Ephesus describes Simeon's practice of praying through the night while his exhausted disciples slept we are told,

He would stand up in the night and lift up the head of David (pray through the whole Psalter), and, until the day break, where he began, there he would end, an, if it happened that he had some time over, he would leave the brothers resting, and would

himself go and recite the Gospel in the hut, weeping, until daybreak, and then he would rouse them to go and perform matins.

It would seem, therefore, that one of the huts in the compound was used as a small chapel, while one or two other huts had been constructed to provide accommodation for Simeon and his brothers. We learn in a later section of this narrative that a local community of Jews had attacked the compound on one occasion and had burned down the huts, but that Simeon looked on this as a blessing,

That the blessed man might have a little breathing-space in his huts, because he was much straitened in them.

We may take this as suggesting that either the huts had been constructed very badly, or were very small, or more likely that over time, and with many followers at one period or another, the space in the compound had become very cramped.

It is of course very interesting to read about the practical situation in which these Fathers chose to live, but Simeon is most interesting because of the means by which he chose to support himself. We know that in the Egyptian desert the production of baskets was often the means of employment chosen by monastics, but Simeon chose an occupation which appears to have been much less common. Certainly the narrative describes his compound as being quite close to the local village, and other studies in the monasticism of Palestine at this time also point to monasteries usually being a feature of a rural population rather than completely isolated. It is this proximity which offered a rather unusual means of employment.

John of Ephesus writes,

Since the task of performing anything in the way of manual work was not open to them, and that they might not continue to eat the bread if idleness, and be despised by themselves and their consciences, the blessed men formed a plan and chose for themselves to teach boys, and this they did out of the window, since a seat was placed inside the window, and hours were appointed for the boys to come, that is, in the morning and in the evening, and when they had taught one class to read the Psalms and Scriptures, and they had withdrawn after being strengthened, another came in of little infants, thirty or forty of them, and they would learn and go to their homes, because it was a populous village and many people used to come out from it. And so the old man continued doing until the time of his end, and the boy-pupils supplied their needs.

This passage shows us that Simeon, and Sergius his disciple, chose to become educators of the local community, as a means of providing for their own needs. It would seem that several classes were organised, of both younger and older boys, who were organised by age. The older boys were taught to read both the Psalms and the Scriptures, while we can imagine the youngest children having an easier course of study, perhaps the alphabet. The numbers of boys attending these classes is significant, and would suggest that a large proportion of the boys from the local village had a relationship with Simeon, and knew him as a teacher, as well as a holy man.

We learn that there was a window constructed in the wall, and that it was possible for Simeon and Sergius to sit by the window and speak with those outside. We know, from elsewhere in John of Ephesus' account, that Simeon had constructed a guest house outside his compound, and it would be reasonable to assume that some sort of shelter was erected by this window to allow the children who came to be taught to be protected from the elements.

During the early period of the Desert Fathers there had been a concern about the presence of children near the monastic settlements, and even women who were family members tended to be received with a great degree of caution. But Simeon, while he seems to have been no less strict in his own ascetic practices, also seems to have been much more welcoming to both children and women, who we learn were allowed to stay in his guesthouse.

This does seem to represent a development in monastic practice, which can be found elsewhere at the same time, by which monastic communities and holy men became a feature of the rural and suburban environment, and more easily accessible to the lay community. The monasteries were becoming, in many places, part of the local Christian context and not completely isolated from it.

It might seem a little surprising that such a committed monastic as Simeon should make himself so much available to the local community. But he was obviously a most holy man, as John of Ephesus was willing to travel all the way from Constantinople to visit him when he was near death. The role of educator which he took upon himself certainly allowed him to develop a relationship with the local village which provided material support in return for the provision of teaching in literacy. But it also ensured that a generation of boys grew up having seen him as an exemplar of the monastic way of life.

There are two other characters in John of Ephesus' work who have used education in some manner in the working out of their Christian life. But it is likely that many others also became educators, while also being entirely monastic in the character of their spiritual ascesis. Further studies will show how far this form of service characterised monastic life at this time, and in which places. Certainly Simeon saw no contradiction between his very severe spiritual life and his service to his local lay community as a teacher.

Natural disasters in the Sixth Century Chronicle of Pseudo-Joshua.

Despite the apparently universal human need to look back to a golden age of long summers, full churches, and ecumenical unanimity, the reality of human history is replete with examples of chaos and catastrophe in every age. There has never been a century, or even a decade, when there have not been devastating storms, calamitous earthquakes and overwhelming floods and tsunamis. These have been a regular feature of all human societies whether Christian or non-Christian, orthodox or heretic, and have therefore demanded an attempt at theological explanation from the Churches long before this present age.

As an Orthodox Christian, a western convert member of the ancient Coptic Orthodox Patriarchate, it is almost impossible to consider reflecting on the use of the Bible in making sense of the human experience of chaos and catastrophe without making reference to the theological considerations of Orthodox writers of the past. Indeed for Orthodox Christians, as undoubtedly for many others, there is a communion in time with these fathers of the past, who are present with us through their writings and through their present and living communion in Christ. Therefore their opinions count. They are not simply a useful quarry for proof texts, but they have something to add to our own thinking. They are always contemporary if we allow them to be, and if we take care to comprehend the universal implications of their historically contexualised thought.

The Orthodox theologians of the past had to ask the same questions which natural disasters force upon our own theological and spiritual consciousness. Their experience of earthquakes, storm, floods and plague are not so dissimilar to ours. They heard of terrible events in far off places, as many of us do. Or they experienced them for themselves in all of their frightening power. We cannot ignore their reflections on such events if we wish to be rounded in our own reflection.

These theological, spiritual, historical and political considerations can be found in a variety of sources. The most comprehensive are the histories and chronicles which Christian authors compiled. Since these are attempts to document events over a period of years and even centuries they contain many references to natural and social disasters of various kinds. These events will also be found recorded and interpreted in sermons and letters, in lives of the saints, in theological treatises, and in the interesting category of writings which record visions and prophecies.

The study of the documentary materials of even the first five or six centuries of the Church would provide an important contribution to our present study of the Christian reponse to catastrophe, and especially the use of the Bible in developing such a reponse. But for the purposes of this short paper only one early document will be considered. This is the Chronicle of Joshua the Stylite[193], composed in about 507 AD, and therefore in a controversial period of Church history as the Chalcedonian and Non-Chalcedonian parties in the Church were drawing apart.

Joshua's Chronicle covers the years between 494-506 AD in some detail, and during this relatively brief period there are a number of natural and social catastrophes. The title of the text is in fact given as 'A History of the time of the affliction at Edessa and Amida and throughout Mesopotamia'.[194] It is likely that Joshua was not in fact the author[195], rather a later scribe, but the original author is

---

[193] Wright, William trans. **The Chronicle of Joshua the Stylite**. Cambridge University Press. 1882.

[194] Wright, William trans. **The Chronicle of Joshua the Stylite**. Cambridge University Press. 1882. p.1

[195] Tombley, Frank and Watt, John trans. **The Chronicle of Pseudo-Joshua the Stylite**. Liverpool University Press. 2000. p.xxiv

clearly local and contemporary to the events which are described. He introduces his account by addressing it to the Abbot Sergius, who had requested that he write about,

"..the time when the locusts came, and when the sun was darkened, and when there was earthquake and famine and pestilence".[196]

Almost immediately we receive a summary of the interpretation which the author seems to wish to place on these recent events. He says,

"..you wish to leave in writing memorials of the chastisements which have been wrought in our times because of our sins, so that, when they read and see the things that have happened to us, they may take warning by our sins and be delivered from our punishments."[197]

Let us have this initial impression in mind, while we consider what were the disastrous events of those times which had induced the unknown chronicler, let us call him Pseudo-Joshua, to take up his pen. These events may be characterised as natural or political. On the one hand there was a plague of boils which became more harmful to the population over the years 496-497 AD. At first it caused irritation and revulsion, but left nothing more lasting than scarring on the affected limbs, but later it intensified and caused blindness in those afflicted.

Then in 497 AD there was an earth tremor which caused some of the civil buildings in Edessa to collapse with a loss of life. In the following year there was another earth tremor which destroyed church buildings in several places with the loss of life of those who had run to them for shelter. In 499 AD a plague of locusts descended on the region, and

---

[196] Wright, William trans. **The Chronicle of Joshua the Stylite**. Cambridge University Press. 1882. p.1

[197] Wright, William trans. **The Chronicle of Joshua the Stylite**. Cambridge University Press. 1882. p.2

consumed everything for hundreds of miles around. This provoked a desperate famine which caused mass starvation. Indeed the situation throughout the region described in the chronicle remained critical until 501 AD when it seems that there was the beginning of a recovery in agricultural production.

The political catastrophes were rooted in the long-standing conflict and tension between the Roman and Persian empires. This was a border region and often suffered from being a contested area. In 502 AD open warfare flared up again and the citizens of Edessa, Amid and the surrounding towns and villages, having just recovered from a natural disaster, found themselves caught between the pressures of supporting their own Imperial troops and their allies, and suffering the predations of the Persians.

In just a few years Pseudo-Joshua and his contemporaries had experienced as devastating a series of catastrophes as any suffered in our own times, with many tens of thousands left dead as a result of disease, starvation and war.

This is the context in which he is able to reflect on his own experiences, and develop a theological understanding of the terrible events which had recently taken place. He is writing from a first-hand contemporary point of view, and therefore, whether or not his understanding is appreciated or rejected in our own times, it must be allowed to speak for itself as an authentic, Orthodox consideration. Certainly not the only Orthodox voice, other voices will require further research and study, but a voice of experience nonetheless, rooted in the Orthodox tradition.

Returning to Pseudo-Joshua's opening opinion. He speaks of sins and chastisement, warnings and punishments. It would be simplistic to assert that he is assuming that all natural and political catastrophes are a direct punishment for particular sins committed. Nevertheless he is clear that there is a connection between sin and chastisement.

A few examples from the chronicle will show that there is a firm connection between the two in Pseudo-Joshua's thinking.

"For who is able to tell fittingly concerning those things which God has wrought in His wisdom to wipe out sins and to chastise offences?"[198]

and

"...these chastisements ... were sent upon us for our sins"[199]

Now this way of thinking is not alien to the Scriptures. Indeed the author of the Book of Hebrews writes,

"For whom the Lord loveth he chasteneth, and scourgeth every son whom he receiveth." Hebrews 12:6

It would seem that Pseudo-Joshua wishes to place his theological reflection on the disasters of his time within exactly such a framework of chastisement. It should be noted that he is writing to an Abbot, and is describing the situation within an essentially Christian civil community. Therefore he is writing about the relationship between the Christian God, the Christian community, and the historical, chaotic and catastrophic context in which that relationship takes place.

This is made explicit when he quotes from the parable of the tares and wheat. The tares or weeds have been sown by an enemy among the seeds of wheat which the farmer has planted. This is not a parable about those who have no knowledge or faith in the Christian God. If that were so then we would read of wheat being sown among weeds. Therefore Pseudo-Joshua has his own Christian civil society particularly in mind as he writes.

---

[198] Wright, William trans. **The Chronicle of Joshua the Stylite**. Cambridge University Press. 1882. p.3

[199] Wright, William trans. **The Chronicle of Joshua the Stylite**. Cambridge University Press. 1882. p.3

Indeed he has in mind very particular sins of his community which he believes have brought about this well deserved chastisement.

He describes this cause and effect at the beginning of his detailed annual chronicles, as though wishing to make it abundantly clear that the ultimate cause of all of the disasters was spiritual. He says,

"At this time our bodies were perfectly sound all over, but the pains and diseases of our souls were many. But God, who finds pleasure in sinners when they repent of their sins and live, made our bodies as it were a mirror for us, and filled our whole bodies with sores, that by means of our exterior He might show us what our interior was like unto, and that, by means of the scars of our bodies, we might learn how hideous were the scars of our souls. And as all the people had sinned, all of them were smitten with this plague"[200].

We must remember that Pseudo-Joshua is sharing in this experience. He is not writing at a great distance of miles or time. Edessa was a famous Christian city, and considered itself especially protected and blessed by God, and yet our author suggests that under the surface there was a spiritual corruption and sickness.

He illustrates this by referring the immediate justification for this chastisement of God to the enthusiastic celebration of pagan rites and luxurious living. In particular during a festival in May of 495 AD, much of the population seems to have participated in such a celebration, lighting the streets in honour of a dancer, Trimerius, who performed in the displays which the legal code of Theodosius had allowed only if they were decent. It would seem that in Edessa at this time they were still a scandal to Orthodox Christians. Not only were members of the population supporting such un-

---

[200] Wright, William trans. **The Chronicle of Joshua the Stylite**. Cambridge University Press. 1882. p.17

Christian theatrics, but they were failing to give thanks to God for the material prosperity which their city enjoyed.

In fact the plague of boils failed to bring the city to repentance. Indeed we are told that both the rich and poor gave themselves to sin. Slandering one another, having regard to people's position, adultery and other sexual immorality. The consequence, as far as Pseudo-Joshua is concerned, was that the Christian community found it more and more easy to give way to sin.

In terms that are perhaps reminiscent of the experience of Christians communities in all ages, he describes how,

"..they neglected also to go to prayer, and not one of them gave a thought to his duty, but in their pride they mocked at the modesty of their fathers, who, they said, did not know how to do things as we do"[201].

This same connection between sin and chastisement is evident in the account of the first appearing of the swarm of locusts. On this occasion they were seen to lay eggs but were not so numerous as to cause major problems. Yet their appearing is described as,

"A proof of God's justice…for the correction of our evil conduct".[202]

What is interesting is that Pseudo-Joshua tends always to understand the experience of the Christian community, however catastrophic, as being an opportunity for repentance and a chastisement, rather than a punishment. The term chastisement appears again and again, whereas the word punishment appears rarely and almost always in the context of God acting against the

---

[201] Wright, William trans. **The Chronicle of Joshua the Stylite**. Cambridge University Press. 1882. p.21

[202] Wright, William trans. **The Chronicle of Joshua the Stylite**. Cambridge University Press. 1882. p.23

enemies of his people. An example can be found when the depredations and aggression of the Persian king are described,

"But we place our trust in the justice of God, that He will bring upon him a greater punishment".[203]

There is a great difference between chastisement and punishment, and on most of the occasions where Pseudo-Joshua refers to chastisement he also indicates that it has a positive element, in distinction to punishment. He quotes the words of St. Paul from 1 Corinthians,

"When we are judged, we are chastened of the Lord, that we should not be condemned with the world"[204].

This is one positive aspect he draws from all of the difficult circumstances he has witnessed. To be chastened is to be the object of God's care. It is those whom He loves that He chastens. Over and over again, just as he links chastening with sin, so he also links chastening to hope for the future.

"The whole object of men being chastened in this world is that they may be restrained from their sins, and that the judgement of the world to come may be made light for them"[205].

To experience hardship, even catastrophe, is therefore a spiritual opportunity. This certainly does not mean that anyone outside any particular circumstances should take it upon themselves to judge others. We cannot say that these other people have sinned simply because they experience some catastrophe, and Pseudo-Joshua does not seem to want to use the Scriptures to suggest that is the case. But he does want to recognise the sin in his own community and believes the various disasters, signs and warnings are all

---

[203] Wright, William trans. **The Chronicle of Joshua the Stylite**. Cambridge University Press. 1882. p.14

[204] 1 Corinthians 11:32

[205] Wright, William trans. **The Chronicle of Joshua the Stylite**. Cambridge University Press. 1882. p.4

means by which God was calling the Christian people of Edessa to repentance.

He understands this chastening in a positive manner by considering that,

"Had not the protection of God embraced the whole world so that it should not be dissolved, the lives of all mankind would probably have perished".[206]

Is this not rather a difficult measure by which to see the hand of God? That though things were bad they could have been worse? Certainly a secular perspective might indeed take such a view. But the Christian faith demands that we consider the corruption of sin and the judgement due to us all as sinners. The 'wages of sin are death'. This is certainly not viewed by Orthodox Christians as meaning that there is an eternal punishment which God will mete out to all who do not know Him. But it is rather understood that apart from life in God there is a falling apart of our world and of ourselves. Therefore it is indeed to be understood positively that God does not allow this to happen as we deserve, but does show mercy to His creation – even as it groans and travails awaiting a rebirth into the age to come.

Pseudo-Joshua seems to be asking all those who experience chaos and catastrophe how they will respond to it. There could be anger which considers all such hardships as unwarranted – but he reminds his readers that all Christians are deserving of chastisement for sins. There could be despair – but he reminds his readers that these sufferings can be a means of repentance and life.

But it would appear that this must be an internal and spiritual judgement based on the reflection of those who are in the midst of chaos. No one should say that some others are the particular object of God's wrath, rather all those who read or hear about a disaster elsewhere should consider their

---

[206] Wright, William trans. **The Chronicle of Joshua the Stylite**. Cambridge University Press. 1882. p.3

own spiritual state. We should ask ourselves whether, if such events indeed might be a chastening of God's people, we are not worthy less of chastening and rather of punishment.

Pseudo-Joshua make this same point. He considers all of the events in the surrounding cities, and has to declare that,

"Not a man of us was restrained from his evil ways, so that our country and our city had no excuse".[207]

Therefore it is clear that the main use which a Christian should make of chaos and catastrophe is to be turned to a personal repentance. Both in those who experience such catastrophes, which according to Pseudo-Joshua should be considered as a chastisement, and also in those who hear about such catastrophes but are spared the experience of them.

Now it would seem rather monstrous if that was all of the theological reflection which Pseudo-Joshua offers. We know, as Christians, that all people, as sinners, deserve the wrath of God, but we are also deeply aware that God has become part of His own creation and that He shares in the pain and distress of all those who suffer. It is rather a mystery, in the sense of something beyond simple human explanation, how we are to hold together the love of God and the sense that chaos and catastrophe might be something positive in His will for us.

When someone has a car accident and walks away with a minor injury we might easily understand that they have been given a wake up call and are being called to look at the substance of their lives. But when hundreds of thousands of people are swept away in a tsunami it is impossible to speak. What can be said. How is this part of a Divine plan.

---

[207] Wright, William trans. **The Chronicle of Joshua the Stylite**. Cambridge University Press. 1882. p.26

Pseudo-Joshua also appreciates this need for silence, and he says,

"Who is able to tell fittingly concerning those things which God has wrought in His wisdom to wipe out sins and to chastise offences? For the exact nature of God's government is hidden even from the angels"[208].

This must give us cause to be very hesitant in how we speak about disaster. We hold the theological certainties that we deserve judgement, that we are loved by God, that He will do all that He can to bring us to repentance and to union with Himself as far as our freewill allows and that this includes what Pseudo-Joshua and indeed St. Paul call a chastening. But beyond that – who is able fittingly to tell.

Indeed several times Pseudo-Joshua indicates that the events which came across the people of the region are not to be understood as directly caused by God, as though God directly caused an earthquake for instance. When speaking of the tribulation caused by the predations of the Persians he says,

"Now I do not wish to deny the free will of the Persians, when I say that God smote us by their hands; nor do I, after God, bring forward any blame of their wickedness; but reflecting that, because of our sins, He has not inflicted any punishment on them, I have set it down that He smote us by their hands"[209].

It seems that we must keep in mind both the direct action of the Persians and their own liability for their barbarity towards the Romans in Edessa and elsewhere, while also understanding that there is a permissive will of God which allowed the Persians to act, but which does not allow us to ascribe the catastrophe directly to God. Likewise it might be proposed that natural disasters are allowed by

---

[208] Wright, William trans. **The Chronicle of Joshua the Stylite**. Cambridge University Press. 1882. p.3

[209] Wright, William trans. **The Chronicle of Joshua the Stylite**. Cambridge University Press. 1882. p.5

God, and used by God, but need not, perhaps even should not, be understood as being directly caused by God.

In our own experience if we have a young child who runs away from us and falls, scraping her knee, then we might use the experience to warn the child that this is what happens when she runs away from her parents. But this would not mean that we had caused the injury, rather that in allowing a certain necessary freedom we made it possible that such an injury could happen.

Bearing in mind the fact that Pseudo-Joshua links the various catastrophes which the Christian people of Edessa suffered very closely to their sinfulness, it is surprising that there is never any sense of triumphalism. He is never pleased that these things have come upon them, and he always unites himself with them. He says that 'not a man of us' was restrained from sin, he does not say that 'not a man of them'. And when he records the suffering of Edessa and Amida he writes 'sadly' and in 'melancholy tales', and with 'words of grief and sorrow'. There is no need for a belief that in some sense disasters come as a means of chastisement to be devoid of a genuine emotional commitment to those who suffer. Pseudo-Joshua insists throughout on the need for repentance among those who are in these circumstances. As far as he is concerned the only positive route through them is a closer relationship with God. But he weeps with them, and prays with them, and hungers with them because he is one of them.

But there is also a sense that not all those caught up in such natural disasters are equally the subjects of God's chastisement. While he often describes the city folk as sinful, when it comes to the village people who flock to the city during the famine he considers them a different case. He quotes the psalms of David saying,

"If I have sinned and have done perversely, wherein have these innocent sheep sinned?"[210].

Clearly we may also consider that there are those caught up in catastrophe who are not the objects of chastisement, though all may use such events in a positive manner. The author addresses these people directly when he says,

"As for those who are chastised because of sinners, whilst they themselves have not sinned, a double reward shall be added unto them"[211].

This passage can be taken in several ways. Both that there are those who suffer due to the direct actions of those who are sinners, and also that there are those who suffer – as the poor in Edessa – because of the chastisement which others deserve. Yet in both cases there is the scope for a positive outcome within a Christian worldview, and not necessarily in a purely material sense. If the martyr is a Christian hero then we cannot always expect material circumstances to be the measure of the 'double reward'.

But as with the perception of chastisment and the call to repentance, this understanding of being an innocent participant is also perhaps best left to those who are in the midst of particular circumstances. If it is not our place to judge others, then we should hesitate to judge entirely, for good or bad, but as those outside such circumstances we should perhaps treat all alike, while also drawing the lessons of repentance for our own lives.

There are yet more lessons which Pseudo-Joshua offers us. The people of Edessa, though the judgement which came upon them is considered entirely justified by him, are nevertheless shown to grow in this circumstance. Their own response to those in need among them shows us how we might act towards those in such situations.

---

[210] 2 Samuel 24:17

[211] Wright, William trans. **The Chronicle of Joshua the Stylite**. Cambridge University Press. 1882. p.5

It has been suggested that according to Pseudo-Joshua chaos and catastrophe calls us to examine our own lives, whether we are caught up in such events or not. It has also been suggested that we might recognise that some are caught up in such situations through their own actions, and others are innocently swept up due to the actions of others.

The Chronicle also shows how we should act towards those in such situations. Pseudo-Joshua is quick to condemn his own Christian city as having lost something of their love for God, but he also commends them as they grow in the practice and experience of such love in the midst of disaster. He describes in some detail the suffering in the city during the great famine, and how many people were starving and dying each day. Yet there is no record of anyone ever reproaching those who were in such despair. Looking back to the events after they had passed Pseudo-Joshua is clear that they were all to be used as a means of bringing folk to repentance, but while in the midst of them there is no evidence that any of the Christian leaders made particular Christians responsible for the events which had overtaken them. No one is to be found saying that the people of Edessa and Amida should not be helped because God was punishing them.

On the contrary it seems that from all sides there was a growing desire to be of service to those in need. A short description of some of the means by which aid was provided, and by which care and respect was shown to those in these circumstances will show the response to chaos and catastrophe which Pseudo-Joshua expects from other Christians. In the first place the Emperor provided 'no small sum of money to be distributed to the poor'[212].

Mar Nonnus, the cleric who had the care of hospitality, organised the Christian brethren under his

---

[212] Wright, William trans. **The Chronicle of Joshua the Stylite**. Cambridge University Press. 1882. p.31

charge to collect the bodies of all those who had died each day. The people would gather at the gate of the 'Hospital' and would help to bury the bodies. The stewards of the Churches established an infirmary for those who were most ill, and if people died there, and many did, then their bodies were also taken with respect and buried.

The Governor converted the porches of the public baths into places where the poor who had come into the city from the villages could sleep, and he provided straw and mats for them to sleep on. These examples encouraged the wealthy in the city to establish infirmaries of their own in their own properties, and many of the poor found shelter there. Even the soldiers of the Roman garrison provided places for the sick to sleep and fed them as best they could at their own expense.

Over a hundred people a day were dying in the city, and the poor from the countryside were even dying on the roads approaching the city.

It would seem that Pseudo-Joshua wishes us to note the change in character within the Christian community. Where there was once a self-centered and indulgent way of life, now there was a concern for others and a re-orientation of spiritual life on God. Indeed he notes that during the famine the people of the city gathered for public prayers asking that the strangers in the city might be spared its depredations. The Christian community prayed,

"If I have sinned and done perversely, wherein have these innocent sheep sinned?"

At this point in his chronicle Pseudo-Joshua records that the time of the pagan festivities which he believed had provoked the chastisement of the city came around. But in this year, 501 AD, the emperor forbade that it be celebrated in any place in the empire, and the lewd dancers were not allowed to dance. Within thirty days of its abolishing the price of food had dropped and sustenance came in the necessary quantities to those in and around the city.

It is clear that Pseudo-Joshua links the removal of that which God might have found offensive in a Christian city to the end of the chastisement which the city needed for its reformation. Yet he notes that the reformation was hardly a voluntary one, and was rather the result of the emperor than the civic authorities of Edessa. But Pseudo-Joshua adds that,

"God, because of the multitude of His goodness, was seeking an occasion to show mercy even unto those who were not worthy"[213].

Of course the objectionable celebrations were a symptom of the spiritual malaise in the city, and were not the only, or even the most important locus of sinful activity. And it is telling that Pseudo-Joshua indicates that he does not wish to enumerate all the sins of the chiefs of the city. Though he includes all of the people of the city in his criticism of their past activity, nevertheless he seems to judge the leaders of the city more strictly, while judging the poor and the strangers as innocent.

It is clear that Pseudo-Joshua cannot be used to support the simplistic view that people sin and so deserve to be punished. He addresses himself especially to a criticism of his own Christian community in Edessa. In that context he uses the Scripture to link the behaviour of the community to a chastising of God. Yet even though this painful experience is considered by him as justified, nevertheless it is to be understood in a positive sense as exhibiting the goodness and love of God within the catastrophic events. This can only be recognised through careful and spiritual reflection and is not to be imposed as an external interpretation on the events which others find themselves overwhelmed by.

On the contrary these events are an opportunity for the Christian community to rouse itself to help those in need,

---

[213] Wright, William trans. **The Chronicle of Joshua the Stylite**. Cambridge University Press. 1882. p.35

and especially to consider that the poor and the strangers among them are the least liable to any condemnation. He commends those who care for these needy in practical ways, and this is one of the means by which the Christian community works out its reflection and repentance in the midst of such events.

The Scriptures are consistently used by Pseudo-Joshua in a positive sense, even when he is suggesting that chaos and catastrophe are a means of God chastening His own people. God chastens those whom He loves, and chastening is a positive training for life and not a punishment unto death.

In the end, faced with chaos and catastrophe, if we follow the theological reflection of Pseudo-Joshua, we must be content to ask ourselves how we should respond. We cannot respond for other people, and especially we cannot condemn other people. It is a blessing if we are brought to repentance by a consideration of the situation in which others find themselves, brought to reflection on all the blessings which we have already received and enjoy. But it is not a true repentance at all if we are not moved beyond spiritual thoughts into positive actions to help those who find themselves caught in such situations.

Of course this is only one author from the sixth century. There are other witnesses of these same events, and witnesses to the position of the Eastern Church over many centuries. Further study will provide much more material to be included in any contemporary reflection on the issues of the use of Scripture in regard to Chaos and Catastrophe. Yet this is perhaps a small contribution.

The Apostle Thomas and the Origins of the Orthodox Church in India

The occasion of Abba Seraphim visiting the Orthodox communities in India earlier this year seemed to be a suitable reason to collect together some of the earliest traditions surrounding St Thomas and present them in a brief paper.

St Thomas is referred to in each of the Gospels. In the Gospel of St Matthew 10:3 he appears in the list of the Twelve Apostles, where his name is given in the seventh place. His name in the Greek text is Θωμᾶς which is the transliteration of the Hebrew word meaning a twin. In the Gospel of St Mark 3:18 he is listed again as one of those whom the Lord ordained to be sent forth, which is the Greek verb ἀποστέλλω, or apostello. In the list of those disciples chosen to be apostles St Thomas is given as the eighth.

In the Gospel of St John we find that St Thomas features several times, and becomes more than a mere name. When our Lord was preparing to travel to Bethany to see the tomb of his friend Lazarus, even though it was clear that the Jewish authorities wished to apprehend him, it is written,

Thomas therefore, who is called Didymus, said to his fellow disciples: Let us also go, that we may die with him. John 11:16

St Cyril refers to this passage in his Commentary on the Gospel of St John. He says,

The language of Thomas has indeed zeal, but it also has timidity; it was the outcome of devout feeling, but it was mixed with littleness of faith.[214]

---

[214] Cyril of Alexandria, trans. P.E. Pusey. Commentary on John. Library of the Fathers, vol 43. 1874. p.115

St John Chrysostom is rather more frank, and while allowing that some have said that St Thomas was being brave when he spoke these words, nevertheless he considers them a manifestation of cowardice. He says,

Some say that Thomas himself wanted to die. But this is not the case. The expression is rather one of cowardice. And yet Christ does not rebuke him but instead supports his weakness. The result is that in the end he became stronger than them all – in fact, invincible[215].

St Thomas then appears in John 14:5, at the Last Supper, and he is forward enough to express his confusion at some of the things which Our Lord is teaching to the Apostles. Christ has said that he is going to prepare a place for his followers, and that they know the way he is taking. But St Thomas says,

"*Lord, we don't know where you are going, so how can we know the way?*" John 14:5

St Cyril also comments on this passage and suggests that our Lord is almost forced into a situation where he must reveal what he does not yet wish to. But Christ 'evades the excessive curiosity of his disciple', and in his kindness gives an answer which provides them with a lesson they do need to learn at that time, saying, 'I am the Way, the Truth and the Life'.[216] Augustine also comments on this passage, and wishes us to consider that Thomas speaks falsely, yet without knowing that he does. He says 'they knew, but they did not know that they knew'.[217]

---

[215] Elowsky, Joel. Ancient Christian Commentary on Scripture, John 11-21. IVP. 2007, p9

[216] Cyril of Alexandria, trans. P.E. Pusey. Commentary on John. Library of the Fathers, vol 43. 1874. p.241

[217] Elowsky, Joel. Ancient Christian Commentary on Scripture, John 11-21. IVP. 2007, p123

St Thomas finally appears in St John's Gospel in the account of the appearance of our Lord to the disciples, in John 20. The doors of the place where they were gathered were shut, and then suddenly our Lord was among them, saying, 'Peace be with you'. The Lord comforted them, and breathed upon them saying, 'Receive the Holy Spirit. Whose sins you remit they are remitted unto them, and whose sins you retain they are retained'.[218] But Thomas was not with them.

This absence from such an important event has led some to suppose that St Thomas was deficient in some grace given by God, and go even so far as so suggest that he was not strictly an Apostle in the Church. Yet St Cyril is extremely clear, saying,

How then, someone may not unreasonably enquire, if Thomas was absent, was he in fact made partaker in the Holy Spirit when the Saviour appeared to the disciples and breathed on them, saying, "Receive the Holy Spirit"? We reply that the power of the Spirit pervaded every person who received grace and fulfilled the aim of the Lord who gave him to them. Therefore if any were absent, they also received him, the munificence of the giver not being confined only to those who were present, but extending to the entire company of the holy Apostles.[219]

St Cyril also uses the example of Eldad and Medad, two of the seventy elders chosen by Moses. They were apart from the rest of the company when the Holy Spirit came upon the elders, but he came upon Eldad and Medad also, even though they were in the camp. Some of the examples of patristic references to St Thomas which follow will show that he was always and universally considered an Apostle, with

---

[218] John 20:23

[219] Elowsky, Joel. Ancient Christian Commentary on Scripture, John 11-21. IVP. 2007, p367

the full authority and grace which all the other Apostolic community possessed.

St Thomas has been given the name of 'Doubting Thomas' because of his response to the report of Christ's appearance to the others. He would not believe unless he saw the marks of the passion in the hands and feet and side of our Lord. Many of the Fathers refer to him having in some degree a lack of faith, though none seem willing to consider him faithless, but the same Fathers also show that God used his weakness to bring about a greater good. St Gregory the Great says that it was not an accident that he was not present, and that he should be given the opportunity of confirming our faith in the truth of the resurrection with his own.[220] When our Lord appeared a second time, when Thomas was present, he gave him the opportunity of confirming his faith, as that of the other Apostles had been confirmed by his first appearance. We should remember that the disciples had already disbelieved the report of the women who came from the tomb, and it was only the presence of the Lord among them that convinced them. Origen points out that the other disciples had also been doubtful on occasion, and reminds us of the incident of Jesus walking on the water when they had all thought that it was a ghost or an apparition.[221] Peter Chrysologus, bishop of Ravenna, gave a homily in which he wondered at the inquisitiveness of St Thomas, and how he dared to probe the wounds of our Lord. But he explains that not only was he curing his own uncertainty, but that of us all, and he was preparing a solid foundation in truth for his future service as a servant of the Gospel.

---

[220] Elowsky, Joel. Ancient Christian Commentary on Scripture, John 11-21. IVP. 2007, p367

[221] Elowsky, Joel. Ancient Christian Commentary on Scripture, John 11-21. IVP. 2007, p368

St John Chrysostom, in his homily on this passage, reflects that all through this period between the first and second appearances of our Lord, Thomas was being instructed by the reports of those who had been present, such that he longed to see the Lord, and desired greatly that what he was being told might be true. He describes how at his appearing to Thomas and the others, our Lord immediately addresses St Thomas's doubts, showing that all through that period of waiting he had been divinely present, and knew already what Thomas desired.[222] St Cyril links our reception of Christ in the Eucharist to this same narrative of St Thomas' touching the wounds of our Lord, and calls us to avoid unbelief ourselves, and be rooted in faith.[223]

There are a great many commentaries on this passage. It would seem that for many faithful Christians there is a sense of identity with St Thomas, who believes as best he can, and who is treated kindly and gently by our Lord, despite his doubts. He is rather impetuous and emotional, not entirely unlike St Peter. He is not afraid to ask the questions which the other disciples hide in their hearts. He receives grace to progress from saying, 'I will not believe unless..' to 'My Lord and my God!'. He receives a full share in the Holy Spirit and in the Apostleship of the Church.

If we knew nothing more of this Apostle then we would already have many lessons to learn from those passages in which he appears in the Gospels. But in fact he does not disappear from the pages of history. The writings of the Fathers describe a consistent tradition, the basis of which need not be doubted as historical.

---

[222] Elowsky, Joel. Ancient Christian Commentary on Scripture, John 11-21. IVP. 2007, p369

[223] Elowsky, Joel. Ancient Christian Commentary on Scripture, John 11-21. IVP. 2007, p369

The earliest witness to a Christian tradition concerning St Thomas is found in the Acts of Thomas. This was a rather Gnostic document, though it was transmitted through a variety of Orthodox communities and in a variety of languages such as Syriac, Latin, Ethiopian and Greek. The most important aspects of the document for this brief study are the historical references which it makes. The Acts of St Thomas would appear to date from the end of the second century AD. They describe the Apostles gathering together and determining which area of the world each of them should take as the place of their missionary endeavours.[224]

By lot, then, India fell to Judas Thomas, also called Didymus. And he did not wish to go, saying that he was not able on account of the weakness of his body, and said, "How can I, being a Hebrew, go among the Indians to proclaim the truth?" And while he was thus reasoning and speaking, the Saviour appeared to him during the night and said to him, "Fear not, Thomas, go away to India and preach the word there for my grace is with thee." But he obeyed not, saying, "Wherever thou wishest to send me, send me, but elsewhere. For to India I am not going."[225]

Now it would seem that the author of this text has rather captured something of the psychology of St Thomas, and describes the sort of emotions which we might imagine him struggling with. Nor is he alone in such feelings of weakness. St Augustine of Canterbury shared exactly the same sense of fearfulness when he planned to abandon his mission to the English, and our Lord appeared to him in a similar way as is reported of St Thomas. Of course these Acts suggest to us that even an appearance of our Lord himself was not enough to persuade St Thomas.

---

[224] Pick, Bernhard. The Apocryphal Acts of Paul, Peter, John, Andrew and Thomas. Open Court Publishing. 1909. p. 225

[225] Pick, Bernhard. The Apocryphal Acts of Paul, Peter, John, Andrew and Thomas. Open Court Publishing. 1909. p. 226

We should also note from this passage in the Acts of St Thomas that he is referred to as Judas Thomas, and in the Syriac tradition from an early date it was considered that his name was Judas, since Thomas or Didymus simply means 'the twin'.

In the Acts, St Thomas is sold as a slave by the Lord to a merchant from India, who had come from the King Gundafor, looking for a carpenter to work on his palace. Now this King Gundafor had been unknown to Western history, and as with many such references in ancient texts was assumed to be evidence that the Acts were not based on any historical facts. But in the 19th century examples of coins featuring this king were first discovered, and it became clear that he was the founder of a dynasty in North-West India, being succeeded by his brother, his nephew and then a more distant relation. The coins are dated to the first half of the first century. Gondophares, or Gundafor, describes himself as autokrator in Greek on his coins, and would appear to have been the ruler of an Indo-Parthian empire that stretched from modern Afghanistan into the Punjab.[226] An inscription has also been discovered which refers to this king, and which appears to date his reign from 21 A.D. to perhaps 50 or 60 A.D. certainly within the lifetime of St Thomas.

Now this evidence does suggest strongly that the Acts of Thomas must have some basis in fact. There is no reference to this king in any later works in the West, and therefore no likelihood that a later writer should accidentally choose the same name as an unknown king and place St Thomas in connection with him. It seems entirely reasonable that this tradition must have originated very close in time and place to St Thomas and King Gondophares.

---

[226] Medlycott A.E. India and The Apostle Thomas. Nutt. London 1905 p.13

In the Acts we read that another king, Mazdei, sent messengers to St Thomas asking him to come and deliver his wife and daughter from demonic oppression. The narrative describes his journey and the incidents which take place in this other Indian kingdom, and then describe his martyrdom.[227] This ancient text therefore allows us to conclude that at a very early date there was information which is at least accurate in regard to the name of an otherwise unknown king, which suggests that the St Thomas travelled to Parthia and North-West India where he was present in the court of King Gondophares, and that he then travelled to another Indian kingdom where he was martyred. The text describes St Thomas as an Apostle, and shows him establishing Christian communities in several locations and providing ministers in each place to serve the congregations of converts.

This would appear to agree with the information which Origen had several decades later. He writes saying, 'When the holy apostles and disciples of our Saviour were scattered over the world, Thomas, so the tradition has it, obtained his portion in Parthia'.[228] The Doctrine of the Apostles from the 3rd century also locates St Thomas' mission in India.

India and all its own countries, and those bordering on it, even to the farther sea, received the Apostle's hand of Priesthood from Judas Thomas, who was Guide and Ruler in the Church which he built and ministered there". In what follows "the whole Persia of the Assyrians and Medes, and of the countries round about Babylon.... even to the borders of the Indians and even to the country of Gog and Magog" are said to have received the Apostles' Hand of Priesthood from Aggaeus the disciple of Addaeus.

---

[227] Pick, Bernhard. The Apocryphal Acts of Paul, Peter, John, Andrew and Thomas. Open Court Publishing. 1909. p. 283-362

[228] Bremmer Jan The Apocryphal Acts of Thomas. Peeters. 2001. p.137

Ephrem, composing hymns in the 4th century, writes about the relics of St Thomas being brought from India to Edessa, where they were enshrined. He says,

But harder still am I now stricken: the Apostle I slew in India has overtaken me in Edessa; here and there he is all himself. There went I, and there was he: here and there to my grief I find him. The merchant brought the bones: nay, rather! They brought him. Lo, the mutual gain! ... But the casket of Thomas is slaying me, for a hidden power there residing, tortures me.[229]

This hymn refers to the tradition, undoubtedly early, that the bones of the Apostle Thomas had been brought from India to Edessa. Indeed a feast is celebrated on July 3rd of 'St Thomas who was pierced with a lance in India, and who body is at Edessa having been brought there by the merchant Khabin'. This form of martyrdom is consistent with that recorded in the Acts of Thomas. Another hymn of St Ephrem says,

A land of people dark fell to thy lot that these in white robes thou shouldest clothe and cleanse by baptism: a tainted land Thomas has purified. Blessed art thou, like unto the solar ray from the great orb; thy grateful dawn India's painful darkness doth dispel. Thou the great lamp, one among the Twelve, with oil from the Cross replenished, India's dark night floodest with light.[230]

There are several other hymns by the same author about St Thomas. Together they show that in his time, the early 4th century, the relics of St Thomas were venerated in Edessa and were believed to have been brought from India by a merchant. It was understood that his mission had been in India, and that he had worked miracles there and

---

[229] Medlycott A.E. India and The Apostle Thomas. Nutt. London 1905 p.23

[230] Medlycott A.E. India and The Apostle Thomas. Nutt. London 1905 p.26

established the Church, but that after his death, and the translation of his relics, such miracles continued to take place in India and now in Edessa.

Fathers from the 4th and 5th centuries continued to speak about St Thomas, and located his Apostolic ministry in India. Gregory Nazianzus says,

What? Were not the Apostles strangers amidst the many nations and countries over which they spread themselves?... Peter may indeed have belonged to Judea, but what had Paul in common with the gentiles, Luke with Achaia, Andrew with Epirus, John with Ephesus, Thomas with India, Mark with Italy?

Ambrose of Milan reports that Thomas has been sent to India, as does St Jerome, St Gaudentius, and St Paulinus of Nola. In the 6th century St Gregory of Tours describes St Thomas as having been martyred in India, and then his relics being removed to Edessa. Even the Venerable Bede, writing from the British Isles, records that India had been the scene of St Thomas' labours.

These are not the local testimonies of the Indian Church, which it might be imagined were embellished over the centuries. But this is the constant witness of the Church. St Thomas was truly and entirely a member of the Apostolic band, and having been allocated the area of India as his mission he would appear to have hesitated and eventually found himself led there by the will of God rather than his own desire. He attended the court of King Gondaphares where he converted some of the residents, and then was called to another kingdom where he also won converts but was martyred by the thrust of a spear. In due course his relics were removed to Edessa, where they remained to be venerated by Ephrem of Syria, and to be known of by other Fathers of these early centuries. Since there is a mention of the relics of St Thomas being taken out of India, this would seem to suggest that the translation took place at an early date. Even if this is an interpolation rather than an original passage it would suggest that the translation was a known fact early in the transmission of the Acts of Thomas. Ephrem of Syria does not write of the translation as if it were a recent event and therefore it may be concluded that it took place before the early 4th century, and quite possibly early in the 3rd century.

This brief paper has only provided an overview of the scriptural and early patristic information about St Thomas. There is a great deal more which could be studied, especially from the Indian Orthodox traditions. But by referring only to the statements made by the Fathers it is possible to show that there is a universal Orthodox tradition that the Apostle Thomas established the Church in India, was martyred there, and that his relics were venerated from the earliest centuries in Edessa. Those who would doubt his Apostleship find themselves speaking against the weight of universal Church tradition and the explicit teaching of St Cyril.

The Orthodox Tradition and the Councils of the Church

This morning I would like us to spend a short time considering the Councils of the Church and their relation to our Orthodox Christian Tradition. There is a limit to what can be said in forty minutes and I will certainly not be describing the details of the hundreds and thousands of councils which have taken place over the history of the Church. Instead we will especially consider what councils are for and how they preserve the Tradition of the Church.

We have been reminded that the Tradition of the Church must not be conceived as simply a collection of doctrines, practices and disciplines which are passed on more or less coherently from generation to generation. Of course these are aspects of the Tradition. But essentially the Tradition is the living, vital and dynamic presence and activity of the Holy Spirit in the Church, and it is this life which Orthodox have consistently sought to guarantee by the careful and deliberate transmission of the Tradition.

On the one hand the Tradition is constant, while on the other the traditions are liable to change in order to preserve the Tradition, the inner life of the Church by the Holy Spirit, in different times and places.

Now it is useful that we have introduced this Education Day by considering the difference between the Tradition and the discrete traditions because we must have a clear understanding as we come to consider the conciliar nature of the Church that what is of greatest and necessary concern is not to preserve every custom and practice, indeed we will see that this has never been the case, but rather to preserve the life of the Church, the interior presence of the Holy Spirit and the unity with Christ, the Head of his own Body, the Church.

If we are able to look beyond the detailed and contingent specifics of the multitude of conciliar events and actions which have taken place, and if we are able to enquire what was the intention of each council in regard to the ever-renewed Tradition itself, then it is often possible to find a continuity even where there are apparent divergences in specific matters. Very often it is the preservation of a practice or discipline which will best safeguard the Tradition, but sometimes a practice or discipline must be modified or allowed to fall into disuse so that the Tradition itself, as life in Christ, is best preserved.

To a great extent the value and meaning of councils in the Church is not simply to form traditions – though certainly the production of conciliar canons was a necessary and important aspect of councils. But to preserve the Tradition – the experience of the divine life in the Church - and to maintain a living continuity with the experience of this divine life through all ages.

Church Councils are by their very nature a gathering together of various leaders and representatives for some common end, the welfare of the Church. Each council builds on that which has already been confirmed by the conciliar activity of past generations without creating something new nor simply repeating what is received. The one Tradition which is received is ever renewed by the continuing conciliar reception in the one Holy Spirit. We see this in the manner in which ecumenical councils deliberately recount and restate the Tradition which they are intending to apply to some new controversy without creating a new Tradition at all. We should not consider only the great and ecumenical councils of the Church, however many we count, when we are thinking of councils. There is sometimes a sense in which ecumenical councils are presented as if they are over and above the Church, or even descend as divine statements without any significant human participation. But they form part of a continuity of conciliar activity within the Church and far from being divine events in which human bishops have no real significance, they must be considered divine-human events in which both divine grace and human weakness are present.

In the same continuum, each autocephalous Church community, with its own Patriarch or Catholicos manifests this same conciliar nature and routinely calls together all the bishops and metropolitans under the presidency of their Patriarch or Catholicos so that the affairs of the autocephalous Church may be conducted for the good of that community. Even within such large Orthodox Churches there are often Metropolitan councils in which the local bishops under the presidency of some senior bishop in a region will meet together. While at the very heart of the local experience of the Church there is the bishop in his own see surrounded by his council of presbyters. The Church is conciliar from top to bottom and in each case there is a desire to express the unity of the Church by the application of the Tradition of the Church to contemporary difficulties in the power of the Holy Spirit.

The councils do not so much create Tradition as transmit it from generation to generation and apply and explain and extend its scope to new situations, if we understood the Tradition as the living and vital presence of the Holy Spirit in the Church. In such a case the councils are a necessary expression and guarantee of this life rather than an accidental means of changing and developing it. Within our Orthodox Faith we perceive the Tradition to be the same whether we consider it in the first century, or the fourth, or the fourteenth. The various traditions and practices and disciplines might take on different forms, the explanation of teachings might become more complex, but it is the same life which is described, the same Faith, there is nothing new to be said, just the one Tradition explained and described in terms appropriate to the times.

Therefore we can insist that the Church is conciliar. We find this reflected in the Scriptures. A passage such as Hebrews 10:25 says…

And let us consider one another to provoke unto love and to good works: Not forsaking the assembling of ourselves together, as the manner of some is.

Or the important teaching of St Paul about the Body of Christ in 1 Corinthians 12 reminds us…

For as the body is one, and hath many members, and all the members of that one body, being many, are one body: so also is Christ.

These are not passages about councils, but they are foundational references to the communal nature of our faith and life in Christ. We are not being saved alone, but belong to each other and must express that unity with one another. In the local congregation this unity was especially manifested by attendance at the local celebration of the Eucharist.

The well-known letters of St Ignatius of Antioch have much to say about the gathering of the congregation around the bishop. In his letter to the Ephesians he writes…

For if I in this brief space of time, have enjoyed such fellowship with your bishop-I mean not of a mere human, but of a spiritual nature-how much more do I reckon you happy who are so joined to him as the Church is to Jesus Christ, and as Jesus Christ is to the Father, that so all things may agree in unity! Let no man deceive himself: if anyone be not within the altar, he is deprived of the bread of God. For if the prayer of one or two possesses such power, how much more that of the bishop and the whole Church! He, therefore, that does not assemble with the Church, has even by this manifested his pride, and condemned himself. For it is written, "God resisteth the proud." Let us be careful, then, not to set ourselves in opposition to the bishop, in order that we may be subject to God.

From the earliest times, even from the Apostolic age, it has been clearly understood that the Church is a community and that we are united with Christ together or not at all. It is therefore entirely consistent with this view of the Church that conciliarity should become a central aspect of the Tradition, both expressing the unity of the Church in Christ, and preserving this unity for the future.

The earliest council is taken to be that which was held in Jerusalem and which is described in the Acts of the Apostles, chapter 15. Paul and Barnabas travelled to Jerusalem...

And when they were come to Jerusalem, they were received of the church, and of the apostles and elders, and they declared all things that God had done with them. But there rose up certain of the sect of the Pharisees which believed, saying, That it was needful to circumcise them, and to command them to keep the law of Moses. And the apostles and elders came together for to consider of this matter.

It is reported that there was much disputing, and we can imagine that the unity of the early Christian community was threatened. For this reason the leaders of the Church, the Apostles and Presbyters, gathered or assembled together. The outcome of this early council is well known to us. Certain canons or rules were established for convert Gentiles. But I would suggest that the most important outcome was the expression of the unity of the Church in the Holy Spirit which the council represented and the agreement expressed about the nature of the Tradition as it applied to this situation.

After the account of the discussion which took place we read...

Then pleased it the apostles and elders, with the whole church, to send chosen men of their own company to Antioch with Paul and Barnabas;

And the letter which accompanied them, sent from the council added...

It seemed good unto us, being assembled with one accord, to send chosen men unto you with our beloved Barnabas and Paul... For it seemed good to the Holy Ghost, and to us, to lay upon you no greater burden than these necessary things.

We see that from the very beginning of the life of the Church there is conciliarity. It is in the gathering together of those with the ministry of leadership and the pastorhood of the Church in the presence of the Holy Spirit that the Church finds itself fitly joined together and able to express the unity in Christ which belongs to us as those who have been united to him in baptism and the gift of the one Spirit. Without the conciliar nature of the Church expressed through the gathering together and unity of the episcopate our Orthodox Church would essentially be congregational. Each local gathering of Christians would do as it thought best, perhaps communicating with those who thought like them. But in such a case the Tradition of the Church would entirely lose its integrity and coherence. There could not be that necessary discipline which preserves the doctrinal basis of our Orthodox Faith, nor that necessary expression of love and submission to one another which joins together Orthodox Christians into one Body of Christ across space and time.

After the account of the Apostolic Council in Jerusalem we find the first documented councils of bishops, as leaders of various local congregations, in the mid-2nd century, and so roughly at the time when the last of the Apostolic men were falling asleep in the Lord. St Polycarp, for instance, who had been a disciple of the Apostle John, was martyred in about 155 AD and represented one of the last of those who had been a disciple of the Apostles and those who had known the Apostles. Yet even before these earliest councils there was certainly communication between bishops for the common good of the Church.

Just as St Paul had written to the churches which he had established and continued an oversight of them by visits and letters, as well as writing to churches such as that of the Romans even before he had visited them. So it seems that the bishops of the major cities and communities corresponded with each other and offered direction to those congregations which seemed to be facing difficulties. The letter of St Clement of Rome to the Corinthians is just one such example of a bishop of one city having a sense of shared responsibility for the community in another place. He writes on behalf of the Church in Rome to that which is in Corinth, and makes no apology for doing so, rather wishing that he had been able to respond more quickly to the correspondence which had been sent to Rome by some of the Corinthian congregation.

Likewise in the years before his death we know that St Polycarp travelled to Rome to discuss various matters with Pope Anicetus, and especially the variant traditions of celebrating Pascha which were held in Rome and in Asia Minor. About fifty years earlier he had himself received a letter from St Ignatius of Antioch as he was being taken a captive to Rome and his own martyrdom in which he says…

Since I have not been able to write to all the churches, by reason of my sailing suddenly from Troas to Neapolis, as the Divine will enjoineth, thou shalt write to the churches in front, as one possessing the mind of God, to the intent that they also may do this same thing -- let those who are able send messengers, and the rest letters by the persons who are sent by thee, that ye may be glorified by an ever memorable deed -- for this is worthy of thee.

It is well known that St Ignatius sent letters to many of the churches in Asia Minor, and to Rome, offering advice and exhortations to unity, and when he found himself unable to complete his correspondence he asks St Polycarp to complete it, not as if such correspondence between churches was a novelty or something unusual.

Indeed the familiar churches of Asia Minor, whose names we know well from the letters of St Paul, were not so far distant from each other that there could not be such communication. Papias, the bishop of Hierapolis in Asia Minor, records how he would question all those who came through his town from Palestine asking them what they had heard from those who knew the Apostles, and those Apostolic men who were still alive in his youth. As far as we can see, there was much communication between Christian congregations and even between Christian leaders from the earliest times.

Hierapolis is only about 8 miles from the New Testament city of Laodicea, and Smyrna is only an hour's drive by car from Ephesus. It is not surprising then that it is in this region of many relatively densely spaced congregations that the first councils of bishops appear to have taken place.

One model for such gatherings must have been the local congregational council of presbyters gathered around their bishop as described by St Ignatius. But the demands of Christian unity must surely have made it clear that in the absence of the Apostles and their close associates, it was the bishops themselves who were responsible not only for the pastoral care of local communities but for expressing and preserving the wider unity of the Christian Church spread throughout regions and countries and indeed the whole world.

The impetus for these first councils was the development of the Montanist movement. In some places, such as North Africa, it seems only to have represented a rigorist movement of Christians encouraging greater holiness and devotion, but in Asia Minor, where these councils took place, it certainly seems to have become a heterodox competitor to Orthodox Christianity. The presence of such a divisive teaching called for the gathering of bishops representing many towns and cities to develop a response that would preserve the unity of the Church and the doctrinal and spiritual Tradition of which they were guarantors.

In a fragment of a work by Apollinaris Claudius, bishop of Hierapolis, where Papias had been bishop a little earlier, and right in the heart of Asia Minor, preserved in Eusebius' Church History, we find it recorded that...

The faithful of Asia, at many times and in many places, came together to consult on the subject of Montanus and his followers; and these new doctrines were examined, and declared strange and impious.

Elsewhere we discover that at least one of these meetings, held at Hierapolis, consisted of 26 bishops as well as Bishop Apollinaris, and these must have represented a significant proportion of the bishops of Christian communities in Asia Minor. The heresy of Montanism was condemned and Montanus and Maximilla, the false prophets of Montanism were convicted of heresy. At about the same time a council is recorded as having taken place at Thrace on the Black Sea under Bishop Sotas of Anchialus, with twelve other bishops taking the same action against Montanism, Montanus himself and Maximilla. We see that the bishops gathered together had examined and considered that which was causing a disturbance to the Church and then gave a judgement together, by this means creating nothing new, but preserving the Tradition as they understood it and had received it.

These very first recorded councils of bishops were clearly occasioned by a present threat to the unity of the Church, and to the integrity of the Apostolic Tradition which the bishops were charged with preserving. There was a practical basis for their taking place, but as in the record of St Polycarp travelling to Rome and meeting with St Anicetus, we should not imagine that bishops were entirely isolated in their pastoral ministry. On the contrary, we can reasonably imagine that local bishops met with each other and corresponded with each other so that these larger formal councils which first appear in the middle of the second century to deal with the challenge of Montanism were a natural outgrowth of such relationships.

Later in the second century there were further councils which were called to try to resolve the issue of the variant calculations of the date of Pascha. A new development seems to have taken place. These first councils were rather spontaneous affairs, and took place on the initiative of local groups of bishops, perhaps under the presidency of the one among them who had the greatest prestige. But in about 196 AD Jerome records that in light of the Quartodeciman controversy about the date of Pascha, Pope Victor of Rome wrote to the leading bishops of various regions asking them to call together councils of local bishops to discuss the matter.

Thus Polycrates, Bishop of Ephesus, and one who must have known St Polycarp, found himself receiving a letter from Pope Victor requesting him to hold a council. He did indeed gather together those bishops within his influence, and it appears that these were a considerable number. They discussed the issue of the date of Pascha but determined to follow the custom which had been passed down to them, believing it to derive from St John who had lived in Ephesus. Eusebius describes this issue and records some of the councils which took place across the Christian world at this time saying…

A question of no small importance arose at that time. For the parishes of all Asia, as from an older tradition, held that the fourteenth day of the moon, on which day the Jews were commanded to sacrifice the lamb, should be observed as the feast of the Saviour's passover. It was therefore necessary to end their fast on that day, whatever day of the week it should happen to be. But it was not the custom of the churches in the rest of the world to end it at this time, as they observed the practice which, from apostolic tradition, has prevailed to the present time, of terminating the fast on no other day than on that of the resurrection of our Saviour.

Synods and assemblies of bishops were held on this account, and all, with one consent, through mutual correspondence drew up an ecclesiastical decree, that the mystery of the resurrection of the Lord should be celebrated on no other but the Lord's Day, and that we should observe the close of the paschal fast on this day only. There is still extant a writing of those who were then assembled in Palestine, over whom Theophilus, bishop of Cæsarea, and Narcissus, bishop of Jerusalem, presided. And there is also another writing extant of those who were assembled at Rome to consider the same question, which bears the name of Bishop Victor; also of the bishops in Pontus over whom Palmas, as the oldest, presided; and of the parishes in Gaul of which Irenæus was bishop, and of those in Osrhoëne and the cities there; and a personal letter of Bacchylus, bishop of the church at Corinth, and of a great many others, who uttered the same opinion and judgment, and cast the same vote.

And that which has been given above was their unanimous decision.

We can see from this passage that the issue of the date of the calculation of Pascha had now reached such a point of controversy with the growth of the Church that it was necessary that it be considered and resolved for the sake of the unity of the Church. What is important here is that councils were called in response to the matter and took place in many different locations. There was one in Palestine, and one at Rome, another in Pontus, and a further one in Gaul, and even one in Edessa. And it would also seem that in each case there was one or more presidents, and a sense of local bishops and congregations being in a relationship with the senior bishop of their region.

This has happened organically, as it were. There are no canons imposing such a form of conciliarity, and it would have been possible for bishops to ignore the initiative of Pope Victor who proposes these local councils as a means of coming to a universal judgement on the matter. Nevertheless it appears that it was received everywhere as the proper means of dealing with controversy. And even in Asia Minor where the issue was most pressing, there was no objection to calling together as many of the local bishops as possible under the presidency of Polycrates of Ephesus. It was already, in some sense, an expression of the nature of the Church rather than some externally imposed organisational programme that was not essential at all.

Of course the bishops of Asia Minor refused to back down from their own customs and Pope Victor of Rome went so far as to sever communion with them. This action was resisted by St Irenaeus who wrote in the following manner…

But this did not please all the bishops. And they besought him to consider the things of peace, and of neighbourly unity and love. Words of theirs are extant, sharply rebuking Victor. Among them was Irenæus, who, sending letters in the name of the brethren in Gaul over whom he presided, maintained that the mystery of the resurrection of the Lord should be observed only on the Lord's Day. He fittingly admonishes Victor that he should not cut off whole churches of God which observed the tradition of an ancient custom and after many other words he proceeds as follows:

For the controversy is not only concerning the day, but also concerning the very manner of the fast. For some think that they should fast one day, others two, yet others more; some, moreover, count their day as consisting of forty hours day and night. And this variety in its observance has not originated in our time; but long before in that of our ancestors. It is likely that they did not hold to strict accuracy, and thus formed a custom for their posterity according to their own simplicity and peculiar mode. Yet all of these lived none the less in peace, and we also live in peace with one another; and the disagreement in regard to the fast confirms the agreement in the faith.

These are interesting passages which Eusebius preserves. In the first place we can see that regional councils were called in response to particular situations, especially those which were likely to lead to heterodoxy, or disunity among Christians. Whereas these larger gatherings were somewhat of a novelty in the middle of the 2nd century, by the end of the same century they appear to be recognised as the normal and most appropriate means of dealing with such controversies. We can also see that such regional councils were already presided over by the senior bishop, sometimes according to age or length of ministry, but in other places according to the importance of their episcopal location.

We can even see that when there were disagreements it was appropriate for local councils to mediate between those in dispute, and that the senior bishop of a region, such as Irenaeus could write on behalf of the other bishops of Gaul.

St Irenaeus' letter to Pope Victor is especially important because it expresses some aspects of the ministry of bishops in council. He speaks about the fact that the difference in calculating the date of Pascha should not be something which leads to a loss of peace one with another – indicating that being at peace was a necessary aspect of the relation of bishops in communion. But he also says that even where there is a difference in the practice or traditions of fasting which different places had adopted, this variation confirmed the Tradition itself, the life and manifestation of the Holy Spirit in the Church, since all agreed that it was proper to approach the Feast with fasting.

In one sense there is nothing more to say about councils. From almost the earliest times, and just as the last disciples of the Apostles passed away, bishops exercised their ministry of preserving the Tradition and the unity of the Church by meeting in councils to deal with those issues which might disturb the Church. This conciliar nature of the Church is not accidental and merely one of the traditions which can be modified in different times and places, but is considered a central and necessary aspect of the Tradition itself. The activity of the Holy Spirit is present in the conciliar service of the episcopate as a source of Grace and a means of Grace for the sake of the whole Church. The Tradition is expressed authoritatively in each generation according to the contemporary circumstances by the unity in council of the bishops of the Church.

Of course the history of the Church shows us an accelerating pattern of councils from the third century onwards. Even here in the British Isles the Church was organised as congregations gathered around their bishops who met together in council. In 314 AD several British bishops attended a large council of the West held at Arles in

Gaul to discuss the Donatist controversy, and they are named as Eborius of York, Restitutus of London and Adelphius, perhaps of Colchester. This council was one of the first in which the Imperial power had a hand, and the Emperor Constantine said of it...

I have assembled a great number of bishops from different and almost innumerable parts of the Empire.

It was to be the beginning of a new relationship with the civil power that was not always to the best advantage of the Church. The ecumenical or Imperial council of Nicaea took place only 11 years after that of Arles in 325 AD with the intention of bringing unity and peace to the Empire, but it was not entirely successful. Just one hundred years later and the ecumenical council of Ephesus equally failed to bring unity, and that of Ephesus in 449 AD and Chalcedon in 451 AD merely illustrated that imperial councils could certainly enforce the will of the civil powers if that were exercised, but could not in themselves bring about peace and unity.

While the succession of councils, and there were a very great many even in these few centuries, produced canons to deal with practical matters, they also issued Definitions or Statements of belief about various controversial doctrinal matters. Nicaea was called to deal with the Arian heresy and though there was agreement found on the wording of the Nicene Creed which gained the support of many, in fact Arianism continued to be an issue for many years. Likewise the council of Ephesus in 431 AD, basing itself on the Nicene expression of the Tradotion was called to deal with the controversy around Nestorius, the Archbishop of Constantinople, but though it led to his deposition it hardly resolved the continuing support for the teaching and terminology of Theodore of Mopsuestia which was at the heart of the matter. And the council of Chalcedon, though representing many bishops with varying agendas and viewpoints, with the Imperial influence always in the background, brought about the first and longest rupture in the communion of those who believe essentially the same even while it also presented itself as being rooted in the expression of the Tradition manifested at Nicaea, Constantinople and Ephesus.

What had happened? St Irenaeus describes the conciliarity of the Church as means of bringing peace and unity in the Faith, but in later periods it can hardly be disputed that they often became a vehicle for party spirits or political ambitions even where the substance of disputes could have been resolved and agreement reached on controversial matters.

There is surely more to a council than that it be held and that it include a variety of bishops. The preservation of the Tradition must require more than that the form be followed even if the Spirit is absent. The history of the Church finds it littered with councils that failed to bring about peace and unity on the basis of the manifestation of the Tradition.

The great St Theodore of Tarsus, was the Syrian archbishop of Canterbury in the late 7th century. When he arrived in England he found the Church in rather a disorganised state. Many sees were vacant, and those bishops present in England often had vast dioceses that were virtually impossible to pastor properly. His first act on reaching England was to call a council.

This council drew together St Theodore with five other bishops, Bisi, Bishop of the East Angles; Wilfrid, Bishop of the Northumbrian people, who was represented by proxies, Putta, Bishop of Rochester; Eleutherius, Bishop of the west Saxons, and Winfrid, Bishop of the province of Mercia.

I refer to this council because in the account which is preserved in the writings of the English Church historian and scholar, Bede, we find justification presented for calling together the bishops of England, as far as was possible. It is interesting to read why St Theodore considered it so important for the council to take place. He says...

It was thought right that we should assemble in accordance with the custom of ancient canons to transact the necessary affairs of the Church.

I wonder if in fact it is St Theodore, with his experience of the well regulated government of the Church in Rome, since he had lived there for many years, who expresses his own desire to see the Church in England equally well ordered. Indeed from what follows in the account it seems clear that he was introducing his own godly ambition for a structured Christian community, even if the other bishops were willing to be guided by him, for Bede continues...

My dearest brothers, for the love and reverence you bear our Redeemer, I beg that we may all deliberate in harmony for our Faith, preserving inviolate the decrees and definitions of our holy and respected Fathers." I then proceeded to speak at length on the need for charity, and the preservation of the Church's unity. And having concluded my discourse, I asked each in turn whether they agreed to observe all the canonical decrees of the ancient Fathers. To which all our fellow-priests replied: "We agree gladly, and we will readily and willingly obey whatever is laid down in the canons of the holy Fathers." I then produced the said book of canons, and publicly showed them ten chapters which I had marked in certain places, because I knew them to be of the greatest importance to us, and I asked that all should devote careful attention to them.

Let me suggest that we can see here the proper relation here between the Tradition which is passed on and the circumstances of each age. St Theodore is moved by the traditions of the Church, the practice of regular assemblies of bishops which he has seen in Syria and in Rome, to call a council in his own time. But it is not with a sterile desire to simply obey a custom or canon. Rather it is with a sense that the difficulties faced by the Church in his own time require the Church in England to be better rooted in the Tradition, the life of the Church. There had been no such regular and routine national councils of bishops in England. The *necessary affairs of the Church*, as it is described, required conciliar action to be taken.

We might even say that the divine life of the Holy Spirit in the Church has so ordered matters that the *necessary affairs of the Church* are undertaken in council. St Theodore is neither holding a council because he wishes to obey a rule, nor holding a council as something he has recently introduced, but he calls this council because it is the way the divine life in the Church is expressed. The council is called because the experience of 700 years of Church life have determined that this is the manner in which *the necessary affairs of the Church* are managed.

It would be possible to imagine a variety of organisational differences in the manner in which such councils are held. Perhaps in some places they might talk place three times a year, and in another just twice a year. These are traditions, as it were, the practices which may change and develop but which do not disturb the essential character of the Tradition itself, which is that councils of bishops must take place, and that the *necessary affairs of the Church* are dealt with in such a context. In fact this very council, while insisting that it would obey what was laid down in the canons then proceeded to breach them by agreeing to meet only once a year in August instead of twice a year as had become customary. I am not going to consider the canons produced at this council, but I believe this indicates that the very gathering of a council of bishops manifests something necessary about the Tradition of the Church. The canon which instructed bishops to meet twice a year was useful and appropriate in many circumstances, but it existed for a higher purpose, and in the case of England in this period it was impossible for bishops to meet so regularly, but it was still possible, even with only one meeting a year, to express that which was most necessary to the life of the Church, that which was the Tradition, even if the traditions were modified. This is entirely how St Irenaeus had considered the issue of the celebration of Pascha. The Tradition might find expression in a variety of ways, but it was still the essential Tradition, the life of the Holy Spirit in the Church.

What is it then about councils that St Theodore thought most important? He says...

I begged that we might all deliberate in harmony for our Faith and I then proceeded to speak at length on the need for charity, and the preservation of the Church's unity.

I would like to suggest that this is the necessary aspect of conciliar activity which creates, preserves and guarantees the Tradition. The harmony expressed by gatherings of bishops in a spirit of love brings about and preserves the unity of the Church in the manifestation of the one Tradition.

Of course there are canons, local and practical decisions made by these six bishops, based on previous canons and modified by their own circumstances. But these are, to a great extent, the outcome or necessary product of the interior character of the council which is harmony in love for the sake of unity in the manifestation of the Christian life. The necessary business and activity of the Church requires that bishops meet in such a context of harmony in love for the sake of unity. Where this does not take place the life of the Church suffers. Certainly the arrival of St Theodore in England brought about a great improvement of the Church through the restoration of the conciliar Tradition. Within a few years there were fourteen bishops instead of only six. In many ways the Church in England as an organised community derives from his episcopacy and the efforts he made to renew the conciliar Tradition in England.

There could easily be a TV programme called When Councils Go Wrong! because in the history of the Church it does seem that the fruitfulness of a council, of whatever scope, is not guaranteed by simply organising it. There are many councils which have made a difficult situation worse. Councils which have failed, for a variety of reasons, to bring about that unity in the Tradition which might have been possible.

But the fact that councils can go wrong is not reason to abandon the conciliar nature of the Church. There are still wonderful examples today of councils expressing the unity of the Church and unity in the experience and manifestation of the Tradition. In 1965 the Churches of the Oriental Orthodox communion held a council in Addis Ababa. The introduction to the texts produced there says...

Although these five Churches have all along recognized one another officially as sister churches holding full Eucharistic fellowship with each other, they have not had a common council or synod after the fifth century. The Addis Ababa Conference has now brought to an end this practical isolation one from another of these Churches and opened up a new age in which they may be expected both to manifest concretely their unity and to play their role together in serving the Christian cause in the modern world.

It seems to me that this expresses perfectly the nature of a true council, since it allowed the manifestation of unity of Faith and Tradition, and the desire for communion in service to the Church and the world.

The great problems which the Church faces today will only be countered with conciliar action in love and humility. Bishops meeting together in such a spirit, in the Holy Spirit, become a gift of unity to the Church and of life to the world. There are divisions between Orthodox Christians which need to be resolved, and it is in council that God has provided the means to such resolution, both within our own Oriental Orthodox communion, and between our communion and others. There are social influences and philosophies which threaten our faithful members, and it is in council together that our bishops will properly address these and come to agreement in the Spirit. There is a need to present a unity to the world of those who belong to Christ, and it is in council that our bishops first and foremost express this unity.

The Orthodox Tradition, the life of the Holy Spirit in the Church, is renewed when bishops meet together in council in unity and love with humility. This expression of unity in Christ is at the heart of the Orthodox Tradition. What councils achieve when they are in accordance with God's will is to manifest that unity which already exists as a divine gift. Everything else is subsidiary to this unity. The creation of disciplinary canons exists to bring about unity in the Tradition. The publication of various statements and doctrinal acts is also to bring about unity in the same Tradition. The gathering of bishops from various places is to practically and spiritually manifest this unity in the one Tradition.

The organic nature of the development of conciliarity in the earliest centuries under the direction of the Holy Spirit should inspire us to be hopeful in this age as in every age. The difficulties which the Church faces can be resolved by the direction of the same Holy Spirit. But it will be by bishops meeting together in charity and humility to discover the will of God for the people of God. That ever renewed expression of the unchanging Tradition manifested for our own times.

May we all prayerfully support our bishops and encourage them in every place we find ourselves as Orthodox Christians to gather together in council for the *necessary affairs of the Church* not only within our own jurisdictions but as bishops of the Church of Christ already gathered together in this place and every other place.

Thoughts About Penal Substitution

It seems to me, from my study of St Cyril and St Severus (which I am not suggesting is comprehensive), that the Anselmian notion of Penal Substitution is very far from their own Orthodox teaching. Indeed I do not believe it is Orthodox at all.

This does not mean that there is not a place for an understanding of God's just and righteous judgement against sin, his hatred and condemnation of sin, his punishment of those who turn to darkness and harden their hearts. But this is not what Anselm teaches. The more I study our own Orthodox Fathers - St Athanasius, St Cyril and St Severus - the more I am filled with their own sense of the deep and abiding love of God for mankind, and the sense that the whole of the Holy Trinity is involved in earnestly desiring the renewal of mankind in life above all else. The idea that one of the Holy Trinity had to somehow become an object of hatred by another is far, far from Orthodox.

I will not fill this forum with extensive passages from the Fathers, but I can do if necessary, and perhaps I will write a paper explaining my understanding. I need to write something for the next edition of the British Orthodox Glastonbury Review in any case. But I will try to summarise my understanding.

God, the Holy Trinity, created man as the object of divine love. Looking upon Adam and Eve He said that what He had created was good. Man was created from dust, and like all created beings was naturally mortal and corruptible (corruptible is not the same as corrupt). But Adam and Eve received the breath of life, the Holy Spirit, who was breathed into them and granted them the gift of immortality and incorruptibility. This blessed life in the Garden of Eden was contingent upon one thing only, that the law of God which said 'you shall not eat of the Tree of the Knowledge of Good and Evil' was not broken. As long as Adam and Eve preserved themselves in obedience they retained the gift of the Holy Spirit, and would have lived for ever in a state of happiness with God.

But Adam and Eve were tempted, and by the exercise of their own free will they chose to satisfy their own pleasure, and by choosing other than God's will they fell into sin. Sin is nothing other than the exercise of the human will apart from God. The Fathers are very clear that sin has no existence at all. It is a wrong choice. A choice for self and not for God. When Adam and Eve chose other than God they broke the one command they had been given, and the curse fell upon them. Dust you are and to dust you shall return.

The Holy Spirit withdrew from Adam and Eve, it cannot dwell where there is sin. Adam and Eve found themselves left in their own human nature - mortal and corruptible. Human nature was not changed. St Cyril and St Severus are absolutely insistent that our human nature has not become corrupted. But our hearts are without the stabilising grace of the Holy Spirit and our wills are shot to pieces, choosing other than God all the time. Yet even when the curse fell upon Adam and Eve our Fathers teach us that this was an exercise of God's mercy and love. It would have been a terrible thing if mankind was allowed an immortality in sin, and so the length of a man's life was cut short by his natural mortality. Even more, God granted that the soul of a man might retain the gift of immortality so that it would always be drawn beyond itself to the spiritual heights of heaven - which is why every man is filled with a yearning for that which is eternal.

Cast out of Eden, man was doomed to suffer, to hunger and thirst, and eventually to suffer a bodily death. Yet there was a greater doom, since having lost the Holy Spirit he was already in a state of absolute death, of separation from God.

Each of us is born into this condition of mortality and corruptibility. But we are not born sinners. We are not born corrupt. Our human nature is as it was when God created it and saw that it was good. Yet because we lack grace and the Holy Spirit we all of us find that our will is turned this way and that and quickly finds itself bound by sinful habit, ignorance and self-love. We are born mortal, but not sinners. We choose to sin.

Yet we are still under the curse and in the power of death. Not even so much the death of our bodies but the death of separation from Life, from God Himself who was the true life of Adam and desired to be the true life of all mankind. The ultimate problem which mankind faces is the righteous judgement laid upon Adam which we all suffer the consequences of. Even if each one of us stopped sinning, or somehow had never sinned throughout our whole lives we would still be lost, not because our humanity is corrupt and sinful - this is absolutely rejected by the Orthodox Fathers - but because we are all in a state of gracelessness, and we all naturally lack the Holy Spirit. Even a sinless man would suffer all of our human frailties and would die. Even a sinless man would be left apart from God for eternity, because all of mankind is in the state in which God's judgement upon Adam left us - we are mortal and corruptible and do not have the breath of Life in us.

When the Holy Trinity willed to save mankind from this state it was not possible that the curse be lifted simply as an exercise of mercy. As has been said elsewhere in this thread, the mercy and righteousness of God must both be satisfied. But the Fathers do not teach that God was so angry, or filled with such wrath, that only a divine sacrifice could appease Him. Far from it. The work of salvation is the will of the whole Trinity, which loves man and wished his salvation.

No mere man could save man, because even a perfectly holy life could not take away the curse which was justly spoken. Rather, it was necessary that a new humanity be created, not by changing the substance of our humanity, but by renewing the divine relationship with man so that the

Holy Spirit could once more take up a habitation in our hearts and souls.

The Word Himself became man as we are, save for sin. This means that he took our own humanity from the Virgin Mary, a humanity which was mortal and corruptible, but not corrupt. It was liable to suffer, to hunger and thirst, and to die. If he was to save mankind then he must unite our own humanity to himself, and not some other humanity that was not in our situation. Being mortal and corruptible it was found in the state of being under the curse of God. He shared our own condition, caused by sin, by Adam's sin, but he never chose other than the will of God, and therefore there was never any sin in him, and though his body was physically corruptible and liable to suffering and blameless passions such as hunger, there was never any trace of the moral passions which we allow to grow and flourish in our own hearts.

The Fathers teach us that one of the reasons why our Lord took our humanity by means of a Virgin Birth was not because he had anything but the highest regard for the sancitity and holiness of marriage, but because he wanted to show that he was the firstfruits, the founder, of a new spiritual humanity in which those who were to be united with him would be sons and daughters of God.

What did the Word do in his incarnation? The Fathers teach us that it was necessary that he lived out our human life in obedience. He is described many times as 'taking up the fight which Adam lost'. So we must understand the incarnation as replaying what happened in Eden. In the Garden, Adam, the man who held our human destiny in his hands, blew it in a big way. Now in his earthly life, and clearly in the Garden of Gethsemane, the same contest happens again, but this time Christ, the Word Incarnate says 'Your will be done'. The failure of Adam had been redeemed in the obedience of Christ.

But this was not enough. A perfect human life had been lived in obedience, which was the basis for the renewal of man's relationship with God. But the curse remained. The curse was not an act if God's implacable anger, but a necessary provision for the salvation of man. Therefore it was necessary that the power of death, true death, be broken by an exercise of power by the one who is true life. Death needed to be destroyed from within. And to be destroyed from within it needed to be experienced by one who was mortal and subject to death, therefore the Word became mortal in our own humanity.

We see several features in his death. He died on the cross, which the Holy Spirit had inspired the prophets to speak of as a cursed manner of death. He was lifted up into the air, as Moses lifted up the golden serpent in the desert for the healing of the people. He was unjustly accused of sin when there was no sin in him at all. Even in his burial he was laid in a borrowed tomb, signifying that the death he endured was not his own but was that which was due to us.

If he sacrificed himself, and he said, 'No-one takes my life, but I lay it down', then who did he sacrifice himself to? Certainly not the Father, who had sent him to do this work of salvation - for God so loved the world. Certainly not to the Devil - the prince of this world has nothing in me. But surely he offered himself as a sacrifice of love for us. He did not die INSTEAD of us - because we were already dead. But he died WITH us so that we might live, might experience his life.

What happened when He died? In the first place he experienced that separation of body and soul which we call death. His soul descended to Hades (which I will not attempt to define) and brought out the souls of the righteous to Paradise (which I will not attempt to define). His body was preserved free from corruption - as the Fathers teach us - and as it is written in the Psalms. Then on the third day, by an exercise of his power, he destroyed death. A holy man destroyed the power of death. The curse had not been taken away, in the sense of being quietly forgotten. Rather the Word Incarnate, as a mortal man, died and then came out the other side.

A holy man, a perfect man, could not achieve this. The best he could have achieved was a sad commendation by God, well done, but sorry you are still cursed, you are still separated from God by true death. But the Word Incarnate could not only live a holy life, but he could die, and more than that he could raise himself from death.

But what does it mean for us? It means that a man, the Divine man, representing all of mankind, has made a way through death to life for us all. This Divine man has a humanity which is filled with resurrection life, true Life, and with the Holy Spirit. Now we can be united with this man and be born again into a new humanity. His life becomes our own. We participate in this life by faith and by the sacraments. These renew in us the presence of the Holy Spirit. He dwells in us not because we are perfect and holy but because Christ is and we belong to Christ. By faith we cast ourselves in humility before God alone and ask Him to have mercy on us. By baptism and chrismation God unites us to Christ and we receive the benefits which He has won for mankind. We receive the Holy Spirit who is our life, our true life. Death is overcome for us and in us. Our turning to God in faith and repentance allows God to forgive our sins, but forgiveness of sins is not all that we need. We need both forgiveness AND the life of the Holy Spirit. Our sins are forgiven because Christ, the Word Incarnate, has taken upon himself our death and in swallowing up the power of death over us he has taken away the power of the curse and has made it possible for our sins to be forgiven. He has lived an obedient life on our behalf - as Adam could have done but did not. And so we are able to say - do not look at my sins, Lord, but look at the obedience and holiness of your own son.

So why do we still die? Well the curse has not gone away. It was and is a righteous judgement against sin and against man who sins. It had an effect because of Adam, and that effect persists. We are mortal and die as mortals. But by faith and the sacraments we are united with God and follow Christ through mortal death to life. We have already received the Holy Spirit as a guarantee that we will rise to true life, because the Holy Spirit does not dwell in those who are subject to death. If we have any experience of the Holy Spirit at all then we can have faith that what has been begun will come to fulness and fruition in the life beyond death. Our sins have been forgiven because Christ has offered himself as a man who has done no sin, and who bears the consequences of our sin himself. He entered our death and took it upon himself.

But Christ has made a way for us through death to life. We follow in his footsteps. We are baptised, we fast and pray, we allow ourselves to be despised and treated as dead in the eyes of the world, we suffer and eventually we die. But this is not the end, it is the means of passing beyond the power of the just judgement of God and being restored to the place of blessing and life.

Christ did not die to satisfy God's anger. He died to manifest God's love. He died for us all, not standing in our place in the face of an infinite wrath, though we must not forget that God is indeed angered by our sin, and did indeed bring a just judgement and chastisement upon Adam and us all, but even before the judgement was made God had already - as our Fathers clearly teach - prepared a way of salvation to deal with the outcome of Adam's sin, which he foresaw. He has always acted in love towards us, even before he created us, and even when Adam sinned.

If we are found in Christ then mortal death holds no fears. It is the path to life. It frees us from the power of the curse and brings us to the place of promise. We can experience this now, if we are faithful. Life in the midst of death. Life in the face of death. Life with power over death. If I die surely I will live.

The teaching of Anselm reminds us that we should not diminish the offence of sin in the eyes of God. It is death to us. It is the opposite of life and therefore is anti-God. It repels God. But we should not turn to Anselm to remind ourselves of the cost of our sin, and its offensiveness. He is not Orthodox. He teaches a deformed Christianity. We must always turn back to our own Orthodox and trusted Fathers and see how they explain these things. And we can find much in our own Fathers about the seriousness of sin. We should not base our theology on a Roman Catholic teacher, this will lead to imbalance.

No mere man could save us. The judgement of God against us was indeed an infinite judgement which could not be overturned. But it was always the judgement of a loving Father, not an angry, wrathful and distant deity. Only the Word Incarnate could overcome the divine judgement by participating with us in the outcome of that judgement, by living with us and for us, by dying with us and for us, and by rising to new life in the Holy Spirit for us. God is love, not wrath. 'God so loved the world', not was 'so angry with the world'.

My every sin deserves death and is a slap in God's face. But God knows what I am like. Christ knows what I am like. Yet still I am offered new life in Christ. He allows me to share in his renewed humanity though there is nothing in me that warrants such kindness. All of this demonstrates to me the overwhelming love of God towards us.

Penal substitution as popularly taught does not do justice to God's love, nor is it rooted in the teaching of the true and Orthodox Fathers. This is not the teaching of St

Athanasius, St Cyril or St Severus. Justice indeed had to be served, and the Fathers are constant in this theme, God could not simply overturn His judgement, but this is never because he is so angry, or because he is offended. He knew what we were like before he made us, nothing is a surprise. Even his judgement is a mercy, as St Severus and St Cyril teach us. And even while he was angry with a righteous indignation against Adam and Eve, and against each one of us who follows them in sin, nevertheless he was always loving with a perfect love towards those he had created and chastised them and us rather than punishing us as we truly deserved.

I could write much more, but I hope that this short summary explains at least my own understanding of these things.

God bless all who seek to understand the truth, may the Holy Spirit lead us into truth.

A Preliminary Conversation with an Eastern Orthodox Monk on the Will of Christ

I am most grateful for the emails you have sent, and which provide a useful set of criteria with which to consider the topic of the will in Christ. I am especially glad that you have taken time to consider some of the obstacles to understanding which might be presented, and have explained your own understanding of this subject so clearly and precisely. It does help, because when I engage with some Eastern Orthodox online I find myself presented with views which appear to be heterodox, even by Eastern Orthodox theological authorities, or else reduce themselves to a polemical insistence on counting two wills rather than one.

I have, until now, hesitated to delve too deeply into the teachings of Maximos the Confessor on this subject because I have always thought of him, rightly or wrongly, as adding to the polemical quality of the seventh century, when it seems to me that there was always to a great extent an agreement on the substance of the matter which could have been discovered. Nevertheless, as I have been in any case, preparing material to write a paper on the issue of will in the teachings of Severus of Antioch, it is absolutely necessary that I consider Maximos the Confessor honestly and open-mindedly. Indeed I bought Father Andrew Louth's edition of some of the writings of Maximos the Confessor last night and have it downloaded to my tablet and smartphone and I have been reading the most relevant portions. I will refer to Maximos and Severus in this response because my great devotion to Severus could not be increased by insisting on using the term saint, and my respect for Maximos and for you might be seen as being lacking if I do not use the term saint only in regard to him.

Let me say at the outset that much of what Maximos says is immediately and completely acceptable to an Oriental Orthodox Christology. However, there are also turns of phrase which produce some confusion as to what exactly he means. It would seem to me that those things which I will describe and agree with in this response are those areas where an Eastern Orthodox might have most concerns about the Oriental Orthodox position, and those places where I do have some confusion about what Maximos means are, I expect and hope, to be understood in a manner which is consistent with a Cyrilline Christology.

I am glad that this opportunity to correspond has occurred at this time, as I have hesitated to write anything about Maximos the Confessor, as I must do in a paper on the teaching of Severus of Antioch, as I would not wish to misrepresent him.

I intend in this response to examine several of the writings of Maximos in enough detail to describe both my own understanding of the Oriental Orthodox position, and those areas where there is a need for me to have a greater clarity of his views. I am of the opinion that much of the present controversy about the will in Christ is due to a lack of resort to primary texts, and the application of vague understandings of the issue by online correspondents. I hope to avoid that by having a correspondence and dialogue with you, rather than an argument. Indeed every online reference to this topic ends up in Gethsemane with a polemical resort to counting wills.

Perhaps I will begin by responding to the sections of your own emails, and discover if we have a substantial agreement, and will then turn to the writings of Maximos the Confessor to see if the agreement can be sustained in the context of considering his teachings as an expression of Eastern Orthodox Christology.

In the first email you state,

Without confusion, the statements of the Oriental Orthodox over the last decades have repeatedly affirmed the true and perfect (unaltered and unconfused, yet truly and perfectly and hypostatically united) Divinity and Humanity of the One Only-Begotten Son and Incarnate and Crucified Word of God (contra Diodore of Tarsus, Nestorius, Theodore of Mopsuestia, Theodoret of Cyrus and Ibas of Edessa and all crypto-Nestorians ancient and modern), as taught by St Cyril of Alexandria. This I know of. We ourselves heard this from Pope Shenouda's on lips at St Paisius Monastery in the Summer of 1997.

So, we have no doubts regarding the facts of explaining what "Mia-physitism" means to the Oriental Orthodox Churches (namely, not "Mono-physitism", Synousiasm, or Eutychianism, or Apollinarianism). This is clear.

But we were wondering if you could tell us whether the Oriental Churches have ever made any explicit statements about the controversy (w/in our Byzantine Church) regarding the heresy called "mono-thelitism" in the 7th Century, when our champion (St Maximos the Confessor) defended the truly divine AND human (not merely or simply Divine) and truly VOLUNTARY (and that not merely or simply Divine) character of God incarnate's willing acts, especially in the Garden of Gethsemane on the way to the Cross, saying: "Not my will, but thine be done".

This seems a good place to start. We are agreed then that the Oriental Orthodox INTEND (leaving room to say that we fail), to confess that the humanity of Christ is true and perfect, and is united to the Word in a manner which is unconfused. You have understood what we intend, and you point out, quite rightly, that what is required is a clarification of what type of humanity is truly and perfectly present and united, especially in regard to will.

This has become an important area for clarification, not least since it seems to me that the Oriental Orthodox insistence on 'one united will', however we come to describe that, is confused with the heretical position of 'one only will', however we come to describe that. This is one of my great frustrations, that engagement with other communions comes down, all too often, to insisting on a one word answer to complex questions, where there might well be substantial, and even complete, agreement.

I will say immediately that we do not confess that the will of the Word incarnate is merely or simply Divine. I do think that we need to unpack the word 'voluntary' when speaking of the human willing of the Word incarnate. It cannot help but raise anxieties in my mind, which I am sure exist because I have not yet understood entirely what is meant. I hope that as I work through some of Maximos' own writings this issue might be cleared up.

Before I say more I will respond to the statements you provided in your second email.

1. "Whatever is not assumed is not saved" (St Gregory the Theologian vs Apollinarius).

Yes, this is also axiomatic for the Oriental Orthodox. The humanity of Christ must be the same humanity as ours or we are not saved. This was especially dealt with during the Julianist controversy in the 6th century. As you know, Julian wished to say that the humanity of Christ was already immortal and incorruptible from the moment of the incarnation, but Severus insisted that this meant that not only was the Christ of Julian unable to redeem our own mortal and corruptible humanity, but indeed being immortal and incorruptible he could neither suffer death nor blameless passions. Julian tried to say that he suffered impassibly in his immortal and incorruptible humanity, but Severus responded by pointing out that his suffering and death could not therefore be said in any sense to belong to him as his own natural death and suffering, rather they were an almost docetic appearance of death and suffering in a nature that could not suffer and die.

It is clear from the writings of Severus that the very seat of the confrontation of the Word incarnate with Satan, taking up again the contest in which Adam had been defeated, is the human will. I will try to provide references for all of the points I make in due course, and I have asked online to see if someone can get me a copy of Homily XXII by Severus on the account of the prayer in Gethsemane, as I think this will provide useful material for unerstanding his view.

But it seems clear to me that the Oriental Orthodox tradition has always insisted on the presence in Christ of a human will, as a necessary aspect of human existence. I understand this does not answer all the questions we need to consider about the nature and function of that will. But Severus, as far as I have understood him, and I have been studying him as much as you have been studying Maximos the Confessor, requires entirely that it is a man who is God who wins salvation for us by living perfectly as man in obedience to the divine will, and that sense of obedience requires itself that there be a human will (however constrained or free) in which obedience takes place.

In the writings of Severus, though he does occasionally refer to will, since he writes 100 years before the later controversy, he tends to prefer to use the term rational as meaning a willing and thinking soul, and almost always when he refers to Christ being incarnate it is with a clear statement that he is incarnate in flesh with an intelligent and rational soul.

2. Ergo, just as human "mind or nous" was constituent of the Logos's own humanity taken from the Theotokos, contra Apollinarius, so human will or "thelema" must be constituent of the incarnate Logos's own humanity.

I agree, and I believe that Severus would agree and does agree. He does speak of the human will in several places. I'll just quote one reference here at the moment..

Even less is Christ divided into two natures. He is indeed one from two, from divinity and humanity, one person and hypostasis, the one nature of the Logos, become flesh and perfect human being. For this reason he also displays TWO wills in salvific suffering, the one which requests, the other which is prepared, the one human and the other divine.

There are other such explicit references to the presence of the human will in Christ, but this will suffice to show that the humanity of Christ is not considered as being without a properly human will, however that is understood.

3. Thus, He willed not merely in a Divine way (as if he had never become incarnate), nor merely in a separated Human way (per Adoptionism or the confirmed tendencies of Antiochene thinking), but in a truly "Theanthropic" way, inclusive of BOTH the faculty of Divine Will/Willing which he shares with the Father and Spirit, and of Human Will/Willing, since the Logos became True Man, the God-Man.

I am glad that you use the word Theanthropic, because what we are always seeking to avoid is a sense that the proper activity of the human will defines a second subject in Christ, the man Jesus. Severus speaks of the Theandric activity which he finds in Dionysius..

As we have already developed in full breadth in other writings, we understood and understand the statement of the utterly wise Dionysius the Areopagite, who says, 'Since God has become a human being, he performed among us a new theandric activity' of the one composite activity..

This theandric activity is understood by us as referring to the activity in union of the humanity and Divinity and not the creation of a new ousia. This is by way of agreeing with your statement that the theanthropic way of willing, which we mean when we speak of one will, is a way of willing that includes and preserves the integrity of both the divine and human faculty of will.

Severus describes the willing in human way when he says..

But because the Emmanuel is by nature also God and goodness itself, although he has become a child according to the economy, he did not await the time of the distinction (between good and evil), on the contrary. From the time of swaddling clothes, before he came to an age of distinguishing between good and evil, on the one side he spurned evil and did not listen to it, and on the other he chose good. These words 'he spurned' and 'he did not listen', and on the other 'he chose' show us the Logos of God has united to himself not only to the flesh but also to the soul, which is endowed with will and understanding, in order to allow our souls, which are inclined towards evil, to lean towards choosing good and turning away from evil. For God as God does not need to choose good; but because for our sakes he assumed flesh and spiritual soul, he took for us this redress.

This seems to me to show that Severus understands that it is the human will of Christ which must be the active faculty in this choosing good. He says in the middle of this passage..

The Logos of God has united to himself... the soul which is endowed with will... in order to allow our souls... to lean towards choosing good.

This must be understood surely as insisting on the presence of a functioning faculty of human will which has been explicitly and necessarily preserved in the humanity of Christ for a particular purpose in the economy. It is not accidental, a vestigial organ like the appendix, but a necessary aspect of the nature of humanity which serves a necessary purpose in union with the divine will, and as the own human will of the Word incarnate.

The insistence on the human will being necessary, 'in order to', seems to me to speak of a proper and natural functioning of that faculty of will, however that is understood.

4. Note: In EO dogma, truly human "freedom of will", which the Incarnate Logos DID indeed take upon Himself is NOT to be found in the so-called "gnomic will," or "halting

between two opinions," or deliberative and wavering "dialectic between good and evil".

I am still struggling to understand exactly what is meant by 'freedom of will' in this context. I am obviously affected by the sense of human freedom of will meaning a freedom to choose evil, when I do understand that it means the freedom to choose God. I have said myself in other conversations that Christ is truly and humanly free to choose God, when others have wanted to say that his freedom of will means that he must be free to choose evil. This is one area I need clarity concerning the formal teaching of Eastern Orthodoxy rather than the pop polemics of some I have corresponded with in past years.

In terms of freedom of will, I am also trying to fit this into the Definition of the Sixth Council..

..his human will follows and that not as resisting and reluctant, but rather as subject to his divine and omnipotent will. For it was right that the flesh should be moved but subject to the divine will, according to the most wise Athanasius. For as his flesh is called and is the flesh of God the Word, so also the natural will of his flesh is called and is the proper will of God the Word, as he himself says: "I came down from heaven, not that I might do mine own will but the will of the Father which sent me!" where he calls his own will the will of his flesh, inasmuch as his flesh was also his own. For as his most holy and immaculate animated flesh was not destroyed because it was deified but continued in its own state and nature (ὅρῳ τε καὶ λόγῳ), so also his human will, although deified, was not suppressed, but was rather preserved according to the saying of Gregory Theologus: "His will [i.e., the Saviour's] is not contrary to God but altogether deified."

This seems to me to speak to a proper subordination of the human will to the Word Himself whose flesh and will it is, not so that it does not exist and operate, but that it does not exist and operate independently. I need to understand how to interpret 'moved but subject to the divine will' in terms which make sense of the notion of freedom. I have corresponded with some EO who wish to deny any sense of 'being subject', and indeed one, when shown this statement, insisted it was monophysite heresy.

I don't believe that the human will was suppressed by union with the Word whose human will it is, and I do believe it is deified, beyond the experience of those saints whose own entirely human wills were made freely subject to the divine will. But the idea of some human subject willing to be subject to some divine subject is naturally unacceptable. I can appreciate saying that the Word incarnate wills in his humanity to be subject to the divine will.

There is also, however, the teaching that as the Word incarnate willed, so he suspended some aspects of the natural operation of his own humanity. I think of the fasting for forty days, of which St Cyril says that the Word chose to not allow His humanity to feel any hunger until the end of that period, when He willed that His flesh be moved by the natural human desire for food. I need to understand how you incorporate this sense that the humanity is not a mere humanity, or a humanity outside the purpose of the economy. But that as the Word incarnate wills He can suspend all manner of properties of His own humanity for a season, without those properties always being natural to His humanity. I mean that it seems to me that St Cyril refers to the Gethsemane account with a view to showing that the Word incarnate allowed His humanity to be moved by the natural operation of his human will, which seems to indicate that the natural operation of the human will is not an absolute, but is subject to the divine will.

I suppose I am thinking that when the human will operates it does so freely and naturally, but it is not absolute in its operation, and at some level the Word incarnate chooses not to feel hunger. Would you wish to understand the restriction of the blameless passion of hunger to be at a lower level than the will, such that the will is not being suspended in its operation, rather one of the movers of the will is being suspended? How would you understand St Cyril on this point in regard to the human will in Christ?

I am glad that you exclude all thought of deliberation in Christ, and this is in accordance with the passage from Severus of Antioch already quoted, which refers to the infant Christ as always choosing the good. This is one area of concern, since others have not expressed it as well as you. Some EO do seem convinced that there is a deliberation in Christ or else there is no freely operating human will.

5. That is to say that Kazantzakis, the modern Greek novelist and Nestorianizer and blasphemer, is entirely heretical in his views of Christ's human mind and willing faculty, for the Logos Incarnate could NEVER have sinned and could NEVER EVEN have "entertained" thoughts of sin in his mind. Rather, He possessed the true freedom of the one and Only-Begotten Son of God in a way BOTH truly Divine AND truly Human -- in true and unconfused union -- that is to say "Theanthropically".

There is a lot of discussion online about whether Christ could sin, or even entertain thoughts of sin. Some EO do seem to think that this is necessary. I don't doubt that they are speaking in an heretical manner. I think that I am comfortable with my own understanding of the one will of the Word incarnate, standing for a theandric and composite will, in the sense that it is always the one Word of God incarnate who wills all things both humanly and divinely and therefore in complete accord. The human willing of Christ is the expression and manifestation in a truly human manner, of the divine willing.

6. The Incarnate Logos's own human mind and human faculty of willing, constitutive of His own true humanity (contra any kind of Apollinarianism that truncates His human properties), were deified from the very moment

of His conception in the womb of the Theotokos, and never susceptible to the slightest possibility of any "fall" or "blameworthy passion".

Certainly we would agree that the humanity of the Word incarnate was deified from the instant of the incarnation, and that this necessarily includes the human mind and faculty of willing. There was nothing lacking in the humanity of Christ and he was entirely consubstantial with us.

I suppose I have some anxiety about what is meant by deification in this context. Is it that you are saying he his deified by the indwelling Holy Spirit, as if he were a bare man, or that he is deified by the union with the Word of God Himself? This is not to deny that the Holy Spirit 'came upon' the Virgin Mary, and that the Word is 'incarnate of the Holy Spirit', and that the Holy Spirit also descended upon Christ in the Jordan 'and remained upon him'. But I am not comfortable with any idea that if the Holy Spirit were not present then the union with the Word of God would not have been sufficient to entirely transform the humanity, not from its nature, but into the glory of the Word.

Of course we are in complete agreement that there was not the slightest possibility of a fall, nor any movement of any blameless passion whatsoever. This rejection of the possibility of sin is based on the exercise of the human will in always choosing the good, and not from an external coercion, but this freedom is dependent on the union, and is the proper human expression of the divine will which is goodness itself.

7. So, the Incarnate Logos possessed as His own (in perfect and unconfused union) all the qualities and energies of Divinity and Humanity, therefore He possessed the truly human capacity to will and choose.

Certainly the Word incarnate possessed the truly human capacity to will and choose, but not in independence from the Word incarnate Himself as if the human will marked the presence of some other subject. The willing and choosing of the good by the human faculty of will is always, as you say, the 'own' willing and choosing of the Word in His own flesh and according to His own human will. Severus of Antioch teaches us to reject division, but never to refuse to confess the distinction between those natures of which Christ is. If there was no human will then there would be no true humanity, simply an animated body, moved by some external force. But we do wish to avoid at all and any cost the slightest sense that there is another subject in Christ other than the Word of God incarnate. The one who says, 'if it is possible', is the same Word of God incarnate and no other.

8. We interpret as follows, "nevertheless, not my will [my natural, good, laudable and truly human desire and will for "self-preservation"], but thy will be done [that very Divine Will which I share with Thee and the Holy Spirit]".

This is how I interpret the passage, based on the commentary of St Cyril. I have not always found that other EO, or even OO, accept such a view. And there is a tendency among some to want to find two willing subjects in Christ. But this denies the hypostatic union, as far as I can see. The desire for 'self-preservation' is indeed natural and blameless. St Cyril says..

He sent from heaven His Son to be a Saviour and Deliverer: Who also was made in form like to us. But even though He foreknew what He would suffer, and the shame of His passion was not the fruit of His own will, yet He consented to undergo it that He might save the earth, God the Father so willing it with Him, from His great kindness and love to mankind.

Here we see that humanly he did not naturally will the suffering and shame which was about to come upon Him, nevertheless he willed to undergo it, 'the Father so willing it with Him'.

In this instance we would still wish to speak of the one will of the Word incarnate, even though we see the human faculty of will being naturally and freely moved. It seems me that the movement to avoid death is not the same as the choice to do the Father's will. The faculty of will was certainly moved by the blameless passion, but it was not acted upon, and therefore it was not the expression of the one choice of the Word of God incarnate.

How would you speak of this? He is not deliberating between two different actions, as if manifesting a gnomic will. He is making a determined choice to do the will of the Father, while recognising and expressing the movement of his will by the desire for self-preservation. But this movement of the faculty of will is not the same as the choice made by the faculty of will, otherwise we must say that he hesitated between two comparable options. And we would surely have to say that every blameless movement of the faculty of will must be the same as a choice, when it is clearly not. Our Lord was moved in his faculty of will by the blameless desire for food, but willed not to eat. Both are movements of the will, but both are not choices.

How do we understand the fact that there are physical aspects to the movement of the faculty of will, such that I might be hungry. But there are also intellectual aspects, such that I might desire to study more than satisfy my natural hunger and so I will to continue my study rather than eat. But there are also spiritual aspects, such that I might be moved by a desire for prayer, and so submit both the physical and intellectual movements of my faculty of will to the spiritual movement, and so will to give myself to prayer. Which of these is actually WILLING, and which are only movements of the faculty of will. I might, for instance, be only a little hungry, or I might be very hungry indeed, and surely these various states will exert a different movement in the faculty of will, but the actual choice I make is different and belongs to me as a subject, though still exercised within my own faculty of will, more than the simple movement of the faculty of will, which could be caused by many, diverse, and simultaneous passions.

I'd appreciate some insight here.

I hope you can see that generally speaking I don't see a great difference between the substance of what we seem to believe about the human will of Christ. There are still things to explain, but certainly there should be no doubt that recognising two wills is not problematic, even though we speak of one. And that human will is the active faculty in freely choosing the good in a human manner, since, as Severus of Antioch says, God does not need to choose the good.

I'd like to look at a few passages in Maximos the Confessor, as in the end an understanding of this issue cannot be constructed without reference to him. I'll just refer to a few passages in this response. The first is Opuscule 7 from the translation by Father Andrew Louth.

In one passage he says..

It has been confessed and believed in an orthodox manner that the only begotten Son, one of the Holy and Consubstantial Trinity, being perfect God by nature, has become a perfect human being in accordance with His will, assuming in truth flesh, consubstantial with us and endowed with a rational soul and mind, from the Holy Mother of God and ever Virgin, and united it properly and inseperably to himself in accordance with the hypostasis, being one with it right from the beginning. But the hypostasis was not composite nor the nature simple. But remaining God and consubstantial with the Father, when he became flesh he became double, so that double by nature, he had kinship by nature with both extremes, and preserved the natural difference of his own parts each from the other.

There would be no problem with the first sentence. Nor with the third sentence. The humanity of the Word incarnate is certainly perfect and true flesh, and is consubstantial with us and is endowed with a rational soul and mind. He has certainly also remained God, and although we do not use the term double or feel comfortable with it. It can be understood in this passage as surely referring to the diversity of natures from which is the one Christ.

The second sentence is rather confusing, since we would want to say that the hypostasis of the Word of God does become composite in the incarnation, meaning that the identity of the Word of God is expressed both humanly and Divinely. The Fifth Council says..

If anyone shall not acknowledge as the Holy Fathers teach, that the union of God the Word is made with the flesh animated by a reasonable and living soul, and that such union is made synthetically and hypostatically, and that therefore there is only one Person, to wit: our Lord Jesus Christ, one of the Holy Trinity: let him be anathema. As a matter of fact the word "union" (τῆς ἐνώςεως) has many meanings, and the partisans of Apollinaris and Eutyches have affirmed that these natures are confounded inter se, and have asserted a union produced by the mixture of both. On the other hand the followers of Theodorus and of Nestorius rejoicing in the division of the natures, have taught only a relative union. Meanwhile the Holy Church of God, condemning equally the impiety of both sorts of heresies, recognises the union of God the Word with the flesh synthetically, that is to say, hypostatically. For in the mystery of Christ the synthetical union not only preserves unconfusedly the natures which are united, but also allows no separation.

Since the word composite is synthesis in the Greek texts then it would seem to me that the Fifth Council agrees with the Oriental Orthodox position that the union is composite and hypostatic. How then does Maximos insist that the hypostasis is not composite? From the Oriental Orthodox point of view it could be said that his hypostasis remains that of the Divine Word, and certainly it is not meant that his identity is based in some confusion of nature, but the idea of the composite hypostasis means that the identity is expressed in a union of two natures which continue in their integrity.

Who does this sentence address when it speaks of the partisans of Apollinaris and Eutyches? If it means the Oriental Orthodox communion then it is based on a complete misrepresentation of what has ever been taught among us. How do you handle something which is stated by an ecumenical council but is wrong? If there were partisans of Eutyches still around in 553 AD then it is correct to address them and condemn them, but if it is intended to target the Oriental Orthodox (using that term as shorthand) then it is neither accurate nor just. There has never been a confusion of natures among us. Severus of Antioch says, 'We do not reject recognising the distinction between those things of which Christ is. God forbid!'. I raise this issue because I am not convinced that Maximos the Confessor also properly represents those he is opposing. How do we handle the right people opposing the wrong people for the right reasons?

Maximos goes on to say..

He was the same at once God and man. Those who irreverently think that there is a natural diminishment in what has come together present him as imperfect and as suffering the lack of what is naturally his. For unless the Incarnate Word guards without loss the properties of both natures without sin, according to the teaching of the divine Fathers, out of which and in which he properly is, even after the union, then he exists as a defective God. His Godhead is then altogether imperfect. And his humanity is also defective, since it is altogether diminished in what is natural to it.

Well I certainly agree that the humanity and divinity must remain perfect in the integrity belonging to them otherwise the Word is not God, and/or he is not man. Who are those who diminish him? Again, if he intends the

Oriental Orthodox then he is mistaken. And I am not yet confident that speaking of one will is the same as refusing to recognise that the humanity also has the proper and natural faculty of will.

I start to particularly disagree with him in the following passage..

For either, as making a whole out of parts, we melt down the two essential wills and the same number of natural energies and recast them by composition as one will and one energy, as in the myths, and there is manifest something completely strange and foreign to communion with the Father or with us, for he does not have by nature a composite will or energy, nor do we.

This strikes me as a rather unfair statement made without a desire to understand what his opponents might mean, and it seems no different at all to the criticism which St Cyril faced when he spoke of 'one incarnate nature of the Word'. I know exactly what those who speak one one composite will mean, and it is certainly not how Maximos wishes to describe it. Those who speak of one composite will mean no more than that the human and divine will are so united that they express a divine-human willing of the Word incarnate. There is no creation intended of a third nature, as Maximos must surely have been aware. The human will is consubstantial with our own human will, and the divine will is consubstantial with the will of the Father, but we may still, and must still, confess a composition as the Fifth Council determines, which is not a confusion, or a mixture, but a true union.

Maximos goes on to reiterate that the humanity of the Word incarnate must have all those properties of our own humanity. And this is of course entirely acceptable and agreed. He then says..

How again, if the Word made flesh does not himself will naturally as a human being and perform things in accordance with nature, how can he willingly undergo hunger and thirst, labour and weariness, sleep and all the rest? For the Word does not simply will and perform these things in accordance with the infinite nature beyond being that he has together with the Father and the Son..

It is a little confusing in this passage that the Word, in the last sentence, is opposed to the Son, and I wonder if there is a translation error. But the substance of this passage is entirely acceptable to the Oriental Orthodox. Severus of Antioch would ask how he could suffer for us if it was not in a flesh which was able to suffer, and how he could be obedient if not according to a will that could choose the good. So it is entirely necessary that the humanity of the Word incarnate have the human faculty of will. It is not only as God that he wills, but he wills, we would want to say, always in a composite manner as the Word of God incarnate, which composition describes the union and not any mixture or confusion.

He says…

If then his humanity has a rational soul then it possesses the natural will. For everything that is rational by nature, certainly also possesses a will by nature.

This is also agreed. And as I have mentioned earlier, Severus is always careful to speak of the Word having united to himself flesh with a rational soul.

Therefore as God by nature he willed what is divine by nature and belongs to the Father… and again the same, as man, he willed those things that are naturally human.

This is not quite so straightforward. I think I am anxious because he appears to be setting up two exclusive categories of willing. That God the Word incarnate willed humanly is not in dispute, but what does it mean to say that the Word of God willed only human things humanly? And only willed Divine things divinely? I am not comfortable with that. When our Lord walked on the water he did so in a theanthropic manner. It is not human to walk on water, but it is not divine to walk at all. We surely understand this as an action of God the Word incarnate in a complete and perfect union of his own humanity and divinity. When our Lord says, 'I will, be healed', is this an exercise only of the human will, or is it the human manifestation and expression of both divine and human willing?

I would want to try and think that there was in the Word incarnate a perfect unity of will and willing such that at the same time in the humanity he wills the object of this union of will as far as is appropriate and possible, and in the divinity he wills the object of this union of will as far as is appropriate and possible. This is not to suggest that the human faculty of will was changed into what it is not, but I hesitate to even suggest that the human faculty of will was occupied with earthly things only, and the divine faculty of will had not thought of the human movement of will but was busy with holding the universe in place. In some sense I would want to say that he was humanly willing the universe to be held in place by his own divine power to the limit of his human faculty of will, while also divinely willing to resist the temptations of Satan in some sense by his own human will to the limit that was appropriate to the freedom of his humanity. It is not the reality and integrity of the humanity I am afraid of losing, but the composite and hypostatic union.

I agree with Maximos that in the humanity of the Word incarnate there is no resistance to the good, and so his humanity is always naturally turned to the good. And I have no hesitation in again affirming that the perfection of humanity requires the presence of the human will and energy. But again I would insist that this is not a duality of independent wills and energies, but is an expression of the natural and proper diversity in the natures of which Christ is.

Maximos comes to describe the Gethsemane incident, and he doesn't express himself as I had expected, from correspondence with some Eastern Orthodox.

For that he has by nature a human will just as he has an essentially divine will, the Word himself shows clearly when in the course of the economy that took place for our sake he humanly begged to be spared from death… in order to manifest the weakness of his own flesh. … Again the human will is wholly deified, in its agreement with the divine will itself, since it is eternally moved and shaped by it and in accordance with it, is clear when it shows that all that matters is a perfect verification of the will of the Father… giving himself as a type and example of setting aside our own will by the perfect fulfillment of the divine….

This is all agreeable. The use of the words type and example are consistent with St Cyril. There is no problem with understanding this passage as a manifestation of both human natural weakness which the Word assumed to himself, and also a perfect obedience of the human will to the divine will. What we would want to avoid is any sense that there is in Christ some area which expresses a contrary will to the divine, and therefore is a second subject. The expression of blameless passion is not the same as a deliberate choice against the will of God, and this is what we would want to exclude.

Indeed when Maximos says..

The will can properly be said to have become truly divine in virtue of the union, but not by nature.

I would entirely agree, and would consider this as a very good statement of concord in the substance of our Christologies, even if the terminology is different. I note with gladness that Maximos refers to St Gregory and says…

..he completely excludes any contrariety from the mystery of Christ, as if there were two beings willing opposing actions.... He points to the innate movement of Christ's human will and its essential and natural difference from the divine will of the Father and completely excludes confusion.

Yes, absolutely there is no contrariety and there cannot be two beings willing opposing actions. In regard to 'natural difference', there is indeed a difference of will, but it is a difference according nature, but in regard to the object of will there is no difference even while the things that are willed are diverse.

Maximos goes on to defend the dogma of the 'difference and the union'. This is where it gets rather frustrating. The Oriental Orthodox understanding of St Cyril's Christology is built upon the idea of the 'difference and the union'. Why then was there such misunderstanding? He goes on to insist that the presence of diversity in the Word incarnate requires that those things of which Christ is must be counted, and they must be counted as two. But this seems to me to be a difference of position that has no meaning that is worth division.

Of course there are two natures, wills and energies. But we do not count them in regard to the Word incarnate because we are concerned that to count them is to divide them. This has never meant that they have not been distinguished en theoria which you know does not mean 'in theory' as some polemicists online insist, being unaware that the Fifth Council uses this term. Of course there is a proper and natural human energy, but it is not proper to an accurate Christology to so describe this proper human energy as though it acted always and only independently of the divine energy. Indeed it never acts independently, just as the proper and natural human will never acts independently. This being so, it seems to us entirely proper to speak of one will and energy which is composite or theanthropic.

How is this practically different to what Maximos says, rather than just semantically different? It begins with the union, which Maximos confesses, and understands the difference, which Maximos confesses.

Maximos then turns to the Dionysian phrase, theandric. Why does he dismiss the idea of a theandric energy and will , since this is what Dionysius says, and it is what is meant by those who speak of one will and energy. He says..

For by the word theandric the teacher obviously refers periphrastically to the double energy of the double nature.

Well of course Dionysius means to refer to both the human and divine energy, but it seems disingenuous of Maximos to exclude all sense of one or a new theandric energy, as Dionysius writes, and instead simply use the term to indicate two natural energies, which one could equally say are obviously not intended. Indeed Maximos agrees that Dionysius speaks of this energy, and not these energies. I would not want to suggest that anyone means by theandric a confusion of mixture, which is why it is frustrating that Maximos will not consider that his opponents do not mean such a confusion or mixture, or simple divinity, but wish to describe the unconfused union. Maximos says that when Dionyisus speaks of this energy he does not harm the natural difference and does not propose an essential identity. Why then does he not extend the same explanation to his opponents?

He quotes his opponents as saying, if he has one energy, the same is also theandric. I don't have any problem with this phrase within my own understanding and terminological usage. Theandric refers to the union of natural energies and does not refer to a single energy. It seems rather unfair then for Maximos to continue and say..

But what if the Word incarnate possessed one natural energy and no-one objects. How is the one natural energy to be divided into two?

Who are these who would say that the Word incarnate possessed one natural energy without intending in any sense to describe the union of natural energies? Were there such in the controversy or is this just a straw man?

Certainly Maximos should have been able to find common ground with the Oriental Orthodox based on the substance of what I have read. He then seems to make a controversy where I am not sure or convinced there is one. Later I will consider the statement of Cyrus at the time of the union in Egypt between the two communions to see whether it should be read as speaking of one natural energy, or one united and theandric energy.

Maximos then returns to his point that neither the Father nor humanity have a theandric energy and therefore it must be an energy that is not consubstantial with either. I find it very hard to believe he did not understand what was meant. Why then does he act as though the term theandric must refer to a new and confused union of energies rather than accept that it could well mean what he insisted that Dionysius had meant, to refer to the union of energies. He then says that this energy could only be one if it were referred to the hypostasis, but that this would make him alien to the Father. None of this seems fair. He presents only two options, neither of which were held by the Oriental Orthodox certainly, and therefore I must question if they were held by the monothelites, or all the monothelites. He refuses to allow that speaking of one theandric energy, or even one energy, could refer to the union of diverse natural energies.

Of course based on his own interpretations of what must be meant it is the case that the opposing Christology must fail, but I am not at all convinced that he has properly considered all the possibilities of meaning. Certainly neither of the two options he produces are ones which I hold, and yet I do not wish to use his terminology either.

Indeed he quotes from St Cyril who says, the energy shown to have kinship with both, and has to find another exception to his criticism when a single energy is described. He says of St Cyril..

[this] is not affirmed by the teacher to destroy the essential difference of the natural energies out of which and in which the one and only Christ God exists, but to maintain their exact union.

Of course the term one energy affirms the union and does not disregard the difference. But if St Cyril and Dionyisus are allowed this usage then why not Maximos' opponents? Why must their use of 'one' and 'theandric' be considered only according to obviously and manifestly deficient Christological premises? He says..

Then, as he showed that the natural energies of Christ the God, who is composed of both are perfectly preserved, that of his Godhead through the almighty command, and that of his humanity through the touch, he proves them both to be thoroughly united by their mutual coming together and interpenetration, showing that the energy is one through the union of the Word himself to his holy flesh and not naturally or hypostatically.

This is an entirely acceptable statement of the Oriental Orthodox understanding of the union of energies in Christ. How then can one who makes such a statement, and even speaks of 'one energy' then go on to condemn others who also speak of 'one energy'. If it is the case that some others truly believed in a single and confused energy, or simply a divine energy, then that would be a valid condemnation, but certainly the Oriental Orthodox have never confessed such a thing.

Maximos continues to speak of the natural difference which remains after the union. This is always the teaching of the Oriental Orthodox. He says that this teaching drives away reduction and division, and he is perfectly correct. But he then returns to accuse those who speak of one energy as having affirmed an Apollinarian or Eutychian confusion of essences. Who are these people who make such a confusion?

He does accept that the Fathers speak of one incarnate nature of God the Word, and the theandric energy. But he will not allow that the same necessity of confessing the union which leads to these terms may also properly be applied to the will so that a theandric will is also a proper term. This does not diminish or deny the natural faculty of will in the humanity, but expresses the union of all aspects of the being of the humanity in a perfect hypostatic union with the divinity.

I was going to consider Opiscule 3 which refers to Severus of Antioch, but I will not do so just now.

It seems to me that I am in agreement with your own eight statements, and I am in essential agreement with Maximos. I am confused by him in some places, and frustrated in others but I think that I have understood the substance of his position and agree with it. My issue with him is the way he treats others in his argument, rather than the substance of his own arguments, with which I tend to agree. He says, for instance, that Severus teaches that Christ is non-existent. I have to say that this strikes me as the argument of one who is not seeking to engage with another and does not properly understand the other.

I will in due course produce references from the Oriental Orthodox Fathers and St Cyril, not least because I want to write a paper on this subject. But I believe it will be very helpful to have your own response to this response. Do you think there is a degree of agreement, at least between my own position and yours? Would you consider it a substantial degree of agreement? What about the issue I have a little anxiety around? My criticism of some aspects of Maximos the Confessor's text should not be considered as intended disrespectfully, not least because his value as a spiritual father is undoubted. Indeed I hope that I could also consider the writings of my own master, Severus of Antioch, with enough honesty to see where he has not properly understood another's point of view. In those days it was not at all easy to conduct a lengthy conversation, and I am grateful for the opportunity to refer my own questions about Maximos' meaning back to you for further comment.

Let me quote again a passage from Severus,

He also displays two wills in salvific suffering..

I will also say that I have made reference to Cyril Hovorun's volume Will, Action and Freedom. It is useful for references, but it is defective in that he depends entirely on Grillmeier for his appreciation of Severus, and Grillmeier is unfortunately completely lacking in an understanding of the Oriental Orthodox, or even Cyrilline, Christology. Therefore Hovorun tends to view every reference to 'one' as referring to a simple one, when the very basis of our Christology is that the unity and union of natures in Christ, through producing a real, natural and hypostatic union, does not damage or eliminate the difference in natural quality of those things of which the one Christ is composed.

I hope that this response is of some interest, and that you will in turn be able to consider it with your spiritual father and allow us to continue this dialogue as far as we are able. It is an encouragement to me to engage in that detailed study which I have long wanted to do.

Can the Oriental Orthodox receive the Eastern Orthodox Councils?

At the beginning of the 21st century it seems that the relationship between the Eastern and Oriental Orthodox communities is as close as it has been for centuries. There certainly remain those within the Eastern Orthodox community who perhaps view the Oriental Orthodox community through a prism of lack of knowledge and misrepresentation, some of which is due to the lack of proper explanation by the Oriental Orthodox themselves. But increasingly it has become impossible for Eastern Orthodox to doubt that Oriental Orthodox have always confessed the perfect and complete humanity of Christ. In a growing number of congregations around the world there is a pastorally based reception to communion of lay members from other Orthodox communities. While formal agreements allowing communion between various Orthodox communities, and even proposals for reunion from senior Eastern and Oriental Orthodox hierarchs, suggest that an opportunity to explore the possibility of unity has now presented itself as both a challenge and encouragement.

Despite the positive outcome of the dialogues between the Eastern and Oriental Orthodox communions over the last decades, it seems clear that an outstanding and significant issue remains the status of those councils not received by the Oriental Orthodox. These form such an important aspect of the life and witness of the Eastern Orthodox communion that they cannot easily be ignored. Recent agreements produced by the theological dialogue between the Eastern and Orthodox communities have appeared to skate over the need for a formal response from the Oriental Orthodox to these later councils.

Nevertheless, the Oriental Orthodox and Eastern Orthodox have been able to produce a Joint Agreement which confesses a mutual confidence that the same Christology has always been held by all. That being so, it must be the case that the later councils of the Eastern Orthodox, and even the most controversial texts such as the Tome of Leo, are all able to be understood in an Orthodox manner. These joint statements have been accepted by the Holy Synods of almost all the Oriental Orthodox churches and therefore represent a formal and official view of the Eastern Orthodox.

This seems to be a moment in history that calls for generous efforts to resolve centuries old disputes. If it is necessary to go that extra mile in the name of truth and love, then such demands must be embraced.

I have been a member of the British Orthodox Church within the Coptic Orthodox Patriarchate for over twenty years. Even before I became Orthodox I was engaged in the consideration of the controversy between the Eastern and Oriental Orthodox communities, and it has continued to be one of the most important areas of my own research and study. To be able to write about the unhappy separation of those Orthodox Christians who believe and practice the same faith requires some detailed understanding of the controversial issues, and of the historical consequences of events taking place over 1500 years ago.

This paper is part of a wider project to consider and respectfully present proposals aimed at encouraging the reconciliation of the Eastern and Oriental Orthodox communities. In this particular study it will be considered whether the Oriental Orthodox can receive the Eastern Orthodox councils in some formal manner. I believe it is both possible and necessary, and that such a reception can take place without the Oriental Orthodox abandoning our own consistency of faith and continuity of history.

It will be necessary to consider the Tome of Leo, the councils of Chalcedon, the Second of Constantinople, the Third of Constantinople and the Second of Nicaea. If we must accept them for the sake of reconciliation then how are we to accept them without sacrificing our own integrity?

This paper will describe one perspective in the following pages.

There are two aspects of each of these still controversial councils and texts. On the one hand there is the actual historical event itself, situated in a particular context and represented by a variety of particular narratives, whether positive or negative. On the other hand there is the present interpretation of the different doctrinal, canonical and disciplinary components of these councils. Is it necessary that all of these components and their historical representation be viewed in the same way?

Clearly any event or text can be and is often understood and described in a variety of manners. The Formula of Reunion of 433 AD brought about the union of St Cyril and the moderate Antiochians. A certain lexical compromise on both sides allowed the Orthodox Christology of St Cyril to be confirmed together with an appropriate breadth of language that allowed the Antiochians to be comfortable in expressing the same truths.

But when Ibas of Edessa wrote his letter to Maris the Persian he understood the Formula of Reunion in an entirely different manner. According to his interpretation of the correspondence between St Cyril and John of Antioch he wrote,

For Cyril has written Twelve Chapters, as also I think Your Piety knows, in which he says that there is one nature constituting the Divinity and Humanity of Our Lord Jesus Christ….But how impious such statements are Your Piety will have been quite persuaded…The Lord had willed the subduing of the heart of the Egyptian.

It is well worth considering the letter of Ibas to Maris the Persian, and noting that he viewed St Cyril's Twelve Chapters as error. More than that, he understood that the Reunion was on the basis of St Cyril rejecting his error and adopting a Christology which was consistent with the teaching of Theodore of Mopsuestia. This could hardly be further from the truth, not least because St Cyril was engaged in writing a work against the Christology of both Theodore of Mopsuestia and Diodore of Tarsus. But it does illustrate the fact that a single text can be understood in a variety of ways.

If we were able to have a conversation with Ibas it would not be enough for us to say that we agreed with him in accepting the Formula of Reunion of 433. We would have to ask him how he understood this text, and what Christology it was endorsing. In this case we would find that though we both seemed to accept the Formula, in fact what we were confessing were entirely contradictory and irresolvably different interpretations of what the Formula represented.

What is actually believed must take priority over the endorsement or criticism of various texts, such as the Formula of Reunion because apparent agreement can actually mask an absolute disagreement. While apparent disagreement can in fact obscure a fundamental agreement.

Now if it has already been established over decades of dialogue that the Eastern Orthodox communion shares the same Faith as the Oriental Orthodox communion then it is not possible to insist that those fundamental, but controversial, texts and councils which are necessary to the Eastern Orthodox tradition actually and materially represent a false and even heretical Faith. The Eastern Orthodox cannot both profess the fullness of the Orthodox Faith and also profess error in these texts and councils.

Therefore it must be possible to accept these texts and councils in a manner which is consistent with the Orthodox Faith, and if it is possible to accept them in an Orthodox manner then it must also be possible for the Oriental Orthodox to receive them as Orthodox. This surely requires more than a simplistic assent to them without an appropriate process of reception, just as simply passing over them in silence has not proved satisfactory.

But what do we mean by accepting these texts and councils? In the first place we do not mean that we will be able to accept the current narrative which many of the Eastern Orthodox use to locate these texts and events in an historical context. We have a different view of what happened in many cases, and we believe that our variant narrative is as justified by historical evidence as any other. It is not possible for us to say, "Sorry, we have been wrong about everything all along", because we do not believe this to be the case. But neither do we wish to demand of the Eastern Orthodox that they abandon their own understanding of history as a necessary precondition for reconciliation.

What is surely required is a certain degree of self-reflection that allows all sides to understand how the various views of texts and councils came about. This self-reflection must also extend to an appreciation that different views on historical events is not a dogmatic matter.

There is some controversy at present, for example, within both Eastern and Oriental Orthodoxy, about the consideration of the Emperor Constantine as a saint. It has been noted that he was not canonised until relatively late, and as part of a cultus that focused on the city of Constantinople. There is also the issue that he was baptised only shortly before his death, and had been complicit in the murder of family members. Is he a saint or not? Does it matter that he became a saint only centuries after his death? These are questions that often lead to heated arguments. But the example is raised because having different views about an historical person, even one whom many consider a saint, does not lead to a breach of communion, and is not considered as having a dogmatic character. Is the Emperor Constantine a saint or not? There are those who are committed to Orthodoxy who hold both opinions.

Those who believe that there is no scope at all in Orthodoxy for any difference of opinion on any matter are fortunately in a tiny minority. For most of Orthodoxy and for most of the time, there has been a understanding that there must be unity in dogmatic matters, while allowing a variety of opinions, within the boundary of the Faith, on other matters.

In regard to the controversial texts and councils that Eastern and Oriental Orthodox must come to terms with, there are various aspects that warrant different approaches. In terms of historical context there will perhaps remain, for a while, distinct narratives that colour the reception of the event itself. Modern scholars such as Richard Price, in his outstanding editions of the Acts of Chalcedon and of Constantinople II, have assisted in the process of developing a more neutral and objective history of these events. The understanding that these events were more complex than the brief paragraphs used to describe them in works of catechesis will help to produce an appreciation that in fact different views of the history usually represent the fact that there were different agendas that were actually being played out at these events, and that there is no one monolithic history.

If it is required that Oriental Orthodox accept unchallenged the popular Eastern Orthodox historical narrative then reconciliation will continue to be stalled at an official level. But there is no reason why this should be so. When St Cyril and John of Antioch were reconciled with each other it was not on the basis of John of Antioch confessing that he was wrong to hold another separate council in Ephesus in 431. It was not on the basis of confessing that everything he remembered of the events was in error. It was on the basis of accepting the dogmatic substance of St Cyril's council. It was entirely reasonable for John of Antioch to continue to believe that St Cyril had acted improperly at Ephesus, and for him also to accept the deposition of Nestorius and the use of the term Theotokos in relation to the Virgin Mary.

To accept these texts and councils does not require the acceptance of a particular history. But these councils also produced disciplinary statements. These are also problematic for the Oriental Orthodox since they name some of our own Fathers such as St Dioscorus and St Severus. But it would seem to many, including Eastern Orthodox, that these disciplinary resolutions are also not a matter of dogma. At the council of Ephesus, John of Antioch was deposed by St Cyril and the bishops with him, yet St Cyril was reconciled with him and did not act towards him as a bishop who had been deposed, even though an ecumenical council had disciplined him in such a manner.

Likewise, Theodore of Mopsuestia died in the peace of the Church, and even St Cyril did not demand that his name be removed from the diptychs of the Antiochian Church for the sake of unity, even though he considered him a heretic. Nevertheless at Constantinople II he was condemned and the approach taken by the Fathers of the previous generation was modified. There are those Eastern Orthodox who will insist that any action taken by the Fathers may not be challenged, but this was clearly not the view of the Fathers themselves, who used different approaches in different circumstances.

St Dioscorus was clearly not condemned for heresy in his lifetime but was deposed on a procedural point. He was anathematised centuries after his martyrdom when those who so condemned him could have had no real knowledge of his teachings, which can be seen to be entirely Orthodox by the documentary evidence available to us. Likewise, St Severus was engaged in dialogue with the Imperial Church late into his life, and during the 6th century it had been recognised on several occasions during such official conferences that there was no Christological difference between those who accepted Chalcedon and those who rejected it. St Severus was willing to accept the Henotikon as far as it went, which makes the accusations against him of being both a Nestorian and a Eutychian especially objectionable.

What we require of the Eastern Orthodox is a willingness to consider again whether the condemnations of St Dioscorus and St Severus are properly attached to their persons, even if the errors purported to have been held by them are certainly liable to condemnation. There will be a need for the Oriental Orthodox to consider again the persons of Leo of Rome and the Emperor Justinian. The case of the Emperor Constantine surely shows that agreement in the canonisation of various figures is not necessary for agreement in faith, especially not if there is an agreement in the rejection of those errors some believe these figures held, and agreement in the acceptance of those truths which others would wish to insist they held.

These are not dogmatic matters, they are liable to revision because they depend on the attribution of error and truth to a particular person, and not on any acceptance of error or rejection of truth. To a great extent this has already been understood. When I read the writings of Maximos the Confessor, for instance, I find myself agreeing with his positive statements of truth and with his negative criticism of error. But I know that he is entirely wrong to attribute error to St Severus and that he has mistaken and misrepresented what St Severus taught. At the time in which Maximos wrote, the works of St Severus had been entirely proscribed and destroyed within the Empire. They are preserved to us thanks to the copies made into Syriac even while he was alive. To disagree with Maximos on a matter of truth and error would have a dogmatic significance, but to disagree with him when he attributes error to St Severus is a different matter altogether and is to do with opinion not doctrine.

The very fact that the Alexandrian Churches, Greek and Coptic, allow intercommunion of laity, and that the Syrian Churches, Greek and Syriac, experience even closer ties of mutual fellowship, indicates that the issue of the status of those controversial persons is not considered to be a doctrinal issue. If the veneration of St Dioscorus absolutely meant that the Oriental Orthodox accepted the heresy of Eutyches there could be no such intercommunion. Likewise if the veneration of Leo of Rome absolutely meant that the Eastern Orthodox accepted the heresy of Nestorius there could be no such intercommunion. Metropolitan Hilarion, one of the most senior hierarchs of the Moscow Patriarchate, also believes that issues such as these are secondary to the profession of the same doctrinal substance.

What does this mean? If the historical perspective is not dogmatic, and if the disciplinary actions are not absolute, then to properly consider the status of these texts and councils within the Oriental Orthodox communion means to reflect on the Definitions and official Statements of each council, and those canons which these councils produced.

Such a reflection may even comprehend even the most controversial texts such as the Tome of Leo and the Definition of Chalcedon. We are not asking ourselves do we agree with everything that has happened in history around these texts, but we are asking whether the manner in which the Eastern Orthodox understand the words of these texts is a manner in which we can agree.

If we were to consider the Sentence and the Capitula of the Second Council of Constantinople we would discover that there is little in which there could be any disagreement at all. If we were to consider the Definition of Chalcedon there are aspects which it is well known would cause some concern. What is required of us is not to imagine ourselves into the minds of those who accepted this text in the 5th century, nor even to imagine ourselves into the minds of our own Fathers who had reasons enough to reject it then. But to discover how the Eastern Orthodox today, with whom we are challenged to rediscover our fundamental unity, actually understand this text and all the others.

Once again it must be insisted that since we confess that the Eastern Orthodox have the same Christological Faith as ourselves then even the Definition of Chalcedon must be able to be understood in an Orthodox manner. And if it is understood in an Orthodox manner then we can receive that interpretation as Orthodox ourselves.

What should we do? I believe that a document must be compiled which contains all of these authoritative texts which cannot be ignored if reconciliation is to take place. These texts must be glossed or explained with various notes so that it is clear how we are willing to receive each passage, and which errors and false readings we wish to exclude. This would not be a very lengthy document, the output of the various Eastern Orthodox councils is not excessive and deals with particular issues. This document, however it was produced, and I am researching just such a volume myself, with an introductory essay and doctrinal and historical notes, could be received in due course by each of the Synods of the Oriental Orthodox Churches. This comprehensive text would be accepted as Orthodox, and as consistent with the Orthodox Faith as professed in the first three Ecumenical Councils of universal acceptance.

Would this count as accepting these texts and councils as Ecumenical? The latter councils after Chalcedon might perhaps be considered ecumenical under such a process, to the extent of receiving the doctrinal statements and canons. It would remain problematic to use the term ecumenical of Chalcedon, even under a narrow consideration of the texts as understood by the Eastern Orthodox at present. There might be greater consistency in allowing that the acceptance of a comprehensive document as being Orthodox allows for the reception of all the doctrinal substance of these councils, including Chalcedon, when properly understood.

It would then be possible to say to our partners in dialogue that we do accept all the ecumenical councils, even if we do not count them all as properly Ecumenical.

This will not satisfy all Eastern Orthodox. Some do wish to see the complete submission of all Oriental Orthodox to the historical narrative commonly presented among those who accept Chalcedon. Some will continue to demand the condemnation and rejection of St Dioscorus and St Severus as the cost of an asymmetrical reconciliation. But these are not the majority. There are also those Oriental Orthodox who believe that our own historical views of Chalcedonians are immutable, but this is to fail to properly research our own engagement in efforts for reconciliation in the 5th to 7th centuries.

What is clear is that we cannot hope to achieve reconciliation without properly coming to terms with the central place which these texts and councils hold in the Eastern Orthodox tradition. If there is a need to go that extra mile then we must take it, while preserving our own integrity. We will discover that even the most controversial texts can be understood in a variety of ways, and that in fact we already share agreement in those things which these texts strive to explain.

There is continuing hope for reconciliation. But we will not move forward without honestly considering how to understand these things in an Orthodox manner. I hope to return to this theme in much greater detail in further and more substantial papers.